Pelican Books
Slums of Hope?

Peter Lloyd is Professor of Social Anthropology in the University of Sussex. He was born at Bournemouth in 1927 and educated at New College, Oxford, where he read geography. After research at the London School of Economics he was awarded his B.Sc. in Social Anthropology at Oxford in 1953, and his Doctorate in 1958. From 1950 to 1956 he held a Research Fellowship at the Nigerian Institute of Social and Economic Research, and then, after three years as Land Research Officer in Western Nigeria, he founded the Sociology Department of the University of Ibadan, and became Senior Lecturer in Sociology there. He joined the University of Birmingham in 1964, becoming in 1966 Reader in West African Sociology.

Professor Lloyd has visited the U.S.A. on many occasions, and has lectured at several American universities. He is a member of anthropological, sociological and African Studies associations in both Great Britain and the U.S.A. His publications include *Yoruba Land Law* (1962), *The New Elites of Tropical Africa* (1966), *Africa in Social Change* (1967), *Classes, Crises and Coups* (1971) and *Power and Independence* (1974). In addition he has contributed to *Peoples of Africa*, ed. J. L. Gibbs (1965), *Political Parties and National Integration*, ed. J. S. Coleman and C. G. Rosberg (1965) and *Social Change: the Colonial Situation*, ed. I. Wallerstein (1966). He is co-editor of *The City of Ibadan* (1967). Peter Lloyd is married, and his wife, Barbara, is Reader in Social Psychology at the University of Sussex.

Peter Lloyd

# Slums of Hope?

## Shanty Towns of the Third World

Penguin Books

Penguin Books Ltd, Harmondsworth,
Middlesex, England
Penguin Books, 625 Madison Avenue,
New York, New York 10022, U.S.A.
Penguin Books Australia Ltd, Ringwood,
Victoria, Australia
Penguin Books Canada Ltd, 2801 John Street,
Markham, Ontario, Canada L3R 1B4
Penguin Books (N.Z.) Ltd, 182–190 Wairau Road,
Auckland 10, New Zealand

First published 1979


Made and printed in Great Britain by
Hazell Watson & Viney Ltd, Aylesbury, Bucks
Set in Linotype Times

# Contents

# Tables

# Foreword

A book and its message both grow out of the author's experiences. For many years I studied and worked among the Yoruba people of Nigeria. Great differences in power and wealth existed in traditional Yoruba society, but top positions were usually open to those of humbler birth; polygyny prevented the successful from passing their status on to all, if any, of their children. It was an open society and was seen to be so. Pre-colonial attitudes towards social mobility proved compatible with modern society, in which most political leaders and members of the newly dominant groups have come from poor rural homes. More recently I have carried my interest in urban migrants to South America, spending some time in Lima, Peru. Here the peripheral shanty towns look so despairing, yet the desert environment and a permissive government policy have enabled residents to convert many of the older settlements into respectable working-class neighbourhoods.

These experiences have given me an image of the city immigrant living in material poverty, but enjoying a stable family life, law-abiding and rationally pursuing future goals for himself and his children. This view contrasts starkly with the conventional image of a slum population, and indeed that conveyed of third-world slums in the popular descriptions of the social anthropologist Oscar Lewis. Yet my own picture is corroborated by that of many other anthropologists (for example Leeds, Lomnitz, Lynch, Mangin, Mayer, Safa) who, like me, have seen a shanty-town community at close quarters.

The first purpose of this book is therefore to offer a corrective to the conventional picture of the third-world shanty town. Secondly, I wish to stress the universality of this picture. The physical environment and culture of the shanty towns differ from one country to another. Yet the process of cityward migration is universal. (In the third world most movement is within countries. In Europe, with its recruitment of labour from the Mediterranean areas, the Middle East, North Africa and further afield, it is international.) It stems from the economic development of the industrial nations, which draws ever-remoter areas into its field of dependency. Recent theoretical interest centres on two themes – the structural relationships of dependency and the changing structural patterns within the dependent nations. The first is a matter of debate among economists, and, if the mechanisms of dependency are not fully understood or agreed, their consequences in the third world are obvious and undisputed – slow industrialization, changes in rural society, rising populations and migration to the cities. And these are, in turn, causal factors in the growth of shanty towns.

We all view the world in structural terms – we seek a patterned regularity in events observed. Macro theories – of dependency, as of other relationships – tend however to become too abstract for empirical verification; they become ideologies. *In extremis* the structure becomes equated with reality; laws are established which are seen, not as our rationalization of situations, but as existing in the real world. The theories thus become highly deterministic, seeing man's behaviour as governed by these laws, and allowing man little or no role in making the world in which he lives. An alternative approach views the world as man-made – and as consciously made by man, though this does not mean that every action produces the intended effect. It thus becomes important to see how men view the world within which they live, how their behaviour is governed by their image of their society.

The third purpose of this book is, therefore, to plead that we should try to understand how the shanty-town dweller sees his society. I say plead because so few studies have been made that one cannot give, at this stage, a definitive description. Some may retort that the shanty-town people have so little control over their destiny that it is not worthwhile inquiring into their views and attitudes; and indeed there is much justification in this, for economic policies are certainly not decided by them.

Yet they do have a potential for action and if this potential is to be harnessed or developed, their view of their world is certainly important.

To all those who have helped me to understand the shanty town I owe a great debt of gratitude. Firstly to the people of these communities in Nigeria and Peru where I have carried out my own research, for their forbearance and tolerance, and indeed the interest shown, in projects which nevertheless constituted an intrusion into their lives. Secondly to my colleagues in these projects – Gavin Williams and Adrian Peace in Nigeria, Cristina Herencia and Sonia Becerra in Peru – upon whose loyalty the success of the research ultimately depended. Thirdly to my students in the University of Sussex who have helped to develop and formulate ideas at first so inadequately expressed. Fourthly to the University of Sussex, the Nuffield Foundation and, in greater measure, the Social Science Research Council which have generously financed my recent field trips to Nigeria and Peru. And finally to my wife Barbara, to Rachel and David, who shared some of these trips.

# 1 Prologue: The Shanty Town

Primitive man is haunted by fears of natural disasters – of floods, droughts and earthquakes, whose incidence he cannot predict and against whose terrors he can but propitiate his gods. Modern man is haunted by the misery and squalor in which millions of his fellows live, the causes of which may be obscure to him though they are undeniably the product of his own activities. Among the spectres of poverty few can today match the sprawling slums peripheral to almost all the cities of the 'third world' – the nations of the tropical latitudes so often newly independent after decades, or even centuries, of colonial rule. The standard of living in most of these slums is probably no lower than in the rural areas from which their inhabitants have recently come; nor is it perhaps very different from that obtaining in the countries of the industrializing West two centuries ago. But it contrasts starkly with the technological affluence of the urban populations of the industrial nations and, even more pertinently, with that of the elites of the third world. The endless spreading slums form a terrifying backdrop to the striking modern architecture of the city centres – their office blocks for a thriving bureaucracy, lavish hotels for visiting experts and businessmen, sumptuous supermarkets and department stores for the rich. For the gap between rich and poor is, today, in these countries, so much greater than in the West. A smaller elite shares a major share of income gained; the remainder is distributed among a much larger mass.

The people living in these slums are mostly recent immigrants. At one time it was possible to view them as temporary sojourners in the city. Their squalor mattered little, for were they not saving hard-earned cash to take back to their idyllic rural homes? But today it is accepted that the reverse movement

Table 1: Income distribution in poor nations

| Country | Per capita GNP in US$ | No. of examples | Poorest 20% | Poorest 60% | Highest 20% | Highest 5% |
|---|---|---|---|---|---|---|
| | 50–74 | 5 | 10 | 33 | 49 | 30 |
| *Tanzania* | *54* | | *10* | *29* | *61* | *43* |
| *Niger* | *74* | | *12* | *35* | *42* | *23* |
| | 75–99 | 6 | 7 | 28 | 53 | 24 |
| *Kenya* | *75* | | *7* | *21* | *64* | *22* |
| *Nigeria* | *76* | | *7* | *23* | *61* | *38* |
| *India* | *77* | | *7* | *36* | *42* | *8* |
| | 100–199 | 9 | 5 | 27 | 56 | 27 |
| *Bolivia* | *117* | | *4* | *27* | *59* | *36* |
| *Philippines* | *187* | | *4* | *25* | *56* | *27* |
| *Ivory Coast* | *192* | | *8* | *30* | *55* | *29* |
| | 200–299 | 8 | 4 | 20 | 65 | 39 |
| *Brazil* | *215* | | *4* | *23* | *61* | *38* |
| *Peru* | *225* | | *4* | *17* | *68* | *48* |
| | 300–399 | 5 | 4 | 18 | 67 | 39 |
| *Zambia* | 306 | | *6* | *27* | *57* | *37* |
| | 400–499 | 5 | 7 | 34 | 67 | 36 |
| | 500–699 | 3 | 5 | 25 | 52 | 21 |
| | over 700 | 3 | 6 | 33 | 46 | 21 |
| *Venezuela* | *968* | | *4* | *30* | *47* | *23* |
| 5 Western Industrial States | | | 4 | n.a. | 46 | 10 |

The above figures have been taken from Kravis (1973), pp. 61–79.

The very poor countries show a less marked inequality of income distribution than do those which have some development. The figures for individual countries show different degrees of skew; this often reflects the proportion of the total population engaged in near-subsistence agriculture; thus the top income holders of India are large in absolute numbers, small in relation to the total population.

The five industrial countries aggregated in the final line are: France, Netherlands, Norway, United States, United Kingdom.

to the countryside is insignificant compared with the waves of migration into the cities. The urban explosion will continue; and most of the migrants and their children in turn will become city dwellers.

Migrants and shanty towns are part of a universal process which began only a few decades ago with the intensified penetration of the tropical world by financial capital and the rapidly advancing technology of the industrial nations. A world economy is being created in which most of the rich live in the latter, most of the poor in the former. But just as the industrial societies have their own relatively poor, so do the third-world nations have an elite whose wealth matches (and in many cases exceeds for given skills) that of their Western counterparts.

Each nation, however, struggles with its own problems. External observers contemplate the diversity of slum profiles – the inner-city slums and the vast peripheral squatter settlements; the sea of matting huts stretching across arid hillsides that constitute the Peruvian *barriada*; the pavement settlements of Indian cities or the collection of huts on a vacant city plot; homes constructed from sacking, packing cases, rusting sheets of corrugated iron, the detritus of the city; the settlements on steep hillsides or swamps, land deemed unsafe for permanent housing.

Three thumbnail sketches by sympathetic Western observers illustrates both the squalor and the diversity of the shanty town.

There is a typical bustee out near Calcutta's second university at Jadavpore. It starts on the edge of upstanding middle-class houses and it trails off into the railway lines; so many bustees do. The huts are made of wattle, they have tiled roofs, they have mud floors. They are so congested that there is nowhere more than an arm's space in the dirt-track lanes that separate one row from another. And open drains run down the middle of each lane, so that you tend to walk them at the straddle. People sit in these lanes chopping wood, cooking at open fires, even buying and selling at tiny stalls. As many as seven or eight sleep in one room of a shanty. There is no electricity, which means that there are no fans; and the fan in Calcutta is a minimal necessity of life for any European, no luxury for any Indian. There is a stand-pipe providing water for 125 people. There is also the khatal. The khatal is the rich man's method of stabling his cattle upon the premises of the poor. Every bustee contains them; it is one way of acquiring a minute income from the rich man, and there is also the consideration of dung which can be collected, shaped into small pots, placed upon the baked earth for drying in the sun, and then used as fuel for the fires. (Moorhouse 1971, pp. 99–100)

The barrio of La Laja [Ciudad Guayana, Venezuela] consists physically of three uneven-shaped blocks of small one-storey houses separated by two wide unpaved streets ... these two main streets serve, if not quite as plazas, at least as semi-enclosed public spaces. Both are used for parking cars and trucks, of which there are likely to be a half dozen in the barrio at normal times. The larger of the two streets has the two-classroom school building at one end and the old school, converted into a community centre, at the other ... Those who feel inclined sweep the streets, especially the part nearest their houses. City trash collection was introduced in La Laja ... and barrels for trash were provided ... but this system has not yet completely supplemented the older method of getting rid of trash by throwing it on the beach or in the brush beside the road to the highway.

There are in the barrio more public water sources, each consisting of two faucets mounted on a cement block... Water is usually turned on for only a few hours in the day; there were often days when no water came at all.

Sewerage runs off toward river or lagoon in earth channels which in a few places have been lined with cement. When channels be come clogged the residents of adjacent houses sometimes clear them out with a spade....

Houses in La Laja are constructed of one of the two main building materials: cement blocks or *bahareque* – earth mixed with manure and straw... Of these two materials *bahareque* represents the traditional and rural, cement blocks the more modern and urban... Houses built originally out of *bahareque* may be rebuilt in cement blocks by building the new walls around or inside the old, and then removing the *bahareque*. This process can be seen going on a good deal of the time ... by now, over a third of the dwellings are cement block.

Almost all houses had a cement floor; most had corrugated iron roofs, though a few were thatched. Only one had glass windows.

All families have at least one fifty-gallon metal drum for water. This is filled either from the public tap, using a hose ... or from one of the water trucks which sell water... Cooking is usually done with kerosene, although two people use bottled gas Most kerosene stoves are simple two or three-burner table models, but a few families have elaborate floor models with oven. Refrigerators are expensive and not general, but are greatly valued. (Peattie, 1968, pp. 13–17)

Downtown Nairobi is beautiful, with its tall buildings, modern architecture and flowering trees... Four miles from the downtown area, along the sides of the Mathare River, live some 10,000 to 20,000 urban squatters. The area ... is ugly. The houses, crammed together in an apparently haphazard fashion dictated by the uneven terrain of the valley's walls, are built of mud and wattle and have roofs made of cardboard, flattened-out tin cans, or even sheet metal. A visitor entering the area is struck by the lack of social services; the roads are makeshift, garbage is piled high in open areas, and children play in the dust...

The inhabitants of Mathare are generally urban misfits and rural outcasts. They lack the skills necessary to find jobs in the modern economy, while at the same time there are no meaningful rural alternatives to which they can turn...

The squatters in Mathare are highly marginal in every sense of the term. Not only are most of them jobless and landless, but their daily existence is highly insecure because of the constant threat of arrest and harassment resulting from the most important local economic activity, the illegal brewing and selling of *pombe* (locally made beer)...

Mathare Valley Village 2 has about 2,000 people living in 700 rooms... The village is long and narrow, running along the hillside for about half a mile, with an average width of about 100 yards. A single path ... is lined by small sparsely stocked shops. Most rooms are about twelve feet by ten feet, and have at least one wooden window which provides light, a wooden door, and unfinished mud walls. Furniture consists of a bed or two, a table, several chairs and stools and sometimes a chest.

The most striking aspect of Mathare 2 however ... is that it is highly organized and politically integrated, apparently in response to the particular set of conditions facing the residents. There is a clearly identifiable group of community leaders who direct the village committee. [The village runs a cooperative society, maintains nursery schools and has a social hall for dances which finance the schools and pay beer fines]. (Ross, 1973, pp. 5–8)

No one would challenge the literal accuracy of these descriptions, nor would one doubt that the insanitary conditions pictured lead to a greater incidence of disease. But would the residents of these shanty towns highlight the same features were they, rather than these sympathetic Western observers, to describe their environment? One suspects that they would not. They too can make the adverse comparison with the neighbouring affluent suburbs; but the shanty-town dweller will also make the comparison with his home area, equally lacking in modern services and in many ways providing a much tougher environment. Water and drainage are certainly desired; but their absence is not likely to be seen as one of the foremost characteristics of the shanty town. The images of the Western observer are a response to his own expected reaction were he to be suddenly thrown into the shanty town. For some city immigrants the move is equally traumatic, for others much less so. At one extreme an indian from the Peruvian Sierra who migrates to Lima may leave a small Quechua-speaking community at an altitude of 12,000 ft for a huge Spanish-speaking city at sea level, enveloped in a low damp cloud for nine months of the year. At the other extreme the Yoruba from a large provincial town finds in the suburbs of Lagos an environment climatically and culturally similar to his home – it is just busier. Yet whether these contrasts are great or small, their effect is usually mitigated by advance knowledge of the city and by the reception given to the new arrival by his already established urban kin. Again the shanty-town resident may well stress the sense of solidarity and cohesion experienced within this small community, contrasting this adversely with the anonymity seen in the planned housing estates.

We of the affluent West look with horror on the processes which we have generated. But what do we know about the feelings of those involved in it? What views of the society and its glaring inequalities are held by the peoples of the slums? How do *they* assess their present squalor and their former rural life against the opportunities to particapate in the technologically modern world? What are their reactions, and how do these relate to the development of the shanty town?

## THE URBAN EXPLOSION

Cities there certainly were in the third world before the recent industrial impact. The capitals of the Indian states with their temples and royal courts often reached a considerable size. Smaller in scale were the cities of savana Africa – the now lost Mali and Songhai, the decaying Timbuktu, the still commercially prosperous Kano. In Latin America the cities of the Aztecs and Incas are mere archaeological ruins. The colonial powers built their own capitals either as annexes to the earlier cities or in new locations, tending here to choose their seaport of entry. These developed modestly as centres of the territory's commercial activity and of its nascent administration, the personnel of which were often as numerous in the provincial hinterland as in the capital. A settled expatriate elite – for example, the Spanish in Lima or the French in Dakar – replicated in the capital the society of their own homeland. But all of these cities, both traditional and colonial, remained relatively small in comparison with the extent of their hinterlands.

The urban explosion has occurred within the past few decades, in many states occurring on a massive scale only after the Second World War. Its causes, in the most general terms, are the increasing industrial activity in the capitals and the spread of social services – at first roads, then education and health facilities – in the rural hinterlands. The figures in Table 2 exemplify the rapidity of its urban growth. Naturally, the smaller the city the greater its proportional rate of growth in the first decades. Later rates of growth look more modest, yet in absolute numbers they reflect a continuing mass movement citywards. Ultimately the flow must moderate as the cities accommodate an increasing proportion of their nation's population; but experts continue to predict steady growth during the remaining years of this century. In Africa and Asia men predominate among the migrants. They come to the city when young, either to save money for marriage or leaving a young

Table 2: Population growth in selected cities 1950–70

| *America* | 1950 | 1970 | *Africa* | 1950 | 1970 | *Asia* | 1950 | 1970 |
|---|---|---|---|---|---|---|---|---|
| Bogotá | 607 | 2500 | Accra | 173 | 750 | Baghdad | 540 | 1250 |
| Caracas | 694 | 2147 | Algiers | 551 | 998 | Bombay | 3335 | 5100 |
| Kingston | 260 | 560 | Dakar | 186 | 600 | Calcutta | 5153 | 7350 |
| Lima-Callao | 947 | 2500 | Khartoum | 230 | 450 | Delhi | 1737 | 3100 |
| Mexico City | 2234 | 3541 | Lagos | 267 | 800 | Djakarta | 1452 | 4500 |
| Rio de Janeiro | 3052 | 7213 | Nairobi | 135 | 500 | Istanbul | 983 | 2600 |
| São Paulo | 2449 | 8405 | | | | Karachi | 1086 | 3246 |
| | | | | | | Singapore | 1022 | 2113 |

Figures, in 000s, from Table E of Davis, (1969).

family at home, but ultimately they bring their families to the city. In Latin America, where young women are employed as domestics, the sex ratio is more nearly equal – and in some areas women migrants predominate. The youth of the migrant leads, in turn, to a growth of city population by natural increase. Thus, in cities of recent expansion, one third of the growth may be attributed to natural increase, two thirds to immigration. In cities which have been expanding for a longer period these proportions become reversed.

Much of the increased city population lives in the shanty towns. In the 1960s these contained a quarter of the population of such cities as Manila and Djakarta, a third of that of Mexico City and a half of that of Ankara and Lima. These proportions are furthermore growing; while the rate of city growth is frequently twice that of natural increase, in some states the shanty towns are growing at rates above 10 per cent, that is at double the growth rate of the city. It has been estimated that by 1990 three quarters of Lima's population will be living in shanty towns.

The greatest rates of growth have occurred in the national

capitals. Generalization is difficult, for some states have many long-established provincial cities, others very few. In some, industrial centres located near a mineral resource have developed in the hinterland, but these have often shown no abnormal growth in recent years. Industry, dominated by multinational companies, has preferred the capital city – often a seaport, close to the political leadership of the country, with technical skills and services more readily available, and the city elite providing a greater part of its local market. The governmental bureaucracies, administering the expanding social services, are largely located in the capitals. So instead of a hierarchy of urban centres, evenly spaced along a continuum, we find the capital city embracing an ever-increasing proportion of the national population, far out-distancing its nearest rivals.

### *Migration*

The urban migrants come from all corners of their nation – and sometimes beyond it. In most cities we find a preponderance of people from the adjacent provinces; but the flow of migrant workers from Malawi and Mozambique to the Republic of South Africa shows that distance can be but a trivial hurdle. There are, it is true, some areas to which knowledge of the modern world has yet to penetrate and these send no men to the city. But from the rest of the country they come both from the most and the least economically developed areas. From the latter, areas without cash crops or mineral resources, men must migrate to earn cash to pay for limited imported necessities and their taxes. While the richer areas provide more opportunities to earn money locally, they have also given their sons more education, raising their aspirations beyond the levels which the local community can satisfy. Throughout the third world the development of agriculture has lagged far behind that of other economic sectors, the apparent breakthrough with fertilizers, new high-yielding strains and the like being of limited or dubious success. The opportunities seen to exist in the city far outweigh those apparent in the rural area. In addition, men are being forced off the land in many places. Improved rural health facilities produce a rapidly rising rural population and thus increasing land shortage; fallow periods are reduced, causing deteriorating fertility; a man may in theory be entitled to as much land from his descent group as he is able to cultivate, but in practice he can be allocated much less. Many new developments favour the richer farmers who buy out their indigent neighbours and rely increasingly on daily paid wage labour. Traditional ties of dependence, such as the Indian *jajmani* relationship between men of high and low caste, assuring the poor of security, are ruptured. State schemes of rationalized land holding and collective and co-operative farms have often resulted in the eviction from the land of those with tenuous legal titles – men in a status of tenancy, or absentees who intend ultimately to return and claim their dormant rights.

In attempting to bring order to an apparently chaotic picture, scholars search for a universal pattern of migration. A step process is postulated in which the migrant successively moves from village to provincial town or mining centre and from thence to the city. This is then replaced by a chain process, as succesful city immigrants encourage their rural kin to travel directly to the metropolis.

Again the migratory process may be seen in terms of the length of stay of the migrants. At one end of a continuum are the seasonal migrants – young men who leave home in the agriculturally slack season for a few successive years. In the past their spare time might have been spent raiding; now they earn to buy a bicycle or blankets. Then there are the 'target' workers who spend a year or two in the city. Their needs are greater – money for bridewealth, for more land, for a sewing machine. But these two categories return to settle in the rural area as traditionally oriented farmers. Increasingly, however, the migrants are spending most of their working lives in the city. They say that they plan to return to their villages but at this stage it is impossible to say how many of them will do so. Among those who are successful in the town some will be able to use their savings to establish themselves in their home area as wealthy farmers or traders; others cannot move to an equivalent job in the village – and by the time that they retire their own children will be adult and established in the city. Though the village may represent the ultimate social security for the poor migrant, he is reluctant to return without visible signs of success; and his urban sojourn may have deprived him of many of his rights to land and status in his home community.

These changes in the pattern of migration are taking place in countries which are themselves rapidly developing. Thus the image of the city presented to the migrant from a near-by area several decades ago is very different from that offered to his more remote counterpart today. Certain political regimes have seemed to discourage migration, others to encourage it with promises of more jobs, better city housing. The mere enumeration of 'push' and 'pull' factors – the opportunities he perceives in the city and the resources available to him to achieve these (his education, his kinship ties), contrasted with the opportunities open to him if he stays in his village – seems too crude a method to describe the choice made by each individual migrant. It is these choices which determine both the rate of migration – how many people leave for the city and for how long – and its incidence – who goes and when: young men about to marry or unable to get a farm of their own, girls seeking to avoid an arranged marriage, and so on.

On arrival in the city the migrant's most urgent needs are accommodation and work. From each continent the evidence is that the newcomer depends initially upon his kin or others from his community. Either his arrival has been planned in advance or he seeks out his relatives immediately upon entering the city. They feed and lodge him. In many cases they are largely instrumental in finding him work, in most they will describe the job market to him.

### *Settlement types*

The residential milieux into which the humble migrant comes are however immensely varied, though universally squalid – the outcome of the poverty of the migrants, the state's lack of resources to cope with housing problems on this scale and the inability or unwillingness of private landlords to supply the deficiency.

Inasmuch as the cities were, until recently, relatively small, their centres have little decaying residential property into which the migrants may move. In fact much of what previously existed has been demolished to make way for planned ultra-modern developments, not only catering for the new need for offices, shops, hotels, etc., but also raising national prestige through the splendour of its capital. Recent private investment in housing for migrants has been extremely small. The nature of the economic development of the third-world nations has been largely inimical to the growth of a flourishing entrepreneurial elite. In India landlords have built tenement blocks. Subsequent rent-control legislation has led them to provide minimal maintenance, and the quality of the accommodation provided has deteriorated rapidly.

In Lima, the *callejones*, narrow alleys leading off the street and lined with single rooms, provided accommodation in the heart of the city until the 1930s, when this type of development was halted. In Lagos and other Nigerian towns successful early migrants have purchased land from local owners and, over a number of years, built imposing houses. The owner may occupy the upper storey (until in his affluence he moves to an even better property), leasing the ground floor to migrant tenants. Most migrants here are in fact housed in this type of dwelling. But such a development depends upon a number of factors – the existence of a local entrepreneurial talent (absent over much of Africa) with wealth generated in local commercial activity (absent, for instance, in a mining settlement); the ability of local landlords to acquire land and develop it without restriction (impossible where the state controls all vacant land); the willingness of such a landlord to share his housing with other migrants (possible where all have similar rural origins, unlikely where caste or major ethnic differences exist – where the landlords for instance are of European stock, the migrants Indians).

In the colonial period, governments, the public corporations and many industrial enterprises located far from established centres of population were obliged to provide accommodation for their own employees. Thus a variety of forms of 'barracks' or 'compounds' are found within the urban areas. But the ability of governments to provide further housing has been limited. The third-world countries have neither the money nor the technical skills to mount a city housing programme on the scale demanded by the recent immigration. Furthermore, the absence of an effective policy for housing the very poor reflects in some cases a desire to discourage immigration, in other cases a preference, in allocating scarce resources, for benefiting the richer classes. A very rich country, such as the Republic of South Africa, with a rigid control of urban population and movement, may with techniques of prefabricated construction, build townships providing a high standard of accommodation, however much they lack individuality or personal freedom. Elsewhere, housing estates or 'urbanizations' are built to such high building standards that they are beyond the reach of all but the highest-paid employees; rules prohibit the sub-letting of rooms to lodgers, thus depriving the owners of a secondary income; the development of local marketing or artisan trades is impeded, again preventing the owners and their kin from establishing secondary occupations. With too little to spend, the authorities lend to those who will repay with most speed and certainty, to the established migrant with a good job.

Too poor to purchase land and build a house within a reasonable time, unwilling to continue to pay rent for decaying accommodation or perhaps unable to find a room for his own family, the migrant is impelled towards the illegal occupation of land, to become a squatter. Within the city, shacks constructed of waste materials – whatever is best suited to keep out rain or sun – are erected on any vacant lot. Individually of small extent, these sites grow by slow accretion. G. Moorhouse describes one such settlement in the heart of Calcutta:

For five hundred yards or so there is a confusion of packing cases, corrugated iron, straw matting, odd bricks and wads of newspaper arranged into a double-decker sequence of boxes. Each box is approximately the size of a small pigeon loft, with room in it to squat and only just to kneel . . . each box is the sleeping and living quarters of a family. The rest of their life is conducted on the pavement where they cook and play and quarrel together. (1971, pp. 95–6)

More striking are the vast peripheral squatter settlements, often founded by 'invasion'. Classically these are a Latin American phenomenon. They are the creation of migrants already established within the city – would-be migrants dispersed throughout the rural areas could never organize in this way. After months of secret preparation a group of families, at night or during a public holiday, invades a large area of vacant land and within a few hours has demarcated it into substantial plots on which individuals erect a temporary shelter. Attempts by the police to halt the action may be brutal but not sustained. As the occupants feel more secure in their position and save, so they construct more durable houses. Thus in Lima, *barriadas* formed twenty years ago as a sea of crude matting shelters are now well established with many good-quality houses, differing from the housing estates largely in their greater variety of style and affluence. Such settlements are well laid-out but of very low density; in many senses they represent an unproductive use of scarce city land (they tend too to be far from the loci of employment). Local entrepreneurs develop a transport system of buses and taxis, but until the government recognizes their existence, these settlements lack water and electricity, schools and dispensaries.

Unable to provide cheap housing yet willing to acknowledge the migrant's desire to build his own house, governments have recourse to two solutions. In 'site-and-service' schemes, the public authority lays out the area with roads and services, the site owner then constructing his house with materials centrally provided. Here the degree of control exercised can yet stifle individual initiative. Alternatively, the existing squatter settlement can be recognized and services provided; it is 'upgraded'. The *barriadas* of Lima have become the *pueblos jovenes* – young towns. But the tasks of improvement are still immense and efforts are likely to be concentrated in a very few areas to the neglect of the remainder.

The city slums are far from static. In the inner city, apartments decay further, and the illegal shanties are hardly capable of improvement. Some of the peripheral squatter settlements improve noticeably over a decade, others seem to stagnate. And all the time people are moving in and out of the slums.

Some are seen as 'bridgeheads' – places where the new migrant first settles, close to his kin and employment so that he can seize upon an opportunity suddenly presented. Later, with a steady job he moves to an area thought desirable for permanent residence and the raising of a family. A progression from city centre to peripheral settlement and perhaps then to a housing estate is thus postulated. But the settled shanty-town dweller becomes an obvious host for the new generation of migrants, who thus move directly from village to the peripheral area. The physical characteristics of each individual slum vary enormously – we may associate each with a population which is making a success of urban life or failing hopelessly. Yet within each such area the variety in the characteristics of the individual inhabitants is often equally great – the recently arrived and the long-established, the relatively successful and the failures, the hopeful and the despairing.

### *Work*

The quality of slum housing is but a reflection of the poverty of the migrants. They come to the city with no savings and, in most cases, few skills beyond bare literacy (or less), only to find that the opportunities for wage earning are far exceeded by their numbers.

A feature of modern capitalism is the increasing concentration of industry using advanced technology in the existing industrial centres. The export of manufactured goods has killed many traditional crafts in the third world; yet there are exceptions to these rules. The location of specific resources has governed the siting of certain industries in the poorer nations. Cheap labour for the assembly of partially manufactured items can outweigh the increased costs of transporting these items and the finished product across oceans. The large cities with their limited markets provided by their more affluent citizens attract import-substituting manufacturers. Thus the manufacturing sector in most of the third-world countries has, in the past three decades, grown quite phenomenally, though its beginnings were so small that it still does not account for more than a small part of the national income. Nevertheless the flow of investment capital from the West to the third-world countries is still minute compared with flows within the industrialized world. Furthermore, the new investments in many a third-world country are annually exceeded by an outflow of wealth in the form of profits accruing to multinational corporations, and debt repayments. The economic growth of the third world depends upon that of the industrialized nations – though some of the former states are strengthening their bargaining power and now speak of 'negotiated dependency'.

Much of the new industry is capital-intensive. One Latin American estimate suggests that in the 1940s 1 per cent growth in industry resulted in 0·6 per cent more jobs; in the 1950s the proportion of new jobs had fallen to 0·26 per cent. In some African states the numbers in wage employment actually fell for a short period as modern methods of road construction, for instance, replaced the traditional labour-intensive practices. In the modern industrial establishments, and especially those of multinational corporations, conditions of work tend to be good: wages are high (relative to earnings in other local sectors, though not to Western wage levels) and labour turnover tends to be low. The skilled workers in these firms have been termed a 'labour aristocracy'. They are the favoured ones – but they are only a very small minority of the total wage-earning labour force, most of whom are unskilled workers in these firms or in the public services, or are employees of smaller oriental or local companies, domestics and the like.

Alternative modes of employment open to the migrant are varied. He may become a self-employed artisan, and if successful employ not only family labour but also journeymen and apprentices. He may trade – at levels ranging from peddling a tray full of articles through the streets to wholesaling. Professional services – laundry, barbering, prostitution – also serve the needs of the slum population. With continued immigration to the cities it is this sector of the economy which is expanding most rapidly. A few successful persons are fully occupied by their work. Others find that custom comes very intermittently. The divisions between employment, underemployment and unemployment become almost impossible to define or measure. Census figures often fail to distinguish clearly between the wage earner in manufacturing industry and the self-employed artisan. They do disclose a growth in the tertiary or service sectors which embraces many of the activities just cited.

The contrast between the modern factory worker and the self-employed artisan or petty trader is so stark that the designation of the dual economy seems obviously meaningful. Differences exist in scale, in levels of technology, in the relationships between those engaged in production. Yet a more precise division is fraught with difficulties of definition. If we speak of traditional and modern sectors, where do we place the artisan who repairs radios? His relationship with apprentices is traditional, but his craft is modern, albeit relatively labour- rather than capital-intensive. A division between wage earners and self-employed is not valid either, for many artisans, traders and professionals employ assistants – in fact at extremely low wages. The terms 'formal' and 'informal' economy are no less ambiguous than others, but they are becoming increasingly accepted as economists recognize the existence of the latter and consider its present and future role in the economy. I shall use these terms in this book. Other terms used to express the same dichotomy are organized/unorganized, reflecting much the same characteristics as formal/informal, and enumerated/unenumerated, reflecting the dearth of statistical data concerning the latter sector. One corollary of this is that the formal sector is a recipient of state aid and recognition, whereas the informal sector generally is not.

But the dichotomy implied by the concept of the dual economy is misleading, for it obscures the interdependence of the two sectors. The growing informal sector has emerged because the city-based formal economy has not been able to absorb the waves of immigrants. It is argued furthermore that the low wages of the formal sector (and corresponding profits) are possible because the informal sector supplied to its workers cheap goods and services. Economists are divided however between those who see the informal sector as parasitic – it should be abolished or absorbed within the formal sector – and those who claim its potential for development. Hitherto, governments have tended to cramp its development with petty restrictions concerning licences, etc, whereas they could encourage it by providing credit, while large factories might recruit artisans to make certain parts in their local workshops. A developing local entrepreneurship is envisaged – but this is countered by the fear that as soon as a local businessman has established a profitable enterprise serving a growing local market, he will be taken over or squeezed out by the larger companies mass producing the same product. Many proposals for the development of the informal sector seem politically impracticable given the existing involvement of national elite and leaders in the formal sector. The measures here suggested seem mere palliatives, shoring up the existing structure, maintaining the gap between rich and poor but spreading poverty a little more evenly.

While analysts contrast the structural differences between formal and informal sectors, the migrant himself sees them as alternative but interlinked routes to success. A good wage-earning job is valued for the security it provides, the savings which it permits. But self-employment is often valued above commitment to the factory and the worker aspires to set up his own business, using his savings and skills learned from the employment. Manual work in a factory provides little scope for advancement; in self-employment the successful man can rise not only to wealth but also to positions of prestige and leadership within the community.

While the 'problem' of the slums is usually seen by governments in terms of housing policies and the provision of social services, their long-term future clearly depends on the rate and mode of economic development. Will the small-scale enterprises be fostered and protected? Will the modern sector enterprise expand sufficiently to absorb, as wage labour, the majority of migrants? Or will the slums grow increasingly impoverished as neither sector of the economy provides the migrants with an opportunity to achieve a reasonable living standard?

## ATTITUDES AND POLICIES

We look upon these slums as external observers from the affluent, industrial West, and most of the vast literature is by authors sharing the same viewpoint. Our own reactions have come to dominate our analysis of the situation. Emotionally we contrast the squalor of the slums, negating all our own standards of privacy and cleanliness, with an image of idyllic rural life in which disease resulting from such factors as an inadequate water supply, fears of witchcraft caused by interpersonal tensions, are conveniently excluded. We feel guilty that man should have fallen so low. We fear the spread of diseases from the insanitary shanties to the decorous suburbs. The 'invasions' of squatters are deemed as an assault upon private property (and we overlook the obvious desire of the squatters to own their own home) and the affluent live in terror of the unstructured violence of the mob. These fears are increased by Western radicals who, in hope, predict that the urban poor will spearhead, or at least sustain, the coming revolution.

Scholarly explanations, some of which will be outlined in the following chapter, in part reflect these 'gut' reactions. The immigrant poor are described as marginal to society – not fully integrated with it. The cause of their poverty is associated with the values which they hold – values which are the product either of their traditional society or of their present poverty. The 'culture of poverty' is seen as a self-sustaining system, a vicious circle. The process of adaptation to urban life is seen in terms of contrasting structures, the urban and the rural, which compete for the allegiance of the migrant.

These attitudes are in turn mirrored in the policies adopted towards the slum settlements. Complete eradication was often demanded, though infrequently practised. An evicted population would merely move to a new corner of the city and liberal opinion would be outraged by the severity of the action. It is easier to ignore the slums – in many cities they do not feature on the town plans except as unexplained blanks. The attempts to frustrate invasions are often token. It is cheaper for the government to lose land than to provide housing, and it may not be unwilling to snub the owners of private land so seized. Voluntary agencies in turn invade the slums, directing their energies largely to the education of the poor, to the inculcation of those values which will enable them to take advantage of the opportunities which urban society is supposed to offer.

Changed attitudes have developed during the past decade. Political leaders, anxious for the support of the numerically increasing slum population specifically at election times, have promised and implemented schemes of improvement such as those outlined above. On the academic front the picture of slum apathy and violence was countered by descriptions of vitality, achievement and petit bourgeois conservatism given by social anthropologists who lived among the poor. In particular an alliance between William Mangin, an American anthropologist, and John Turner, a British architect, who advocated the development of self-help policies in Peruvian squatter settlements, both reflected and reinforced a change of policy in Peru which extended throughout Latin America and beyond. The rival viewpoints proceed from different ways of explaining man's actions in society. One sees him as blindly accepting the fate thrust upon him, responding emotionally to its strains; the other portrays him as rationally calculating the possible outcome of the opportunities offered to him and seeking his own self-interest. But equally it may be argued that observers are focusing upon two different types of slums. Mangin and Turner, and many of the subsequent commentators, have described Latin American squatter settlements, formed by invasions, which have undoubtedly improved in quality. It seems hard to transpose many of the generalizations derived therefrom to the worst of Calcutta's hutment areas.

Western concepts of poverty have frequently distinguished the 'deserving' from the 'undeserving' poor. The former accept the dominant values of their society. They aspire to better themselves or, at least, to achieve respectability in fulfilling social norms. The latter reject these values. In the eyes of the 'middle classes' the former merit assistance, the latter punishment. This dichotomy is parallelled by the classification by Stokes of 'slums of hope' and 'slums of despair'. The former are peopled by the upwardly mobile, the latter by the downwardly mobile. In each case a subdivision is made reflecting the degree of mobility actually possible rather than that expected. The slums of hope will become integrated into the mass of the working populations; the slums of despair will remain, the homes of the dregs of society, the dropouts. Though seeking a universally valid classification Stokes remarked that his slums of hope seemed to embrace many third-world settlements, 'the home of the stranger, the in-migrant, the recent arrival ... attracted to the city by the social or economic opportunities the city offers ... [or] driven from their homes in the countryside by economic, political or social upheaval' (1962, pp. 189–90). The designation seems particularly appropriate to third-world shanty towns, as will be demonstrated in later chapters. In many cases the migrants have come from societies with a strong emphasis on individual achievement: their journey to the city was a conscious move for self-improvement, their success in finding work and establishing a home in the city a demonstration of their achievement – and those goals unattainable by themselves might still be available to their children; many of the social relationships in which they are enmeshed stress individual patronage rather than collective action.

Yet the term slums of hope seems to raise a number of paradoxes or contradictions. The shanty town, at least in its early stages, presents a picture of such primitive living conditions that it is hard to imagine its people as happy, achievement-oriented and hopeful. It is so much easier to assume that such poverty would lead to social disorganization, with its attendant violence, apathy, broken families. Undoubtedly these do exist – yet those who have lived in such areas stress the former attitudes as being more prevalent. They also prefer to stress such characteristics, for it is through these that self-improvement or mobilization is possible.

But is the hope justified – will it last? A new generation of shanty-town dwellers is being born in the city knowing little of rural life and of their parents' feeling of achievement in having broken with it, and successfully establish themselves in the urban area. Will the economy expand so as to provide the improved social mobility anticipated – or will there be stagnation?

The emphasis on hope and achievement is convenient too for the upper classes, for it suggests a lower class which is willing to integrate itself into the dominant culture, and furthermore to raise itself by its own bootstraps, thus necessitating no major redistribution of income. Yet these attitudes of the poor do not appear, in practice, to be incompatible with a distrust of government, though in the circumstances political opposition is weakly articulated and difficult to mobilize.

## METHODOLOGIES

The term 'slums of hope' needs a big question mark. In posing such a question we quickly realize how little we know of the migrants' hope and frustrations – how *do* they see the world in which they live? And furthermore why should we want to know this? I would give two answers.

Inasmuch as we are trying to work with people in the shanty town we must be able to communicate with them. At the very least this means understanding (or not misunderstanding) the concepts used. Thus I have heard Western-educated Nigerians use the term 'working class' to refer to senior civil servants (who work harder than others), and when a recent newspaper article referred to 'working-class wives' it clearly meant professional women who work for a salary rather than in petty trade or craft. Our goals may be valued differently from those of the shanty-town dweller. How often have community development schemes, sponsored from outside, failed, as the recipients could not understand what was being done for them? And how often have the organizers then blamed the failure on the recipients, ignorance and traditional attitudes? Middle-class radicals too can make the same mistakes. As Hector Bejar has written, the Peruvian left 'has always approached reality from the point of view of its own pre-conceived systems . . . The ideals proclaimed by the guerillas appeared remote to the peasants ... guerillas must act not only for the distant objectives of the revolution but also for the immediate ones of the peasant and not only *for* the peasants but *with* them' (1970, pp. 126, 116, 118).

Secondly the actor's view of the situation is an essential ingredient of our own analysis of the same situation as external observers. This raises a dichotomy – our view and his. We are all trying to do the same thing – to find patterned regularity in the world about us, to predict confidently the outcomes of observed and intended events. How do we relate these two images? At one extreme it is argued that both images are equally valid. Some would go as far as to assert that reality exists only in the mind of the observer. The dichotomy is also presented in the distinction between subjective and objective views of the world. Here the difference lies not merely in the position from which actor and observer view a situation. The subjective view of the actor is held to be biased by his personal preferences. In contrast the observer uses superior concepts, tested in the world of scholarship, and has access to information 'scientifically' or 'objectively' collected. At its most arrogant objectivity suggests a correct view of reality, subjectivity an incorrect one, a false consciousness perhaps.

My own stance lies between these extremes. We view, as external observers, a world peopled by actors. We see the world as presenting certain opportunities for action. We then ask how far these opportunities are perceived by the people themselves. How do they evaluate different goals? What routes do they see to their attainment, how do they assess and marshal their resources in striving for the goals, and in the end what do they do? We see what were the consequences intended by the actors; but from our own rather different analysis of the situation, our access to different types of information, we may well predict a different course of events. However, if we are to be able to predict how the actor will act in a given situation we must try to assess *his* view of that situation. In other words, we operate with a rational model of a man (man making choices, making decisions) rather than with a normative model (man, robot-like, acting according to the norm of his society) or with a structural model (man blindly swept along by unseen and unknown forces). (For instance Samir Amin (1975) has argued that a study of migration has no place for any discussion of the motives of individual migrants in choosing when and where to travel – economic forces alone determine the migratory pattern).

There are, too, behaviourists who would not deny the relevance of the actor's interpretation of a situation but who believe that it is impossible to establish with sufficient certainty what that interpretation is. Hence we should content ourselves with descriptions of what people actually do, and predict on this basis only. The difficulties are accepted – and in Chapter 3 I endeavour to assess some of them. But just as medical science proceeds not through the statistical testing of new drugs – approved drugs work in an acceptable number of cases with few side-effects – but through the attempts of pharmacologists, biochemists and others to establish why a given compound has the noted effect, so too must we try, however crude our efforts, to establish how observed behaviour comes to be generated.

To see the world through the eyes of one's subjects is the task of the social anthropologist. As Malinowski stated, his goal is to 'grasp the native's point of view, his relation to life, to realize *his* view of *his* world' (1922, p. 25). But the anthropologist who wishes to work in the shanty towns faces problems not shared by his colleagues in a traditional village community. The village is usually a clearly bounded unit, though not of course exclusive; but the slum dweller lives far from his work, his kin are scattered across the city, the pace and rigour of city life give him little time for relaxed talk with the research worker. To the anthropologist himself the discomforts of life in a hut in a remote village are negligible in comparison with residence in most slums. In the village he does not share his life with social equals but on his visits to them in the city he can reassume his Western roles. The anthropologist in the city must simultaneously maintain satisfactory relationships both with informants and with mentors and officials in the local university and government departments. The 'rural' anthropologist will, typically, want to preserve the society which he studies, or at least to shield its members from the vast traumas of Western contact. The 'urban' anthropologist cannot wish to preserve the way of life of his subjects but is likely to become personally involved in schemes to alleviate their poverty and distress. Detached observation is replaced by active participation, and a host of ethical problems then loom larger. How far may one use one's subjects for scientific research?

Having settled upon a role and a method of research the urban anthropologist must next face the problem of seeing the world through the eyes of his informants. This has not, in the past, bothered the social anthropologist working in the traditional manner. His society seemed exotic, he recorded behaviour and the actors' explanations, but nevertheless he tended to slant his own written account either towards his society's image of itself or towards his own analysis of social life. For the urban anthropologist, less involved with witchcraft and rituals, more with familiar issues of housing, education and jobs, it becomes much harder not to impose one's own concepts and propositions in one's explanation of one's subjects' attitudes and activities. How far can one go in presenting the world view of another, and an abstract one at that, while excluding, as far as is possible, one's own self? The issue is so complex that one must, I feel, justify one's own position and mode of analysis, and this I attempt in the third chapter.

Finally, the problem of generalization. The traditional social anthropologist lives in one village for a year or so, visits one or two others, finds them basically similar and presents a monograph valid for the entire ethnic group. The urban anthropologist is immediately aware of the uniqueness of his own field work site. The slums range from municipally or employer-owned apartment blocks to the hovels constructed from debris by their owners. Some are long-established, others recent; some are slums of hope, others of despair. The characteristics of the inhabitants vary equally widely – young, old, recent migrant, second-generation, educated, illiterate, skilled manual employee, self-employed petty trader. Conclusions deriving from one's own little area seem dubiously valid for any other area within the city, let alone cities in neighbouring states or other continents with vastly different cultural backgrounds. Yet one sees the urban explosion as a universal phenomenon, generated by factors which are common and not restricted to particular nations. Superficially the character of the migrations and of the migrants themselves, as disclosed in the literature, has a number of features in common. One is tempted in summarizing these findings, to present a picture of an 'ideal' or 'typical' shanty town, a yardstick against which the 'deviations' of others may be measured. This, however, is not my intention in this book. Inevitably generalizations must be made. But the purpose of such statements is to present a variable which seems to me to be a significant one. Thus in the following chapters, in which I describe the social backgrounds from which the migrants come, the manner of their migration to the city and their establishment, the work they do, their economic relationships and their aspirations, and the political activity in which they participate, I shall on one hand be attempting a summary and generalization, and on the other hand setting out a number of factors which are of significance in our task of presenting the slum dweller's view of this world.

The world is complex. The simple dimensional explanation is inadequate. Peasant revolutions, it is claimed, are the work of middle peasants – but such a generalization closely fits only a few cases. The main thrust of revolutionary activity in third-world countries is expected, variously, from skilled workers, the lumpenproletariat and the peasants; these expectations are then defended more often in terms of ideology than of empirical investigation. But we can go too far in the other direction and believe that the multiplicity of variables makes prediction impossible. I think that a limited number of variables are important, and it is these which I have outlined in the following chapters. I am, therefore, not only trying to give an overview of the third-world shanty town, showing how attitudes of hope and achievement derive from the present and poor experiences of the migrants and are demonstrated in their daily activities and modes of co-operative organization; I am trying too to provide a framework of analysis which will enable the reader to assess a given situation and to draw his own conclusions.

I intend to limit my discussion to what I shall term the shanty town. This I define as a settlement composed of recent migrants (thus excluding second-generation migrants in long-established communities) who are poor (thus excluding the highly skilled workers, clerks and professionals, usually well educated). These poor migrants live in houses largely constructed by themselves, whether all are owner-occupiers or some live as tenants of richer members. Thus I exclude the inner-city tenements, the compounds built by employers for their own workers, the housing estates built by large construction companies and state agencies. As so defined, the shanty towns of the third world vary widely; yet in excluding other types of settlement we may focus upon those which do have much in common.

The literature on third-world slums is vast and increasing, but the contribution of social anthropologists is as yet extremely meagre. Urban anthropology is now established as a recognized arm of the discipline, but it attracts few adherents though their number grows. The vivid accounts given by Oscar Lewis have, by their lack of rigorous analysis, made less impact within the profession than their popularity outside it would suggest. At a recent international anthropological congress over two thousand papers were presented, yet less than twenty dealt specifically with the third-world slums – one per cent of the papers to describe the life of a quarter of the population embraced by anthropology. Nevertheless much of that written in other circumstances is germane to our account. Governments and international aid-giving bodies have called for statistical surveys to illuminate for them the nature and scale of their problems. And inasmuch as we extrapolate attitudes from experiences, data on the mode of migration, or nature of employment, for instance, are essential. Surveys carried out by university departments of the social sciences account for most of the literature on Indian slums. It is perhaps paradoxical that the most academically significant work in Africa has been carried out in the central and southern states in which laws of residential segregation have often prevented the social anthropologist from living among his subjects of study. The literature from Latin America is far richer; but sociologists and political scientists anxious to account for the degree of organization apparent in a land invasion (contrary to the conventional image of apathy) or the conservatism of slum dwellers have, in their scientific questionnaires and in their general approach to the issues studied, clearly imposed a framework of their own concepts on to the situations studied. Very few scholars, and most of them are social anthropologists, have made any attempt to present the view of the world held by the subjects of their studies.

The ideas expressed in this book reflect strongly my own experiences in towns of Western Nigeria and more recently in Lima. It is through eyes coloured by situations in these areas that I have viewed the literature. However, as I hope will be abundantly clear, I do not attempt to provide a definitive description of third-world shanty towns, nor, even less, prescribe policies of action. I shall raise more questions than I can ever answer. I invite the reader to set aside for a brief moment his own preconceptions of these slums, his own ideas of the solutions to their problems and to ask instead how their inhabitants view the world in which they live and what they are doing about it.

# 2 Poverty: Attitudes and Policies of Dominant Groups

Before describing the characteristics of the shanty town and attempting to see how such settlements might look to their residents, we ought first to consider how the outside world looks at them. The attitudes of the dominant groups in society, expressed in their public utterances, their overt behaviour, in the ideologies propagated by church or political party are all part of the environment in which the immigrants' own ideas are formulated – they may consciously reject them, but many (domestic servants for instance) only too readily expound the views of their employers. Equally influential are the policies pursued by the dominant groups – punitive slum clearance, obstruction to or encouragement of individual effort, charitable works to alleviate suffering or planned attempts to raise the levels of social consciousness. These policies reflect, in turn, the social opinions of the dominant group, the political persuasion of contemporary governments and their resources. Here I wish very briefly to outline the diverse character of the dominant groups in third-world nations and of the policies adopted, and then to examine how popular attitudes are reflected in academic approaches.

In the third-world nations the dominant groups control the national power structure, they are in alliance with international capitalism and often own and control smaller local enterprises. Their control of the economy, such as it is, is exercised through the alliances, ownerships and control of the state bureaucracy. Yet these groups have very diverse social origins. Do these, one wonders, correlate with the attitudes expressed towards the shanty towns or the poor in general?

## DOMINANT ELITES

At one extreme one finds the dominant elite of the newly independent tropical African state composed of men and women who have come from the same villages as the residents of the shanty towns. High-ranking politicians and civil servants have among their close kin not only those who are subsistence farmers but also petty traders and artisans in the city. At the other extreme lie the Latin American states, together with South Africa and Rhodesia, where the dominant elite is racially distinct from the mass of the indigenous population. Here however a contrast lies between the South African regimes, which practise apartheid, and those in Latin America, which refuse to give official recognition to racial categories or which positively glorify the historical heritage of their indigenous peoples – populist policies which may, however, be belied in everyday social interaction. Let us elaborate these distinctions.

Tropical Africa was colonized in the latter half of the nineteenth century. Although commerce had affected the development of the indigenous Negro societies in the previous four centuries, they remained economically backward. Because of the climate, permanent European settlement was, in most areas, on a very small scale (Dakar in Senegal and Kenya are among the exceptions). The ruling elite of the colonial state thus consisted of the expatriate administrative officials allied with other expatriate traders and missionaries. The British preferred a policy of 'indirect rule' – local government through the institutions of the indigenous people. The French ruled 'directly' through African appointees. In practice this divergence in policy was more theoretical than real. Both colonial powers trained cadres of junior executives. The British saw their colonial structure as something which would wither away when, in the distant future, the African peoples gained independence. They tended to despise the African who sought to emulate the British way of life and its values. Yet many educated Africans did so, and these formed the nuclei of the early nationalist parties – one of their main grievances being their non-acceptance in white colonial society. The French 'assimilated' those who became full acculturated, but the numbers who passed this test were small. The latter too were among the early nationalists, and today it is they who develop the tenets of *négritude* – the definition in Western terms of these concepts seen in the traditional culture which are held to be valuable and relevant in contemporary society.

In these colonial territories a small number of men managed to gain a high standard of education. These came variously from high- and low-status homes in indigenous societies. In Buganda for example, a precariously placed ruling elite espoused Western influence and missionary education and sent its sons to school. Elsewhere missions were welcomed by peoples low in prestige – the slave-raided rather than the raiders – and they quickly accepted education. The rich traders and chiefs of a community would perhaps send one or two children to school, valuing their skills in writing and arithmetic but fearing the damage that proselytization might do to their families' reputations. The poor saw in schooling an avenue to success alternative to the indigenous one which denied them opportunities. The provision of education remained very low until the Second World War. But in the pre-independence decade the expansion was phenomenal. While educated parents tended to ensure that their children received as good an education or better than themselves, thousands were drawn into the educational system from humble homes. Thus in the past three decades one has witnessed the rapid upward mobility of a few, often from homes of illiterate subsistence-farmer parents to high positions in government. Yet those who have made this move are able to perpetuate their own status in that of their children – they ensure that the children attend fee-paying primary schools, the more prestigious secondary schools and overseas universities and so qualify for elite offices and occupations.

The early nationalist movements were composed of professional men residing in the cities. Parliamentary government tended to discriminate against these as members of legislatives were expected, *de jure* or *de facto*, to be natives of their constituencies. With the demise of colonialism, Africans moved into positions in the administrative structure vacated by the Europeans, assuming the salary scales of the latter – and in some cases their furnished homes. In the early post-war years the African elite comprised the elected politicians together with the civil servants and professionals – teachers, doctors, lawyers. Later this category has diversified with the growth of national armies and the emergence of a military elite, and also with the expansion of manufacturing industry and commerce, with some Africans taking positions in the multinational companies, becoming a 'comprador bourgeoisie' and occasionally, though still few in number and influence, developing their own businesses. Competition for power between these groups within the dominant elite is today potential rather than significant – differences of interest are muted by the realization of a common privileged status, ties of kinship and schooling.

Those who have succeeded in reaching this elite tend to justify their success in terms of their own hard work. They look upon their poor relatives as unfortunates, the black sheep of their families. Yet they are disposed to help them towards their own success both from feelings of family loyalty and from fears that the poverty of the poor may lead to criminality which would damage the reputations of their elite kin. The poor, for their part, applaud the success of their kinsmen, see it as an example to be emulated and hope to manipulate the, perhaps rapidly weakening, ties to their own advantage.

A very different picture is presented by the Latin American state. The Spanish and Portuguese conquerors, though few in number, settled there. The land and its people were allocated to them and they maintained their style of life through the surplus extracted from farm and mine. Spanish (or Portuguese) institutions were imposed upon the country and indigenous language, religion or forms of community government persisted by default rather than by design. The white population lived on its estates, in the larger provincial towns and in the national capital. In the beginning of the nineteenth century the locally born and resident whites revolted against the European colonial rulers and, following the example of the United States, declared their independence. But although these states gained their freedom half a century or more before the African peoples lost theirs, the patterns of recent economic development have been substantially similar.

The 'Latin' colonizers, unlike their Anglo-Saxon counterparts, permitted miscegenation and there developed over the centuries a substantial mestizo population. In many states this now substantially outnumbers those designated as indian. In Peru however almost one half of the population has in recent censuses been described as indian, most of these still speaking Quechua and having little knowledge of Spanish, and many of them continuing to live in indigenous communities preserving traditions of Inca and pre-Inca cultures though with substantial Spanish overlay. While in the urban society one sees the mestizo trying with success to enter white society, in the rural area his accentuated preference for Spanish life styles, though often severely constrained by a low income, brings him into sharp conflict with the indian.

In the past century, the process of miscegenation has been paralleled by a substantial continuing immigration from Europe – and not merely from the Mediterranean but also from northern European countries. Though the migrants have settled permanently, they tend nevertheless to retain strong ties of sentiment with their continent of origin and more active ties with kin in neighbouring Latin American states. There has thus developed an elite which is cosmopolitan in its outlook but still very 'white' in culture and orientation, and thus opposed (in a classificatory sense) to the indigenous population.

The Latin American elite is both larger and more structurally complex than its African counterpart. In the nineteenth century political parties tended to represent factions within the elite, military leaders assuming power during periods of impasse. More recently conflicts of interest between landowners and the emergent industrialists have provided the bases for political struggle, with the latter victorious in the long run. The earlier development of industry has been paralleled by the rise of trade unions, which have in recent decades played a more significant role than in Africa where the post-independence government have tended to co-opt the union membership into the national politically dominant elite.

The predominantly urban developments would seem to put the Latin American states well ahead of their African counterparts. Yet the colonial powers in Africa placed more stress on the albeit slow development of the rural area. In Latin America there have been few educational opportunities for the indian (or the poor mestizo) until recently, and in consequence few opportunities for mobility into upper urban strata. In British colonial territories primary education began in the vernacular language, passing to a dominance of English in the final years; secondary schooling was conducted entirely in English. Vernacular languages, understood by both judges and parties, were used in local customary courts, though the records were written in English. In Peru, in contrast, it is only in recent years that a military government has decreed that Quechua should be a nationally recognized language on a par with Spanish, and should be taught in all schools, and this policy, for practical reasons, has yet to be implemented. In the Latin American state, post-primary education has been largely restricted to the children of the upper strata. Those in dominant positions have been able to transfer their status to their offspring and there has been relatively little recruitment from lower strata in either urban or rural areas.

Between these two extremes lie countless intermediate situations. In India, for instance, a longer history of British-type schooling has produced families, such as those of Jawaharlal Nehru and his daughter Indira Gandhi, educated over several generations. A Western-oriented elite dominating the public services contrasts with one more attuned to Indian tradition – exemplified by Mrs Gandhi's predecessor in office, Lal Bahadur Shastri. The national, educated elite contrasts too with the provincial elite of wealthy landowners and traders, active and prominent in the political parties.

These differences in the composition of the ruling groups do seem to have affected the manner in which scholars have presented their problems. Thus in British Africa in the 1950s attention was focused on 'detribalization'. The colonial powers had sought to maintain the integrity of indigenous institutions, yet these were weakened by the migration to the towns of men who were seen as moving from a series of well-defined statuses to a situation where they would experience anomie. Psychological research was directed towards the discovery and measurement of mental breakdown among migrants. Detribalization was seen as a problem. The counter view was developed by the scholars of the Rhodes Livingstone Institute who argued that the migrant assumed roles in an urban structure and by many other social anthropologists who demonstrated that the migrants were adapting to and even manipulating the urban situation. The Latin American emphasis on marginality reflects not the fears of expatriate colonial administrators but those of an entrenched urban elite, culturally European, who see a threatening hoard of aliens. In Peru, the *cholo*, the indian who comes to the city, was distinguished from the *mestizo*, the person of mixed blood; for while the former has adopted many Spanish traits of dress and language he remains tied to his indian community; the mestizo, on the other hand, has always identified closely with Spanish culture and has rejected the indian heritage. Would the process of cholofication produce an alternative national culture or transform the existing culture? The British colonialist, in his attempt to preserve the traditional culture, saw in urban migration a threat to his policies; the Spanish in Latin America had done their best to destroy the indigenous cultures – migration, for the elite, threatened their own city-based culture. Neither of these views is however shared by the educated African.

From the early years of this century, the predominantly white urban intelligentsia of the Latin American cities, oriented culturally towards Europe, provided a fertile ground for radical ideas. Many young intellectuals expounded Marxism, and political parties developed with specifically socialist policies. Novel ideas emerged as these radical leaders reinterpreted classical Marxism in the light of their country's problems. Yet these men remained enmeshed in the class structure of their own societies – their ideas were debated in literary journals, in universities and in cafés, but their personal contact with the poor remained minimal. In Africa the influence of Marxism came much later. Students from French colonial territories studying in Paris came under the spell of radical ideologies as their counterparts from British territories did not. Radical analyses in English come more often from Western scholars than from the African himself, who so often seems to be more preoccupied in creating a niche for himself in the new affluence than in criticizing its structure.

Though scholars may formulate their problems in different ways, one finds a substantial uniformity in the general attitudes of dominant groups towards the shanty towns and their people. Whether they are a long-established oligarchy or *nouveaux riches* they, like the European upper-middle classes of the nineteenth century, fear the 'dangerous classes', seeing in them a threat to their property and to their health. Three quotations, one from each continent, exemplify the range of attitudes.

Mangin quotes an American doctor who, reflecting the views of his Peruvian colleague, wrote:

> In this enormous slum lived some 15,000 people many of whom had come down from the mountains, lured by communist agitators. Why starve on a farm, the agitators asked, when well-paid jobs, good food, housing and education were waiting in Trujillo? This technique for spreading chaos and unrest has brought as many as 3,000 farmers and their families to the *barriadas* in a month. Once they arrive (on a one-way ride in communist-provided trucks) they are trapped in the festering slums with no money to return to their farms. (1967, p. 66)

Less emotional yet no less dogmatic are the remarks of the mayor of Lusaka, Zambia, who said that the squatter settlements which housed nearly half of the city's population were 'a positive threat to the health of our city . . . as a whole'. Seymour (personal communication) also cites a Zambian government report which argued that unless the tide of migration was checked 'the decade of the seventies may see an intensification of misery, the spread of epidemics, and political unrest can threaten the stability of government'. As cholera spreads through Africa the infection of middle-class suburbs from the insanitary adjacent slums becomes a growing fear. A patronizing view is expressed by two Indian sociologists:

> Ahmedabad City is known for the architectural beauty of its lavish homes, mansions and luxurious bungalows of its rich citizens. But very little is known about the ramshackle hovels of the poor. The outstanding physical characteristic of Ahmedabad City is the sharp contrast between its housing for the rich and that for the poor... Out of every ten citizens of Ahmedabad five live in slums... Slums are a matter of culture . . If [the people] lack culture, they will defile and degrade whatever place they occupy, even though it be a suite at the Taj Mahal Hotel . . . no amount of money spent in slums clearance would really solve the slum problems, unless serious efforts are made to change the human attitude and habits. (Bhatt and Chawda, 1972, p. 39)

The attitude of people in the dominant groups towards the poor tends to be negative and pejorative whatever their political or ideological persuasion. The reactionary believes in repression and such punitive measures; he must emphasize deviancy from the norms of society – a deviancy which cannot be corrected by education. The paternalist emphasizes the incapacity of the poor – they can do no better. The liberal believes that with his help the poor can better themselves and succeed in attaining some of the values which he himself holds. The radical, though opposing the existing standards as he sees them and wishing to transform society, similarly expects the poor to accept his interpretation of the changes necessary and to follow his leadership. None of these four favours independent action among the poor, for this threatens either the existing structure of society or his own superior role. An appraisal of the capacity of the poor to act positively is more likely to be made by those completely outside the society studied.

## POLICIES

Government policies towards shanty towns are seen in their most direct forms in attempts to eradicate the settlements and either rehouse the poor or help them to build their own homes.

Policies may be scaled along a number of dimensions – the level of activity, co-operative or punitive aspects, viability. Although there is a general tendency today to involve the poor in building their own homes, the policies outlined below may operate simultaneously as different government departments maintain their own vested interests in certain lines of development.

The simplest policy is to ignore the shanty town, turning a blind eye to its problems and misery. This may be justified by governments on the grounds of the illegality of the settlement and its supposed non-contribution to the economic life of the city. If conditions remain bad, the settlement will, it is hoped, fail to attract new migrants and the flow will decrease. But the flow continues and governments are faced with the creation of new shanty towns. In some states a token show of force meets the invaders while the populist political leaders acquiesce in the movement in order to ensure support for themselves. Clever invaders will minimize repercussions in selecting land the title to which is in dispute and which belongs to an owner enjoying little political support; they will seek the prior support of a political faction. Governments may acquiesce in the seizure of their own marginal land, for the value so lost will probably be less than any costs of rehousing the people involved.

Eradication – the levelling of the settlement by bulldozers – is frequently on the lips of officials yet much less often carried out. It is justified sometimes on the grounds that inner-city land is needed for office development, that outlying areas would be more remunerative if developed as middle-class suburbs. Claims that an area is insanitary or dangerous are seen as punitive and are apt to evoke a lively response from politicians and journalists anxious to discredit the government. Eradication, *per se*, solves no problems, for the residents of the shanty town merely decamp to another equally unsuitable site, though further from the city centre.

The stated ideal is to rehouse the poor. Yet few states have been able to build more than a minute fraction of the houses needed – and those which they do build are occupied by those with high regular wages, as they are beyond the means of the poor. A huge gap exists between rhetoric and performance. The housing built tends to be expensive because architects and planners insist on maintaining standards of construction appropriate to Western cities – and they are generally supported in this. Their efforts, if they get beyond the drawing board, bring them praise in the international professional journals. The houses are expensive too because they are built by large firms without the use of prefabrication. Financial agencies not only have insufficient funds to build as many houses as are needed but they seek a quick return on their investment (in order to build further houses) and so demand large deposits and short-term repayment of mortgages. For the residents are expected to pay the market value of their houses and not to be subsidized by state or municipality. Rehousing schemes which do reach the poor are often unpopular, not only because of the high level of repayments, but also because of a lack of opportunity for extra earnings – from lodgers or from informal sector activities, the estate perhaps being far from the city. Non-payment of rent or mortgage provides a difficult problem for the city, resulting often in the expansion of social service and welfare departments, all investigating why the poor cannot cope. Cynically these schemes may be viewed as providing overall more benefits to the middle strata – in moderately priced homes, in jobs in construction companies and in government offices – than to the poor.

The lack of success of such schemes together with the discovery of the potential for self-help among the poor has stimulated policies directed at upgrading the existing shanty towns. They are formally recognized, legal title to land is, if necessary, granted and services – water, sewerage, electricity, schools – provided. The respective contributions of state and community vary widely. The former must inevitably provide the technical expertise but the latter may be expected to contribute not only communal labour but also bear the financial cost of the services of the state agencies. Once their beliefs about the incapacity or instability of the poor have been overcome, such policies clearly appeal to the dominant groups – they believe that home ownership enhances conservative political attitudes, and the schemes may cost the state (or its middle-class taxpayer) very little. Yet the increasing sprawl of low-density settlements, ultimately raising costs of transport and the provision of services, is both an anathema to the planners and self-defeating for the poor.

The upgraded shanty town remains offensive in its untidiness; and many shanty towns cannot be improved – their houses are too close or irregularly sited, or the land on which they are built is either too steep or insufficiently stable for a brick or cement house. Other settlements lie in zones scheduled for a different use. The compromise is a site-and-service scheme: the state agency lays out plots and roads, installs services and perhaps gives credit for purchase of materials with which owners construct their own houses, probably to certain minimum specified standards. In their intention such schemes seem ideal solutions to the housing problem. Yet hardly any have been successful. In Lusaka, a company announced plans to resettle 16,000 families, almost the entire squatter population of the city, within a year, yet after three years only 600 plots had been reallocated (Seymour, 1975). Inasmuch as governments seek to recoup the cost of the land and to be sure of repayments, such schemes offer opportunities of home ownership only to workers earning a regular and substantial wage – a wage well above the average earned in the shanty towns.

Between these various modes of solving the housing problem a compromise undoubtedly exists; but it is one which would involve a considerable relaxation in building standards, a greater participation of the poor (to obviate those failures due to lack of communication between the poor and the bureaucrats) and a willingness on the part of the state to subsidize the housing of the poor. Such a compromise would not only be costly to the rich – in both material and non-material terms – but would, given the high degree of income inequality already described, be *very* costly. The solution becomes not a technical but a political one.

## POPULAR ATTITUDES

Most academic writing reflects popular attitudes, merely reiterating them in its own jargon. So I shall outline the basic nature of these attitudes before considering their formulation in the scholarly literature. Such attitudes embrace descriptively: the mode by which the poor are categorized, explanations of the cause of poverty either in general or in individual cases, and justifications for its existence; and, more analytically, an account of the process by which poverty is created or maintained. In other words, who are the poor, why are they poor and how do they come to be poor?

Even in the simplest hunting and gathering societies it has been noticed that some men prefer to work hard, to feed their families well, while others in the same band are more dilatory in their efforts, content with a lower standard of living and content to depend upon the charity of the first group. Clearly, all men in such situations have the same opportunities. In slightly more complex societies where wealth and political office are open to all, social inequalities are seen as natural. In several West African societies men will explain that just as the fingers of the hand are of unequal length, so men are dissimilar in their abilities and achievement. In other societies inequalities are institutionalized and perpetuated; all men do not have the same opportunities and against some the discrimination may be severe. Such inequality is sanctioned by myths of origin – such as that of the Bunyoro of Uganda which tells of three brothers, founders of the modern ethnic castes, who displayed different aptitudes which determined their descendants' status as cattle owners, herders and cultivators. The ideology of many religions teaches that man should be content with the status to which he is born. Willing acceptance will be rewarded in heaven or a future incarnation. Poverty and discrimination are ameliorated by the ties of dependence between patron and client. Though the poor do not enjoy their poverty, they are thus led to accept it and collective action to alter it is vitiated. But the relationship between patron and client may be an ambivalent one; the most deprived members of society may be seen as witches, their malevolence directed against their patrons. The idea that all men are born equal, that the inequality which patently exists is the product of man's social order, not of his nature, is a product of the Western enlightenment of the eighteenth century. Deriving from it is a belief that poverty can be eradicated. The poor are thus a *problem*. Such a belief dominates the thinking of the educated members of the dominant group in the third-world states; but the recent immigrant, socialized in the rural areas, will not usually share this same intellectual heritage, may hold much more 'traditional' views about social equality and will not see status as a social problem.

The poor are always a large category. One may divide them into 'poor' and 'very poor', the latter living at below locally recognized subsistence levels, producing little by virtue of low skills or ill health, suffering considerable insecurity because of spasmodic employment, recurrent ill health or financial losses. Some would characterize these as the 'lumpenproletariat', in contrast to a 'working class'. At a less statistical but more emotional level, the dominant members of society frequently distinguish between the 'deserving' and the 'undeserving' poor. The former uphold the values and norms expressed by the dominant groups and accept their own subordinate place in society. They are therefore deserving of charity to ameliorate their situation. The undeserving reject these values. They are characterized therefore as immoral, lazy, impure, and merit not help but punishment, which will either coerce them into reform or isolate them from the rest of the community. How far does this distinction parallel that made earlier between slums of hope and despair? Certainly we have degrees of poverty measured statistically, and the least poor will also tend to be the deserving poor and to live in slums of hope. But we are using three very different measures – statistical in terms of occupation, income and security, conformity to the dominant values in society (as interpreted by the dominant groups) and the estimation of the poor of their opportunities for upward social mobility. Some considerable, but not an exact, correspondence may be expected. We must too, distinguish between a categorizing of groups – the poor collectively – and that of individuals.

When dominant groups throughout the world categorize their poor in similar terms one asks whether the poor do in fact share universal qualities which differentiate them from the rest of their societies. Is there, as Oscar Lewis alleges, a 'sub-culture of poverty'; or are the poor of a nation more like their compatriots than similarly situated people in other countries? One's answer will depend upon what one measures. Cultural traits will be shared within the community. Characteristics such as apathy, aggression and disorganization will be shared by all the poor – for these terms mean little more than 'deviation from the dominant norms and values'. We expect a domestic group to be composed of husband, wife and children. The household maintained by a mother with a succession of lovers or husbands is seen as disorganized, yet it may constitute a perfectly rational attempt to cope with a given economic situation. Statistically, the poor may differ from their affluent compatriots in many ways, and we must beware of our evaluation of these differences in terms of good/bad, moral/immoral.

Poverty may be explained in two ways. Either one believes that opportunities do exist for the poor to improve their lot, but that they cannot or will not seize them because of certain attitudes or values which they hold. These derive either from their present poverty or from their cultural heritage – they do not perceive the opportunities, they believe they are unable to achieve the goals offered or they are too apathetic to want to achieve them. Or one believes that the will to achieve exists but that the opportunities do not. If one believes the former proposition, one will couch a solution in terms of educating the poor, of changing their attitudes. If the latter, one will seek a restructuring of society so that opportunities are more evenly distributed. The former solution is obviously preferable to members of the dominant groups, for the latter threatens their own privileged position. Both propositions are difficult to prove. Countless studies of community development purport to show that the innovators are the better educated, the more modern (and the less traditionally oriented), the more Westernized members of their society; they fail to examine the resources at the innovators' command. Those who fail to innovate are castigated for their backwardness – the fact that the changes advocated would bring either benefits which they do not value highly or even no benefit at all is not fully explored. Equally, those studies which do chronicle the rapid acceptance of innovation often tell us little about the role played by allegedly 'traditional' attitudes.

This crudely presented dichotomy between values and opportunities raises the question of the origin of these values. A dialectic between attitudes and the material conditions of poverty is thus postulated – the vicious circle of poverty is established in which poverty itself stimulates those attitudes which inhibit achievement and thus ensure continued poverty. Seeing the situation in this way one concludes that the poor cannot do anything to help themselves, that all changes in their status must be induced from without. But how far is this paternalist stance justified? Much depends upon the degree to which attitudes are deduced from behaviour by middle-class observers employing their own concepts and evaluations.

Undeniably, the behaviour of the poor is unlike that of the wealthier members of their society: their material style of life is obviously different; so too, very often, is their family size and structure and the composition of their domestic groups. But how far does such behaviour condition attitudes? At one extreme one may allege that the behaviour is simply adaptive to the peculiar conditions of poverty – the dominant values in the society are maintained. The clear discrepancy between values and behaviour is contrasted in terms of an ideal to which one would like to aspire and a norm which most of those around one manage to achieve and which is a realistic target for oneself. Acceptance of the latter does not necessarily entail the denial of the former. To cope with the frustrations of one's ability to achieve the ideal, the local norm may, defensively, be raised to the level of this ideal – thus constituting a rejection of the dominant values of society. Ultimately, these alternative values may become fully internalized, certainly affecting behaviour. But just how far behaviour is conditioned by these internalized values and how far by a conscious adaptation to the situation is very difficult to elucidate. Again, it is argued that the children will be brought up accepting those values held by their parents. Thus poverty is perpetuated from one generation to the next. But, it is countered, does not each generation react similarly in poverty not because of transmitted values but because in each generation men face the same lack of opportunities? These are well-nigh insoluble questions. We can but remember that the questions we ask, the academic studies mounted, the practical policies advocated, reflect overwhelmingly our own ideological positions.

## ACADEMIC APPROACHES

Academic discussion of poverty in general and of that of shanty towns in particular reflects the attitudes summarized above. Let us look in a little more detail at four approaches.

### *Culture of poverty*

Oscar Lewis's formulation of the sub-culture of poverty fits squarely into the general debate on poverty. For this reason, and because his biographical descriptions of shanty-town dwellers in Puerto Rico and Mexico are so vivid and unique, the concept has gained wide currency in both popular and academic writing. Once again, the debate has been largely confined to Latin America, though Lewis clearly intended it to be of universal application.

Under four main heads Lewis lists a very large number of traits which he associates with the culture of poverty. 'The lack of effective participation and integration of the poor in the major institutions is one of the crucial characteristics' – they do not participate in the larger economic system, belong to trade unions or political parties; they display a cynical mistrust of government, the church, the dominant classes. There is 'a minimum of organization beyond the level of the nuclear and extended family . . . the low level of organization [which] gives the culture of poverty its marginal and anachronistic quality'; there may however be a few voluntary associations developed within the slums and a certain sense of community. Family life is disorganized – there is an early initiation into sex, a preponderance of free unions and consensual marriages and mother-centred families. 'On the level of the individual the major characteristics are a strong feeling of marginality, of helplessness, dependence and of inferiority' – the poor cannot defer gratification, the belief in male superiority is widespread, psychological pathology is tolerated, little knowledge of other places and periods exists and people do not see their own problems as part of wider issues. They 'are not class-conscious although they are very sensitive indeed to status distinctions'. When they do become class-conscious and involved in wider political movements they cease to exhibit the culture of poverty. (Lewis, 1967, pp. 47–59.)

But, as Lewis argues,

> the culture of poverty ... is not only an adaptation to a set of objective conditions of the larger society. Once it comes into existence it tends to perpetuate itself from generation to generation because of its effect on the children. By the time slum children are six or seven they have usually absorbed the basic values and attitudes of their subculture and are not psychologically geared to take full advantage of changing conditions or increased opportunities which may occur in their lifetime. (1967, p. 50)

Lewis asserts that not all those who are poor exhibit the characteristics described above. At a guess he surmises that only one fifth of those in the USA who fall below the poverty line could be described as sharing in the *culture* of poverty. He specifically excludes too those in primitive and pre-literate societies, still relatively unaffected by Western influences. Their life is technologically simple but

> they have a relatively integrated, satisfying and self-sufficient culture. The caste system of India gives individuals a sense of identity and of belonging ... providing ... a sense of a past and a future. The Jews have their traditions of literacy, their voluntary associations and their religion. (1967, p. 55)

In Cuba, after the Revolution, Lewis found that although material conditions were little different he 'found much less despair, apathy and hopelessness ... [people] expressed great confidence in their leaders and hope for a better life in the future' (1967, p. 55). In general however Lewis expects the culture of poverty to be widespread where one social system is being replaced by another – as in a transition from feudalism to capitalism, where colonial rule destroys indigenous systems, where (he cites Africa here) detribalization is occurring. Most of the third-world slums are the consequences of such processes and Lewis expects his culture of poverty to be widespread, though he does suggest that landless migrants in Latin America would experience it in greater degree than African migrants, who retain rights in their natal villages and maintain close contact with them.

The very multiplicity of Lewis's traits ensures that many of them will be found in specific slum populations. Yet the concept of the culture of poverty has been strongly attacked. Lewis's chronicled accounts of daily life are selective, and they are subject to no analysis which justifies the use of the concept. Critics have pointed to inconsistencies – many of the poor do have a vision of a wider society, his middle-class actors often exhibit traits associated with the culture of poverty. The traits themselves are of several levels of abstraction. Other anthropologists who have lived in the slums report hope and achievement rather than apathy and despair, pointing often to quite an intense level of associational activity. Finally, the popularity of Lewis's formulation among those who assert that education, rather than a change of social structure, yields the solution to poverty has led his critics to emphasize the contrary position. Thus Portes argues that 'ways of acting in the slum are structurally determined to the extent that individuals continuously look for the most efficient way of improving their positions within the limits and barriers imposed by the existing social and economic organization' (1972, p. 286); man thus adopts a rational utilitarian approach – his responses to poverty are not emotional ones, they are not the product of values to which he was socialized either in the rural area or in the slum.

*Marginality*

The concept of marginality occurs frequently, as I have noted, in the literature on Latin America, though less so in that on Africa or Asia, where, however, it would be equally pertinent. Its technical usages correspond closely to those of everyday speech.

In one sense it merely implies borderline. Its opposite is average or mean. The marginals are those on the fringes of any category, marginal occupations are those which yield near or below minimum levels of subsistence and entail maximum insecurity, and the marginal population is that which is employed in this manner. As such, marginality is a purely descriptive term, defined according to statistical criteria.

In sociological literature the term 'marginal man' is used for a person who belongs to two cultures or societies, being fully integrated into neither. Some theories assert that he is more creative or innovative, for he is not so completely constrained by the values of his society. He may exploit the differences between the two societies. In this way the entrepreneurial success of Jews, of the Chinese in South-East Asia, of Lebanese in West Africa, is explained. On the other hand marginality is said to lend to anomie, insecurity and self-hatred. Marginality is associated with deviance – especially in its pejorative senses. The third-world shanty towns are said to be marginal in that their populations are not integrated into the wider society. Used thus the term is an ethnocentric one implying that the structure of the dominant sectors of the society provides the norm, and those acting according to differing norms are deviant.

Economists describe the inhabitants of the slum as marginal inasmuch as they are not wage earners or useful producers of goods, the goods or services which they do provide could be better supplied in other ways, and they are parasitic upon society and should therefore be eliminated – that is excluded from the town or transformed into wage earners. The fact that these people produce enough to keep themselves alive – a sufficient goal for them – is usually overlooked. Again, it is countered, the parasite is in some senses integrated with his host. The low wages paid to those who are in regular employment are possible only because the 'marginal' population is providing certain goods and services so cheaply.

This usage of marginality has been extended in recent years by economists and Marxists. As already noted the poor are seen as marginal because they earn such a small amount. They are also marginal because the product of their labour adds so little to the gross national product when compared with the contributions of the large modern manufacturing enterprise. Were the poor to stop work, the nation would be a little less wealthy. In a Marxist vein it has been argued that capitalism requires a 'reserve army of labour' to ensure that wages remain low; but only a small degree of unemployment is necessary to perform this function. The levels of unemployment experienced in third-world cities far exceed this, and the excess does not therefore contribute to the maintenance of the economic structure of society: it has no function, it is marginal. So used, the concept of marginality is difficult to apply empirically. Who among the unemployed are to be designated as functionally useful, who are the marginals? As I shall note in discussing dependency, the attention of scholars, Marxists and others, is now focused more on the positive contribution of those in the informal economy, albeit underemployed, to the total economic structure – the manner in which they are integrated – rather than on their degree of marginality.

Just as the term 'sub-culture of poverty' has come, in popular usage, to embrace all the poor, so too has 'marginal' come in Latin America, to be a euphemism for 'poor', 'marginality' for 'poverty'. And so one finds it employed in some contexts to denote a half to three quarters of the population, in others only the bottom 5 or 10 per cent. To questions such as whether the shanty town poor are marginal, whether they exhibit a subculture of poverty and whether they are a social class, one's initial response must be to ask the meaning of these concepts.

Political scientists see as marginal those who do not participate fully in the modern democratic process. It is often difficult to ascertain exactly what manner of participation entitles one to be deemed integrated. Membership of voluntary associations and especially of political parties is one yardstick, a distinction often being made between national parties and purely local associations. Voting at elections is another measure – shanty-town populations may be disenfranchized, *de jure* by their poverty or short residence and *de facto* by their apathy. Less easy to evaluate is the impact made by the shanty-town population upon national politics by their very existence, by the perceived threats of violence or by their actual protests. If protest produces the desired results, then are not the protesters integrated? Not, it would seem, if they do not use the institutionalized channels for the articulation of grievances. Trade-unionists, for example, would be regarded as integrated, but self-employed artisans, with no major association to voice their claims, are not.

When the social origins of the poor are very different from those of the affluent, the cultural integration of the former becomes a matter for concern. To what extent are the urban immigrants adapting or aspiring to the life styles and values of the dominant groups? Insofar as they are not, is this due to their poverty, to their own social origins, to their insufficient contact with new influences or their refusal to countenance them? Racial differences exacerbate the issue, European and indian stocks in Latin America have produced mixed populations of varying size and degree of miscegenation, but the terms used are social, not biological categories, the usage of each varying in place and situation. A man may be considered a mestizo in his home village, an indian in the capital. His self-identification may differ from that of others. One term may carry pejorative overtones, another imply acceptance.

In the sense of integration the term marginality is descriptive and ethnocentric. It locates certain groups – here the shanty-town dwellers – with reference to the dominant groups in the society. They do not quite belong to the society perceived by the latter. The problem posed is 'will they become integrated in time, will they persist on the margins, or will they develop a sub-society of their own, in antithesis and opposition to that of the dominant groups?'

*Radical Approaches*

The majority of scholars who have worked at grass-roots level in shanty towns have probably been politically radical, but they have not felt that a Marxist framework was appropriate for the presentation of their data. There is then no clear Marxist approach to shanty-town studies. Marxists interested in the third world have, indeed, inclined strongly towards structural approaches, specifying the contradictions inherent in the international capitalist system. These tend to be defined at an abstract and ideological level and the role of people and organizations in linking these contradictions, to be discovered by empirical research, is weakly developed. One such structuralist approach, though not exclusively Marxist, is dependency theory.

Earlier approaches to the poverty of third-world nations had focused upon endogenous factors. These countries were poor because of physical environment or lack of resources, or because the people lacked skills or were bound by tradition. With Western penetration a dual modern and traditional economy was postulated, each autonomous and operating within its own laws of development. Dependency theory argues that the continuing poverty of the poor nations is the consequence of their depending upon the capitalist system of the Western industrial nations. The theory has been most extensively developed by Latin American scholars; for here, industrialization through the growth of import-substituting manufacturing was seen at a relatively early date – the 1960s – to be incapable of producing sustained economic development. The new industries, established and often controlled by multinational corporations, tied the poor nations even more to the richer ones. The dependency of poor upon rich is explicit in classical Marxism, but whereas Western Marxists generally had failed to consider the processes going on within the poorer society, the Latin Americans paid greater attention to social developments within their own countries. And yet one of the basic criticisms made of dependency theory is the paucity of detailed evidence of the actual mode of exploitation, and in particular of the working of the multinational companies. Combining elements of structuralism, nationalism and Marxism, dependency theory has appealed, in one form or another, to a wide audience ranging from the conservative rationalists to the socialists. A recent strand of Marxist thought urges us to examine the articulation between the various modes of production, in other words how the small-scale artisans and the big multinational corporations affect each other's operations, and in what ways their operations are related.

Few would argue with the proposition that the poor nations are dependent upon the rich. But the long-term consequences of this dependency are hotly debated. At one extreme it is believed that dependency will cause the poor nations to become poorer still, relative to the rich; at the other, it is held that it is a 'contradiction of capitalism', that the moderate industrialization, promoted in the third-world countries as advantageous to Western capitalism, will in fact lead to take-off into sustained growth. The fact that the poor nations are not benefiting equally from dependency is illustrated by their recent division into third and fourth worlds – those which are growing rich (even though the lowest classes may experience little or no improvement in real terms), such as Brazil, and those that remain stagnant, such as the savana states of Africa: Mali, Upper Volta, Niger.

Some variants of dependency theory have expressed the dichotomy as being between rich and poor nations. A centre-periphery formulation enables this to be extended to embrace relationships with the poor nations – between the metropolis and the hinterland or between urban and rural sectors. The marginality of the shanty town is but one expression of this dichotomy. More orthodox Latin American Marxists have attacked such approaches as denying or obscuring the fundamental class differences within the society – differences which can in turn be extrapolated to an international level.

Radical Western writers on Africa have tended much more to explain developments in this continent in class terms, rather than in those of dependency. While in the 1950s attention was focused upon the ascendancy to power of the African 'middle class' of professionals, in the 1960s the growing disparities of wealth within African nations became more prominent. But the Marxist class terminology, so widely espoused in the West, does have a specific historical genesis in nineteenth-century industrialism and is loaded with imagery. Can it be transposed to the third world? Much of the effort of Marxist scholars has gone into fitting categories of people into the class terms, often with more regard to ideological rectitude than to empirical observation, to see if people so grouped together do in fact act in the same manner or in concert.

The upper class is clearly apparent in the third-world state, though its role could well be more precisely defined; is it for example a 'comprador bourgeoisie'? It is in the lower ranks of these societies that terminological difficulties are encountered. Who are the working class or proletariat? Urban wage earners are clearly embraced in this term. But relatively few are employed in large firms – and even these are not fully committed to wage employment, hoping in fact to retire and become petty entrepreneurs and return to the rural areas. Where does one fit in the self-employed artisans and their own employees, the petty traders; or the wage earners in construction and like sectors, who are irregularly employed and poorly unionized? Does the term lumpenproletariat refer to those who reject the norms of the society – the thieves and delinquents – as Marx used the term, or merely the very poor, who may be striving to adhere to social norms? How far can we use our class terms when the people themselves use very different concepts? In our Western scheme the petite bourgeoisie ranks above working class; yet, as we shall see later, in the third-world state the incomes of wage earners span the same range as those of the self-employed. So extreme is the range that an opposition of interests has been postulated between the 'labour aristocracy', the highly paid skilled workers in multinational companies, and the other workers. Quijano (1972) distinguishes between true petite bourgeoisie and true proletariat and marginal (that is, poor) petite bourgeoisie and proletariat. How far are such categories useful when individuals hold multiple jobs – one in each class category? Again, Marxists assume that one's social position is defined exclusively by one's relationship to the means of production. Crudely, this overlooks the fact that many men are in occupations where collective action is difficult to organize and that activity which is highly organized is differently based – upon ethnic group (the migrants from a single village), or the territorial residential unit (the shanty town).

Marxism certainly has its contribution, and most of those scholars working in shanty towns have been heavily influenced by its tenets. But among the professed Marxists more effort is going into defining structures and categories, according to ideological principles, than into establishing their empirical solidity and usefulness.

*Anthropological approaches*

The social anthropological view of African towns has been dominated by a very different approach – that developed by members of the Rhodes Livingstone Institute in Lusaka, Zambia, who later taught in the University of Manchester. In the 1930s British social anthropology was dominated by a rather rigid structural approach. Reality lay in the values and norms of the society to which men adhered. Deviance was seen as a consequence of personality; it was randomly distributed and curbed by processes of social control. Conflict between the many roles which an individual was expected to perform was solved by the acceptance of one established role – not the creation of new ones. This was a workable paradigm for the 'stable' village society. But on coming to the town the villager was detribalized – he experienced anomie. The anthropologist sought in urban life the relics of tribal patterns of behaviour.

Gluckman's classic aphorism affirmed the autonomy of the urban social system – 'An African townsman is a townsman, an African miner is a miner; he is only secondarily a tribesman' (1960, p. 57). His pupils, Mitchell (1966) and Epstein (1967), stressed the external determinants of city social structures – settlement density, mobility, ethnic heterogeneity, demographic disproportions, economic differentiation. The respective autonomy of urban and rural structures so created led to the concepts of an 'alternative model of behaviour' and 'situational selection'. The townsman adopted urban behaviour in some contexts, rural behaviour in others; on his return to his village he again became a villager. A distinction was made between situational change – the changes made by the individual from rural to urban modes of behaviour as the context directed – and historical change – the slow process of general change of urban modes of behaviour. Mayer (1961), writing of East London, criticized the rigid urban/rural dichotomy, arguing that the alternation concept disguised the general acceptance by the immigrant of urban values and that it under-emphasized the choices which he made – choices which were in fact different for each category of migrants, as he showed in contrasting those coming from educated and Christian rural backgrounds, and those coming from traditionally oriented homes.

From this approach developed the method of 'situational analysis' – norms and values were deduced from the detailed analysis of specific situations (or series of limited situations). This produced a much deeper comprehension of the dynamism of the social process – rather than of the static social structure. But the emphasis remained on the maintenance of the integrity of the social structure – conflicts produced tensions but these were resolved by adjustive mechanisms. Furthermore, the successful applications of this method were made in the rural areas, for the social anthropologists were not, until the 1960s, permitted to reside in African urban areas and to be participant observers; they were unable to produce monographs giving a vivid portrayal of town life. Mitchell suggested that one of the types of social relationships which should be studied in the urban situation was the personal network, viewing this either egocentrically and descriptively, or structurally, in the comparison of different types of network. This approach was subsequently developed by Kapferer (1972) in his study of a small tailoring workshop in Zambia. Gradually the emphasis on the manner in which urban social structures determined the behaviour of the migrant gave way to an actor-oriented approach. Thus Kapferer wrote 'individuals are ... able to shape their own destinies and the destinies of others. Social structures and social systems as far as they are the analytic constructs of anthropologists and sociologists are also the creations, though by no means necessarily identical, of the individuals and groups these social scientists observe' (1972, p. 206) – a view which Leach had emphasized much earlier but which was novel in Central African urban studies. Mitchell himself, in the context of studies of rural–urban migration, now urges the study of decision-making, of the perception by the individual of the opportunities available to him and of his own resources. The intellectual problem now facing these scholars is the successful marriage into a single theoretical framework of the structural and actor-oriented approaches; but one of them has concluded that a reconciliation may be impossible, or that it is a problem not for the field anthropologist but for the philosopher (Garbett, 1970, pp. 225–6).

Policies with respect to shanty towns are made by the dominant groups in the society. They reflect the social origins of these groups, their current economic interests, their interpretation of their own needs and those of the nation. Policies range from repression, to tolerance, and benevolent encouragement. Between the attitudes of the dominant groups and their consequent policies, and the commentaries and analyses of scholars, there exists a dialectical relationship; new interpretations reflect changing structures and further help to change them.

This process, however, must not be seen as a one-sided one. The poor themselves make their own interpretations of the dominant attitudes and policies towards them. And, to the best of their ability, they try to exploit legal loopholes – especially when invading land – and manipulate feelings of guilt in winning middle-class support. These interpretations form a most necessary ingredient for our own understanding of the shanty towns.

# 3 The Actor's View of His Society: Theoretical Considerations

In the opening chapter I suggested that if we are to understand what is going on within the shanty towns we must take account of the manner in which their residents interpret the situation in which they live. It is often said that the poor do not make decisions – things happen to them; but the invasions of land and the improvement so often seen in shanty towns belies this implied passivity. The shanty town poor are creating their environment, though within the externally imposed constraints set by the wider society. Again, if we are to be actively involved in helping the shanty town poor to realise some of their objectives, if we are to engage them in a meaningful dialogue, we must understand their view of the world. (They too need to understand ours – but this already seems to be the focal theme of most programmes of community development and the like.)

To look at the world of the shanty-town dweller through his eyes may not seem too difficult a task. In fact it would seem to be harder to understand an exotic culture, using concepts and symbols so different from our own. The shanty-town dweller uses the same language as the dominant culture in his society. His interests – finding work, paying for a house, educating his children – are similar to those of all other members of the society. The danger lies in the ease with which a middle-class observer imputes to the shanty-town resident his own view of the situation. He expects that the poor will react to poverty in the same way as he would do, if suddenly thrust into such a plight. His expectations are conditioned too by the explanation which he holds of the root causes of poverty, as outlined in the previous chapter. Paradoxically, it is in such situations, where we believe that we can intuitively understand the world view of others, that we need a more rigorous methodology to enable us to avoid the pitfalls described.

## MODELS

When we look to the social sciences for a lead we are disappointed. The phenomenologists seem busy defending their philosophical positions. Berger and Luckmann conclude their seminal work: 'There is a vast area of empirical problems ... [but] we have expressly refrained from following up the methodological implications of our conception of the sociology of knowledge' (1971, pp. 204–10). What empirical work has been done in this area is concerned more with the socially deviant than with the poor. Psychologists are certainly interested in cognition, but their experiments tend either to be artificial, divorced from real-world situations, or to be concerned with the simplest of tasks – children sorting coloured shapes for instance. The social anthropologist has hitherto tended to portray the society which he studied in terms familiar to its members and has thus ignored, or at least has not made explicit, a difference between his own analysis and that of his subjects. He has sought from the people among whom he lives the explanations of the behaviour which he observed; the structures which they present are those of normative or jural relationships. The distinction was made apparent in the diverse approach to the study of law propounded by Gluckman and Bohannan. Gluckman argued the applicability of Western legal concepts in analysing Lozi law and opened his classic work: 'In analysing legal problems in an African society one has to use terms and concepts which have been employed by jurists through two millennia' (1955, p. 44). Bohannan distinguished the Tiv view of their judicial system from his own analysis of it and warned: 'The anthropologist's chief danger is that he will change one of the folk systems of his own society into an analytical system and try to give it wider application than its merit and usefulness allow' (1957, p. 5). Today the cleavage has widened to range the structuralists, be they followers of Lévi-Strauss, Marxist-oriented economic anthropologists or ethno-scientists, against the action anthropologists, followers of Goffman, Bailey and others. While the former analyse a society in terms quite alien to its members, the latter, though focusing upon individual perceptions, often seem too involved with minutiae of interpersonal behaviour as to neglect the total society and any image held of it.

More germane to our own problem are the contributions made within the social-science disciplines to the study of decision-making, for here the actor's definition of the situation is obviously important. Wallace (1965), a social anthropologist, has provided a framework with which to describe the process of driving from home to office, but concludes that his approach cannot be applied to more complex situations. The psychologists Miller *et al.* (1960) have provided a useful framework for the analysis of decision-making; they illustrate it with the example of hitting a nail with a hammer. Games theory deals with interpersonal contests. Decision theory (as seen by economists and management scientists) is concerned with man's control over the natural environment. Our own problems combine these two aspects – we are concerned with men competing with, or manipulating, each other with respect to scarce natural resources. These models, though of undoubted merit, are of relatively little help to us. They are designed to provide a method for the study of micro-situations; we are concerned with a macro-scopic view of the world.

Sociologists have been divided into those who believe that it is possible to experience the definitions of the world of others, and those who hold that this is impossible. Inasmuch as we want to know the actor's definition of a situation we must make an attempt, however crude, to describe it. But what exactly are we looking for?

What we describe is inevitably an abstraction. No individual actor ever sees his world view in its entirety. In each specific situation he employs certain concepts and propositions, and recalls as evidence certain items of information which seem to him relevant. It is the observer who tries to amalgamate these into a coherent picture, discovering in the process numerous apparent contradictions. Some of these may derive from an inability to synthesize; some may reflect a clash between deeply internalized religious views and available evidence; others undoubtedly concern propositions which are specific to certain situations only. Thus we have little difficulty in accepting that 'too many cooks spoil the broth' and that 'many hands make light work'. Similarly, social class and ethnic grouping are alternative modes of categorization. If action is defined in class terms ethnicity is overridden. Yet any individual may act as a member of a social class in one situation, of an ethnic group in another.

Again, as sociologists, we are interested not in the perception of the individual actor but in that view of the world which is shared by a collectivity, whether they be members of a nation-state, an ethnic group or a socio-economic category. In other words, we try to present a generalized picture, emphasizing those common elements which derive from widespread socialization practices, shared experiences in education, migration and residence, rather than from the unique experience of any particular individuals. Thus from the individual images of the countless members of a society, each image expressed partially in numberless situations, we try to present for the subjects of our study a coherent, generalized picture.

To do this we must ourselves provide a framework for our analysis and then decide how to fill all the boxes so created. At first this prescription would seem to contradict our earlier assertions. Should the actor not be allowed to speak for himself rather than respond to questions set in our own terms? Should he not tell us what he thinks about his status rather than indicate whether he sees himself as middle or lower class? Certainly he should. But as we listen to a torrent of words and observe a thousand minute details of action, we realize that ultimately it is we, the observers, who decide what is significant. Formal procedures do not obviate this. It is we who choose these key concepts – whether of class, honour or the like – which seem to characterize an ideology; we who select the categories for a content analysis. Thus it is for us to define what we are interested in. Clearly we cannot describe the total world view and in fact we are concerned only with perceptions of inequality – a large enough area as it is. It may be that themes which interest us seem to be of little concern to our subjects; but conversely can we be sure that those topics which, impressionistically, they always seem to be talking about are those which are of most concern to them? The closer we get to our subjects, the more accurately will we be able to reproduce their picture of their world, but in the last resort the abstractions and syntheses which are made are ours, not theirs. It is probably impossible to experience the definition of the world of others; it should be possible in a simplistic manner to reproduce their definition of the world. To do so the framework which we adopt must be applicable both to our own structuring of society and to theirs. For in fact we are always comparing, implicitly if not explicitly, their image with our own, seeing theirs in contrast to our own even though we may not describe the latter. We must try, therefore, to use concepts which are as culturally neutral as is possible, avoiding those, such as 'class', which are highly specific to time and place. Absolute neutrality is impossible; but at least we may indicate where our own biases lie.

I propose that we should approach the construction of this framework in three ways. The first consists in setting out the heads appropriate to our study – what kinds of data we are interested in. The second in setting this data in two models of society – one in which the actor places himself centrally and the other in which he adopts the stance of an observer, viewing his society from the outside; the third in considering the development of the image of society over time, consequent upon the experiences of the actor.

## SOCIAL INEQUALITY

Our concern is with social inequality: certain valued qualities are unequally distributed. Inequalities may be perpetuated through successive generations, giving a 'closed' society, a highly stratified one; or there may be a high rate of social mobility – an 'open' society as men move from one level to another. Any society may be scaled along these two dimensions.

I see inequality in terms of power and rewards. To power I

give a conventional minimum definition – the situation in which the behaviour of one individual is determined by the actions of another, the more powerful actor leading the less powerful to behave in ways in which he might not otherwise have done. Power is thus an element in almost all human relationships and I would follow Edmund Leach in postulating that in every society men seek power (and, conversely, fear powerlessness). Yet power is most difficult to measure. Few would deny the existence of powerful men in their society and most would agree who they were. Yet at the mass level of personal exchanges it is often difficult to locate power when each actor believes that he has gained what he sought. In what spheres is power exercised – familial, occupational? In what manner is it exercised – through influence or coercion, the withdrawal of resources? These are heads under which we arrange our data, not only making our own assessment of the structure of inequality but also that of the actor. How does *he* define power? How does he see it operating?

For my purpose the most important domain of power lies in the control and allocation of rewards. I use the term rewards in preference to wealth, for the latter refers not only to consumed income but also to the control of property – a form of power. Furthermore, rewards may be material – all forms of income used to establish a style of life – or non-material – leisure, honours. Rewards of a given type are easily scaled, but rewards of different types cannot easily be compared. An income of £10,000 is valued more than one of £9,000, a peerage ranks above a knighthood; but is it better to have £10,000 and a knighthood, or £9,000 and a peerage? To members of some societies the choice may be obvious – one quality clearly outranks the other. But, as we shall consider later, choice between a multiplicity of goals is influenced not only by the degree to which each is valued by the individual, but also by his perceived ability to achieve them. Nevertheless we should attempt to discover both the nature of the rewards which are most highly valued and their pattern of distribution in the society.

Prestige is frequently cited as a third and independent criterion for social ranking. But it assumes so many forms.

Deference I see as a correlate of power; admiration as a correlate of reward. A third form of prestige I would dissociate from social ranking: such is the esteem or respect awarded to exemplary role performances – the honest man, the loving wife, the skilled craftsman. Such esteem may be used by an individual as a resource in the attainment of his goals. But equally it may be asserted as an explanation of low social rank, or in denying the legitimacy of the ranking system – 'I'm poor but I'm honest.'

Thus we first ascertain how power, rewards and prestige are defined by the actor and the pattern of their distribution. Next we must ask how these goals are seen to be achieved – what are the stages on the route to success? What resources are required and how must these be deployed? Furthermore, what are the opportunities available to an individual of a given social position and what are the chances of his success? How far is this determined by one's parentage, how much is open to individual achievement? In other words, these are the topics usually subsumed within the concept of social mobility, its mode and incidence.

The ranking of individuals and the assessment of social mobility itself tells us nothing about the degree to which people of similar rank interact socially. Do they form social groups identifiable to an observer and to the members themselves? Or are social groups formed on the basis of other criteria – ethnicity, for instance, or even perhaps age (itself a mode of social inequality, important in tribal societies, though not considered here)? The issue is one for empirical investigation. Between whom do the more intimate forms of social interaction – intermarriage, certain recreational clubs, commensuality – take place? Who are seen as being 'folk like ourselves'?

These three aspects of social inequality – the patterns of distribution, social mobility and the degree to which social ranking determines the membership of social groups – may be variously combined. Thus at one extreme a society may have great differences in power and rewards, little or no social mobility and a predominance of social groups based upon this ranking – a highly stratified society with probably marked cultural differences between strata. At the other extreme is a society with minimal differences in power and wealth, considerable social mobility and social groups based upon age or ethnic criteria – in many respects a most homogeneous society.

## MAPS AND STRUCTURES

Some students of mine, asked to write an essay on 'Myself and My Society', approached the topic in two contrasting ways. One set began by describing themselves, their values, aspirations, personality. They went on to describe their immediate families, then their more distant relatives, neighbours and so on. They presented a very self-centred or ego-oriented view of their society. The other set took an observer's role externalizing themselves from their immediate surroundings and viewing their society as if from a high mountain peak, describing its major configurations. They ended their essays 'and there . . . is me', thus siting themselves within the structure described. In earlier writing (Lloyd, 1971, Chapter 1) I have termed these two views of society the ego-oriented cognitive map and the externalized analytical structure. I would not suggest that these students consciously operated with these two models of society; nor do I know whether persons in other cultures would answer such an essay question in such terms. I do not assert that these patterns or structures exist in the deep unconscious of man. But I do believe that they are useful in arranging our data on perceptions of inequality. Each model highlights different aspects of our perceptions and reminds us, too, that a simple question may produce different types of responses. While it was felt that the essays cited above told us something about the writers, we did not believe that the student who had chosen an ego-oriented approach could not have written from the observer's externalized position, and vice versa.

The cognitive map, as I use it, focuses upon two principal features – firstly on a pattern of goals and routes, secondly on a network of interpersonal relationships. The individual perceives a variety of goals which are highly valued, both by himself and by other members of society (that is to say, his achievement of them will win him approbation). He has an image of the routes by which these goals are to be achieved, in terms of resources necessary – money, skills, educational qualifications, personal qualities, the patronage of others – and of the mode by which these resources are to be deployed. Against this knowledge he sets his own resources and thus chooses which goals to seek and by which route he might best attain them. One of the individual's most important resources is his personal network. Some people will positively help him – by lending money, for instance, providing information, giving moral support; others will thwart his efforts by denying support or even opposing his interests. The network includes not merely those with whom an actor interacts regularly (as so many anthropological network studies are limited), but also those with whom he interacts infrequently or who are potentially involved in any projected course of action. The relationship between ego and alters may be seen in terms of a power balance, of a current state of indebtedness or credit ('I can get him to do what I want' or 'He owes me a good turn'). Again, with close members of one's network one may predict a response partly in terms of personality – one knows what to expect from a given individual. With more distant members of the network the response is anticipated in terms of role – one expects a bureaucrat, politician or priest to behave in a certain manner. The character of the network may be described according to a variety of criteria, most important for our purposes being the degree of interconnectedness – how much do the members of ego's network interact with each other? – and its range or extent – to what extent are individuals included who are socially distant from ego and what type of relationship does he have with them? Or, in more specific terms, does a humble shanty-town dweller have kin or co-villagers in high office upon whom he can call for help?

The ego-oriented cognitive map can lead to the presentation of one's society in 'us – them' terms. 'Us' is the moral community, sharing values. In using this dichotomy to illustrate a world view common in peasant societies the bounds of 'us' are usually territorial – the village is the moral community. I believe that the dichotomy can be similarly applied in urban areas and that the boundaries should be expressed in terms of social and not merely territorial mobility. Thus, 'us' contains those positions in society between which mobility is seen to be possible. (Thus rich and poor peasants are members of the same moral community when it is seen that the many sons of a rich farmer will, upon the subdivision of the land at their father's death, be poor men. Similarly, wealthy traders may be known to have had humble origins; their children in turn may never equal their father's affluence.) Encircling 'us' are 'them', but the latter term embraces three different types of groups. 'Lateral' are like but separate communities – neighbouring villages or suburbs. 'Superior' are those with a different life style, believed to hold a different set of values; individuals of this group may however reside physically within the 'us' community though remaining marginal to it socially – the squire in his village, the priest, high government officials. 'Inferior' to 'us' are those who by birth are members but who for one reason or another have rejected the values of the society; they are the drop-outs.

Let us turn now to the externalized analytical structure by which a member 'observes' his society. Here our overriding concern is with the categories used by an actor in describing his society: what social divisions does he perceive – social classes, ethnic groups, occupations? Are these defined in terms of wealth or power, of specific interests? Are these criteria achieved or ascribed, as are ethnic categories such as those of tribe, colour or religion? The actor may, of course, use different sets of categories in different situations – class in one, ethnic in another. But equally it may be apparent that one set is used more frequently than another and is more dominant. These categories do not exist independently of the other; they are interrelated. The modes of relationship used by Ossowski (1963) in describing class structures may here be used and extended. Thus classes were described as being opposed in a dichotomous relationship – the 'haves' versus the 'have nots'; as being related hierarchically – as in a ladder formation, the individual moving up and down, in and out of fixed classes; or in a relationship of functional interdependence – each occupational group needing the others to make a viable society. To this we might add the competitive relationship seen in multi-ethnic situations where, presuming the ethnic groups to be similarly structured in terms of power and wealth, their members compete for valued goals. These modes of relationship stress, in varying degrees, the principles of the allocation of power and rewards and the differences in life styles which underlie patterns of social interaction.

Again, while an actor may designate certain social categories in describing his society, the manner in which he sees his own membership of one of these may take a variety of forms. Here, discussions on levels of class-consciousness may be broadened to embrace other forms of categorization. Minimally, one must be aware of the behaviour to be expected from members of other categories. This extends to a recognition that certain opportunities may be available to those of one's own category and not to those of others; members of a category identify their special interests (in terms of privileges to be preserved or deprivations to be overcome). Recognition of collective interests may then develop into an imperative to collective action. Finally this imperative may be seen not merely as a directive for individual and collective action but as a description of a historical process. It becomes an ideological statement about the world.

In observing his society in this manner the actor locates himself in one category. Members of this category may be seen as 'us'. But from this stance the 'us–them' dichotomy implies not only broadly conceived but also opposed groups. The nature of the relationship is thus differently expressed from that postulated in the cognitive map, where the centrally placed 'us' was surrounded by groups of 'them'.

Once again it must be stressed that the formulation of these two models is but a heuristic device. What must be emphasized is that these two ways of perceiving society may co-exist and that in any specific situation aspects of one or both models will be uppermost in an actor's mind. Every individual must have a cognitive map – he could not act without one. His map may or may not accord with that of his peers. It may prove valid or invalid in prediction. However, men differ in their ability to view their own society as external observers. The differences may be ascribed to innate ability, to experiences within the society in a variety of roles, to education and to travel beyond the confines of one's society. The details contained within the models should be complementary, but may well not be, for an individual may not always be aware of incompatibilities – he may not see them as such if he applies them to different situations.

The two models emphasize different elements. The ego-oriented cognitive map is delineating goals and routes and the actor's own resources, stresses individual achievement, the role of patronage in success and similar features. The analytical structure indicates broad parameters within which achievement is possible. It sets out a pattern of constraints. Thus it may remind the actor that certain offices are beyond the reach of lower classes, certain ethnic groups, etc. Again, the cognitive map may be said to stress achievement, while the analytical structure gives greater weight to power. Often scholars may formulate models of different types, or, if following the distinction presented here, include other elements. What matters most is not the details of the models used but the awareness of their multiplicity and diversity. The scholar who asserts that his subjects operate with a single simple model is providing a reflection upon his own questions rather than a satisfactory account of the actor's perceptions.

One final point: our discussions so far have been of observers' and actors' images of the world as they see it. The scholar/observer would often argue that he should not judge the legitimacy of this image; but for the actor the distinction between the world 'as it is' and 'as it might/ought to be' is an important one. The cognitive map stresses the world as it is, though the actor may imagine a different pattern – certain routes to valued goals may be made easier, his own stock of resources, both material or personal, might be improved. But if the analytical structure is seen in terms of constraints upon achievement, then the removal of these might be postulated. The relationship between the perceived categories may be altered. Criticism of one's society may take one of two forms. On one hand the basic structure of society is accepted but it is argued that those who have achieved success have done so by flouting the rules – a stricter observance of an ethical code is advocated. On the other hand an alternative structure is advocated – this implying intellectual skills not possessed by all in equal degree. The distinction may however be more apparent than real. In the former situation men accept that positions of great power and reward must exist. They argue that these should be achieved by scholastic competition (believing this to be a universally valued mode of achievement) rather than nepotism (corrupt practices). Others may present the same situations in terms of a relationship of opposition between powerful/rich and poor, and argue that this relationship should be changed.

## SOCIAL EXPERIENCE

Gluckman, as we have seen, attacked the tendency to consider the urban migrant negatively in terms of 'detribalization' – his relationships in his traditional rural society ruptured, replaced by his anomic wandering in the alien towns. The urban social system is just as real as the rural one and in it the migrant plays a number of specific roles. But, as studies have demonstrated, the image of that urban society held by a recent immigrant can differ radically from that of the men born and bred in the town. Thus, what determines our perceptions of our society is not our current position in it but our cumulative experiences. As our knowledge of our society increases through learning, so too are our perceptions validated or invalidated by the actions by which we attempt to manipulate society. Our knowledge is thereby increased, our perceptions reinforced or altered.

Thus one way of establishing and presenting the image held of social inequality is by a diachronic approach. We reconstruct, albeit in a most generalized manner, the life history and experiences of the typical urban migrant. He is born and grows up in the rural area, still traditionally oriented. He learns the concepts and propositions appropriate to traditional society. His information about his own society and especially the outside world is limited. We recognize, of course, that many rural societies are far less traditionally oriented than they were a few decades earlier, than neighbouring communities still are. Again, our migrant may come from a wealthy or educated home in the rural area, already rejecting traditional norms and values. To this experience of socialization in the home and its neighbourhood are successively added the experience of education and migration, the latter embracing not only the decision to emigrate but also the process of settling down in the town, arranging accommodation, finding a job. In discussing the migrant's successive experiences within the town, there is often a tendency to concentrate exclusively upon his role as a worker – he is a wage earner employed in a modern, highly capitalized, expatriate-managed factory, a small, labour-intensive indigenously owned company, a vast public bureaucracy, or he is a self-employed trader, artisan or minor professional. These distinctions are important and the relationships relevant. But we must also see the migrant as a member of a local community, the residential neighbourhood or dispersed ethnic group. His aspirations may be expressed not in terms of his present occupation but of a variety of other positions available within the community. His demands may be articulated not through his bosses or his workmates but through the community leaders.

We need static pictures or synchronic presentations if we are to compare the perceptions of inequality of one group of people with another or of the same group at two different periods of time. The diachronic approach assists us in the preparation of these synchronic presentations, but furthermore it describes for us the manner in which changes have occurred over time and suggests how diverse experiences result in different perceptions at the present time.

## DATA COLLECTION AND ANALYSIS

In the preceding pages I have argued that the external observer must himself know the actor's world view that he is looking for. He must define the areas which interest him and provide a framework into which to fit the data which he abstracts from his observations. He creates a myriad of little boxes, but how does he fill them so that he can claim to be presenting, as nearly as possible, the actor's image rather than a reflection of his own ideology or personality?

The easy answer is – from the actor's own words, his own explanation of his behaviour, collected according to established methods ranging from participant observation to the questionnaire or structured interview administered by a research assistant of a non-resident researcher. But of how much value is the actor's own explanation? We have already discounted the questionnaire approach in which the actor is asked to frame a response in terms of concepts supplied by the investigator – asking him to which class he belongs, for instance. If we listen to the explanations which the actor gives to those around him we realize that he is attempting to justify his action, to win support, to negate possible sanctions against him. But as scholars we are prone to believe naïvely that an explanation given to us, neutral observers of the situation, is the 'real truth', whereas it is in fact no less an attempt to project a certain image. Plotnicov reports that after a year of weekly interviews with his few selected Jos informants, their self-presentations often changed quite radically. We may attempt to test the veracity of our informants by comparing their avowed intentions with their actual behaviour. A wide discrepancy is often apparent. But how far may this be attributed to the expression of intention in respect of an idealized situation, behaviour in a specific one? We may find ourselves placing more reliance on the observation of behaviour, imputing to the actor motives which are but the rules which *we* use to establish a pattern or regularity in events.

The world view which we try to present is admittedly an abstraction. Should we not ask our actor to make an abstraction for us? But as we have argued he does not hold clearly in his mind a world view such as we seek to present. He formulates images specific to a given situation – images which may well contain apparently contradictory elements. Our task therefore is to examine these situations and the images which they produce – or, in other words, to investigate the making of decisions.

All purposeful activity is the consequence of a decision. In our daily life the making of a decision is forced upon us by the action of others, or of the environment; other decisions are the response to specific opportunities which are seen to exist; some are the result of those few occasions when one assesses one's life and prospects and decides to strive for one set of long-term goals rather than another. In the context of our discussion of shanty towns we are interested in decisions about migrating, selecting a place to live and moving from one suburb to another, finding and changing a job, about the schooling of one's children and alternative ways of spending one's savings – in building a home in the home village or maintaining elderly relatives, for instance.

In analysing a decision the observer must explore all possible avenues open to an actor, not simply those perceived by him; for the actor will probably be blind to certain opportunities, and will dismiss without thought or explanation certain courses of action which, from his own experience or that of his peers, he believes to be fruitless. Again, in collecting verbal descriptions of any decision we should rely not only upon the explanation given by the actor himself but also upon that of all others involved. Such a procedure has its difficulties. Such a detailed cross-examination of informants may prove embarrassing to them; group discussion of hypothetical situations may obviate this. In asking one's informants to probe real or hypothetical situations more deeply than hitherto one may well be causing them to perceive courses of action not previously considered by them and, in consequence, altering their behaviour from what it would otherwise have been. The impartial and uninvolved researcher comes to play the same role as the community development officer trying to educate through group discussions. Ultimately the observer may cast himself in the role of his actor, attempting to see a situation using both the concepts and propositions and the information available to the actor, excluding from his consideration those which are the product of his own culture and experience.

In analysing the decision-making we need, once again, a framework to guide our inquiry.

Activity is directed towards the attainment of 'the good life'. What this good life is will vary from one culture to another. Ultimately it is expressed in the fulfilment of certain psychological needs – achievement, affiliation and such-like – but what, for instance, constitutes achievement will vary – some societies may emphasize power, one mode of rewards will be valued more than another. For practical purposes we must convert these needs into the statuses available in the society. The mere ranking of these statuses is less useful (for it is usually so predictable) than the examination of the qualities ascribed to each status. Thus one occupation is valued for the power it bestows on its holder, another for the wealth which it yields. The good life is attained through a multiplicity of goals. Some of these may be mutually reinforcing – great wealth facilitates polygamy and both may be highly valued. Others may be incompatible – the life of the busy globe-trotting top executive, valued for its power, is incompatible with the life of a country gentleman, the village squire. It might perhaps be possible to rank, in hierarchical order, the valuation of these statuses in a given society; but for its individual members this would be a highly hypothetical exercise – their choice of goals at any one moment being dictated so largely by their present position, their resources, etc. Inevitably, most people will claim to value more highly those goals which they see themselves able to attain – and here too one must assess the degree to which the possibility of such attainment is a realistic or fantasy one (according to both observer and actor).

The actor selects a goal, examines the route by which this is to be achieved and assesses his own resources, both material and non-material, and the mode of their deployment. The picture that emerges in the actor's mind depends upon the concepts that he uses and the information available to him. Certain attributes may be regarded as resources, others neglected. The information available to him – itself a type of resource – comes from his own past experience, from his peers and from experts to whom he has access. In all there is an element of uncertainty – is his information correct, will X support him as he hopes? – and of risk – what factors beyond his control (and perhaps his understanding) might jeopardize his success? For any single goal there may be alternative routes to its attainment and each must be similarly assessed. These are then valuated against each other in terms of the benefits to be received and the costs of their attainment, the costs here including the effect of the proposed course of action upon other goals which he is simultaneously seeking. Other goals are similarly explored and the relative benefits and costs assessed. The attainment of the 'good life' is measured against the constraints upon his chances of success – his lack of resources, the sanctions of others, his own internalized values which might prevent action which was otherwise seen as beneficial.

A plan having been conceived – a strategy for the achievement of a certain goal – its tactical implementation is then put in train. Here the actor relies on his skills in managing interpersonal encounters – a false move and the entire plan, feasible though it may seem, can be jeopardized. In communication with others the actor selects only some of the information available to himself in arguing his case; he stresses certain values in seeking support (perhaps those values which he does not himself support). As others in turn make their demands on him, so he bargains with them, offering concessions which would perhaps affect the success or attractiveness of his plan and leading him ultimately to the consideration of alternative goals or routes.

For ease of exposition decision-making is presented as a linear process. But not only does the actor take many short cuts – ignoring what he believes to be blind alleys, accepting certain propositions as self-evident and not open to examination – but he is also continually looking ahead to tactical problems, looking back to consider alternative goals and routes. The stages which we have set out are, in fact, often telescoped into an almost simultaneous activity.

From the description and analysis of decisions, one obtains the data required for the amplification of the frameworks outlined above. The construction of the cognitive map follows very closely upon this process. The categorization necessary for the analytic structure is gained indirectly.

This chapter has raised a number of theoretical issues. In the descriptions given in the following chapters of aspects of shanty-town life it will not always be possible to formulate separately the observer's interpretation of the situation (my own or that of other scholars) and that of the actor. I can but urge the reader to ask himself 'how would I see this?' and in addition 'how would this look to the actor?' using the concepts current in his society, the knowledge and information available to him. In asking this I am not suggesting that the actor's view is better or superior to our own. I am arguing that our interpretation of the situation will be far richer, and of better predictive value, if we incorporate into our own analysis the viewpoint of the actor.

This is a counsel of perfection – what I think we ought to be doing rather than what I, or any other researcher, has fully applied in practice. While one may try to distinguish one's own interpretations of the situation from that of the people directly involved in it, there are difficulties in conveying to a reader two slightly contrasting images in any but a simple example.

Thus, where I describe the societies from which the migrants come, the migratory process, work and political acting in the shanty town, it is my analysis of the situation which predominates. I set out the parameters within which this activity takes place. But in detailing the experiences of these migrants I am suggesting how their own ideas about the world have been formed; in describing the types of social relationships extant in the shanty town I am suggesting what might be perceived from the grass-roots level. Past experiences and present relationships contribute to the view held by the world. Common elements will recur in shanty towns in all continents; yet the superimposition of cultural differences always threatens to obscure any uniformity.

# 4 Communities of Origin

The residents of the third-world shanty towns have, for the most part, arrived in the cities in the past three decades. They grew up in a rural hinterland in a cultural environment very different from that which they now experience in the city. In the literature they are often referred to as 'urban peasants', the term implying both a continuing adherence to traditional beliefs and attitudes, and a recognition that in the city the relationships which they establish in workplace and residential area are more like those of their rural homes than of the modern city. The same themes are embraced in the designation of the shanty-town dwellers as marginal.

Studies of peasant attitudes derive for the most part from their home villages. A variety of traits are often adduced. Peasants are said to lack any drive for self-advancement or achievement, this stemming from a fatalistic view of the world – a world which they are powerless to change or which is essentially unchanging. Mutual suspicion is rife and this too deadens the achievement drive and also inhibits co-operation and collective activity. Peasants are incapable of planning for the future. They cannot envisage a future different from the present or they are unable to defer gratification. In their hopes for improvement they rely on luck or on the patronage of others. Such traits are discussed to explain observed behaviour in the villages and to account for a continuing lack of social and economic development. They seem equally apposite in accounting for the migrant's failure to adapt successfully to urban life, in failing to take advantage of the opportunities open to him. They attribute the blame for his poverty not to the structure of the urban economic system and not entirely to individual weaknesses but to the cultural background in which the migrant remains enmeshed.

On reflection however these attitudes ascribed to the peasant, though perhaps containing a number of half-truths, are seen to be the converse of those values most usually stressed in accounting for our superiority – individual achievement, teamwork, rational planning. Are we not imposing on the peasants those very traits which seem to us to constitute the most plausible explanation of poverty and lack of success?

Two questions emerge. Firstly, what are the attitudes of peasants towards achievement, planning and the like, and are these universal features of peasant society? Just as two observers of a shanty town may give very different pictures of it, so have descriptions of peasant society varied. Thus in the classic debate between Robert Redfield (1930) and Oscar Lewis (1951) concerning the Mexican village of Tepoztlan, the former, in an idyllic and romantic fashion, emphasizes consensus within the village community; the latter, looking at them twenty years later, saw them as individualistic, suspicious, envious and uncooperative (not unlike his later characterization of migrants in town). In the ensuing discussion it seems accepted that the village was unlikely to have changed radically in the intervening period, but that the two anthropologists were asking very different questions – their divergent descriptions reflected different aspects of social reality. Later in this chapter I shall be looking specifically at the possibilities of social mobility within rural communities, the attitudes towards achievement and the degree of co-operative spirit in the village.

But a second question, raised in the previous chapter, requires prior examination. Are attitudes expressed in the rural area relevant to our study and understanding of behaviour in the town?

## THE RURAL HERITAGE

Common sense would seem to dictate a positive answer. As Hobsbawm writes, 'since the mass of migrants into the cities in many parts of the world consists of men and women from traditional peasant backgrounds, who bring into their new world the modes of action and thought of their old world, history remains a current political force. It would be unwise to neglect it' (1973, p. 20). But a contrary position is also argued. Gluckman challenged the tendency for the social anthropologist who followed 'his people' from their village where he first studied them, into the urban areas, to focus upon the continuance of traditional patterns of behaviour; 'the fact that Africans now live, for longer or shorter periods, in towns will influence their behaviour far more than the fact that they come from tribal homes and cultures' (1960, p. 57). In fact behaviour was seen to alternate, according to social context, between urban and rural modes, the migrant selecting in each situation action which seemed appropriate. This rather simplistic formulation was subsequently attacked by those who felt that it overstressed an urban–rural dichotomy; it obscured the development of new patterns of behaviour which fell clearly into neither paradigm. Again, in emphasizing the determinant force of the urban situation, it failed to indicate that different groups of migrants might react differently to the same situation. Thus, in his study of Xhosa in East London, Philip Mayer (1961) showed that those migrants – 'School' – who came from Christian villages were in the town more completely integrated into urban associations; those who came from homes which still professed the traditional religions, the 'Reds' because they still used ochre paint, remained encapsulated in groups which spent most of their leisure hours thinking of their natal villages and planning their return.

> The social organization of School migrants in town seems to reflect a willingness to move in various directions – they take advantage of their liberty. But that of Red migrants seems to reflect a wish to remain bound by the structure from which their migration could have liberated them. Their way of organizing themselves amounts to voluntarily rebuilding something as like the home system as possible. . .
>
> The Red syndrome, which has been termed incapsulation, has as one feature a 'tribal' type of moral conformism, stressing the

superiority of the original undiversified institutions; such institutions make for multiplex relations and the close-knit type of network; and this again makes for consistent moral pressure and conservatism. The processes are two-way or circular ones. It is by refusing to branch out into new habits that Red migrants retain a basis for close-knit networks: while it is by keeping the networks close-knit that they inhibit cultural branching-out.

In the other syndrome, more characteristic of School migrants, we find a culture which has been more tolerant in principle of the engagement in diversified institutions; accordingly, a tendency towards the single-strand type of relation and the loose-knit type of network. Again this produces two-way or circular effects. Cultural specialization makes for looser-knit networks, while the looseness of the network allows for cultural specialization. The School culture, with its institutional diversification, thus carries within itself its own dynamic of change in the migrant situation.

There seems to be no overriding reasons in the East London situation itself why one syndrome should occur rather than the other. On the one hand, Xhosa migrants in East London have excellent opportunities for remaining incapsulated within their old social systems if they wish. They are mostly not too far away from their homes of origin; they are officially discouraged from tearing up roots there; and they come to town in such numbers that material for building up the community-in-exile is readily available. On the other hand the opportunities for becoming assimilated and incorporated into the urban society are likewise excellent. The migrants are ethnically and linguistically at one with the people they meet in the East London locations; there are no insuperable barriers to prevent them from attaining prestige or high class-standing there – rewards which are offered to those who become urbanized, not to those who resist. Seeing that all these situational factors apply equally to Red and School migrants, one can seek explanations only in the Red–School cultural difference itself.

To the question why Red and School migrants organize their lives in these different manners it seems almost impossible to find an effective answer, for one quickly falls into the tautological trap which awaits any cross-cultural comparison on this elementary level – the trap of saying that people of different cultures act differently because their cultures are different. One of the most revelant features of the Red culture, evidently, is the emphasis on group activities and group judgement, and the evaluation of group friendships as more important than person-to-person friendships. Another is

> the 'tribal' attitude of the Red people (of which their conformist morality is an aspect). If we can define tribalism as a group's belief that a unique and exclusive relation must exist between itself and its institutions, the Red Xhosa are more tribal and the School Xhosa less so. The School Xhosa long ago agreed that certain institutions of another group or groups – notably Christianity and formal education – were to be shared by themselves: the Red Xhosa refused. Thus, in the long run, the different potentialities for urbanization shown by these two categories of Xhosa today can be said to have a basis in the different reactions of an earlier generation to a particular conquest situation, over a hundred years ago. How the differences may come to be eliminated in future, in some changed social situation, remains another question. (Mayer, 1961, pp. 292–3)

We thus have two contending approaches – the one averring that the migrant's behaviour in the city will be conditioned by his cultural background, the other – as described above by Gluckman and as we have already seen, explicit in the notion of the 'culture of poverty' – stressing the determinant nature of the urban situation. In the extreme both approaches badly distort our representation of the social process. There is of course, as Mayer argues, a continued interaction, a dialectic, between man and the world which he perceives – and indeed the world which exists independent of his perception. The migrant, of course, does not arrive in the city with a blank mind. He is conscious of his entire past experience however ready he may be, having made such a dramatic move, to view the world in new and unaccustomed ways. But what facets of his personality, what attitudes and beliefs can the migrant suddenly change upon his entry to the town, and what remains resistant to modification?

Studies of behaviour in the village can, as the Redfield–Lewis debate shows, produce divergent descriptions; questionnaires appear more 'scientific'. But they produce statements about norms – what the respondents think that people ought to or usually do, not what actually happens. Again, in the simple form in which the questions are put, it is usually impossible to ascertain whether the respondent is making a statement about the world as he sees it or is describing an internalized disposition to act in a certain manner. To give a very crude example: peasant fatalism is often inferred from affirmative replies to a question such as 'do you feel that it is impossible to change the world?' But what does the peasant mean? Is he saying that the only way to be better off is to have more land, and that this is not available or that it is controlled by a landowner and that any attack upon him will result in failure, punishment and victimization – a not unreasonable assumption in many areas in the past? Or is he indicating a level of apathy which will inhibit him from benefiting from opportunities for self-improvement which may be presented to him? In short we do not know, for the questionnaires do not purport to tell us, how the respondent will actually behave in specific situations; nor will the behavioural studies predict how subjects will act in situations very different from those described. Some studies of southern Italian villages have shown that, while a high level of apathy and consequent lack of change is evident within the village, many of the young men have in past decades displayed their initiative in emigrating to the United States (Lopreato, 1967).

Studies of neighbouring communities frequently reveal quite striking differences in attitudes. A fascinating example is provided by one such study of two villages at the head of a valley in the Peruvian Andes. A century ago they must have been very similar, but a slightly lower altitude enabled one community to embark on fruit growing and to become relatively wealthier. The other had a higher rate of emigration because of its lack of economic opportunities at home. In the former village a much smaller proportion felt that 'things were changing too quickly'; fewer felt that 'some were born to command, others to obey'; they were less inclined to feel that it was better to work on one's own than in co-operation; they felt more confident in the power of their village council; they had more respect for tradition and age; they were more inclined to think that the government took little interest in their village (and thus that their betterment depended upon their own efforts). Clearly these differences in attitude are a result of a century of change and development. It seems unreasonable to imagine (and one could never prove) that these differences antedated the economic changes and were thus responsible for acceptance of new opportunities in the richer village, rejection in the poorer. The divergence of their paths seems mainly due to an accident of nature – the altitudes of the villages (Matos Mar *et al.*, 1969).

Few attempts seem to have been made which actually demonstrate the potency of peasant attitudes in towns, rather than the assertion of supposed traits. In a study of workers in a Paris car factory, Touraine and Ragazzi (1961) found, from questionnaire responses, that Breton migrants were more likely to believe in their ability to rise in status than were the city-born workers. They gave greater weight to chance factors in this success. They were more optimistic about the future of their children – that they would be better placed than their parents. Like the Yoruba workers studied by my colleagues and myself (Lloyd 1974; Peace 1974, 1975), they aspired to set themselves up in independent businesses and felt uncommitted to continued factory employment. Here the influence of the past cultural environment of the migrants is clearly seen. Yet in a study of Ethiopian schoolboys from ethnic groups with markedly different cultures, William Shack (1976) found uniformity in the prestige ranking of occupations; each group placed the professionals – doctor, engineer, teacher – at the top, the menials at the bottom. This is perhaps an unsurprising finding, yet it serves to keep open the question posed – how far can we ascribe patterns of urban behaviour to the cultural background of the migrant, how far to the urban situation which faces him?

As we have seen, this is not an either/or question. It can be answered only through a diachronic study of the dialectical process of interaction between man and his world. When he arrives in the city the migrant will view his new surroundings in terms of concepts derived from his rural home. Thus he may be more disposed to classify the people he meets in ethnic terms or as mestizo/indian rather than in terms of economic class. He will initially interpret the city according to the information available to him on arrival – information which perhaps circulated in the village as common knowledge. Yet daily, with each new experience, he will devise new concepts and his store of information will increase. Perhaps more resistant to change will be his idea of the 'good life', his occupational goals being valued in terms of independence rather than security. Certain routes to such goals might be seen as right and proper, others as wrong and wicked. Reliance on the help of kin and patrons may be stressed, to the extent that the rural migrant comes to the city possessed of certain skills which may well give him an advantage in certain situations over his urban-born rival.

A conclusive answer to our question may forever elude us. Yet it remains important for us to stress the sequence by which the migrant interprets and responds to the urban situation. For so many paths are in theory open to him. At one extreme a train of events leads the migrant towards tight encapsulation within a little community of people from his home village, a little world in which behavioural patterns deriving from the village are continually reinforced; at the other, village origins may be totally rejected as the migrant endeavours to assimilate fully into the dominant urban culture.

We must therefore look at the rural origins of the migrants – the culture which they bring to the towns is an important element in their reaction to city life. As the next section will attempt to show, these cultural backgrounds can vary widely. This variation, furthermore, affects not only the personality and attitudes of the individual migrant; it also governs the degree to which the village claims the continued allegiance of its emigrants. For the rural–urban ties which are so widely discussed in the literature on migration derive not only from the motivations of the individual migrants but also from the character of the village itself.

## TRIBAL AND PEASANT SOCIETIES

In the rural areas from which many of the migrants come, agriculture is at a near-subsistence level; that is, the farmer feeds his own family and produces but a small surplus for exchange or obligatory dues. The family of man, wife (or wives) and children is the usual working unit. Technology is simple, and though the farmer may have a detailed knowledge of crop varieties and soil types, he lacks the means to exercise much control over his environment – he is at the mercy of climate, pests and diseases. The village community is small and it too is nearly self-sufficient; its contacts with the outside world are few. Thus ignorance and powerlessness are universal features of the worlds from which these urban migrants come. But here the similarities end.

For convenience I have used the term peasant society to characterize the migrants' communities of origin. In an earlier book (Lloyd, 1971) I distinguished between tribal and peasant societies. In fact a distinction must be made along two dimensions. On the one hand we must distinguish between autonomous and dependent societies; on the other between open and closed societies.

The African tribe or ethnic group was, in the pre-colonial period, a politically autonomous unit. It possessed its distinctive culture. Such autonomy was more marked in the chiefless or acephalous societies where each village was independent. In kingdoms the outlying villages were subordinate to the capital yet shared in its culture. Again the group which was constantly raided for slaves by its more powerful neighbours perhaps felt that its political autonomy lacked reality; yet it could retain a pride in its cultural individuality.

The peasant society is, in contrast, a part society – it exists only in conjunction with an urban society. The dichotomy is described in terms of urban/rural, oligarchy/peasantry, great tradition/little tradition. Peasant society is dependent upon urban society and is exploited by it; the town is maintained by the countryside. A surplus is exacted from the peasant in a variety of ways – by labour services to his landlord, by payments of rent, of a share of his crops, by direct and indirect taxes, by controls exercised by urban society over the marketing processes so that the peasant is underpaid for his produce. The peasant is aware of this exploitation and though he may feel unable to change the system he may endeavour to subvert it, by cheating in his payments, or to maximize his advantage within it, by currying favours from his patrons in the dominant sector. He not only feels inferior but realizes that he is regarded as inferior. Dependency creates a personality markedly different from that found in the autonomous communities. The downtrodden peasant is contrasted with the proud tribesman.

Today, of course there are no truly autonomous societies in the sense in which this term has been used in the preceding paragraphs. All have become incorporated into the modern state. And this state exploits the farmers through a variety of taxes and the control of the prices of foodstuffs and export crops in a manner not unlike that used by the medieval urban oligarchy. The farmers of all the third-world countries are now peasants, as this term is usually defined. But an essential difference often exists, as has been noted above: the new Western-educated elite, the urban technicians and bureaucrats of the new states, have often come, in their lifetimes, from tribal villages. The urban–rural dichotomy, the cultural cleavage, is developing rapidly; but it is a new phenomenon and not one which has persisted for centuries.

An approach which focuses upon the external relationships of the community tends to neglect its internal structure. Here we must distinguish between those societies which are open, homogeneous or relatively unstratified and those which are closed, heterogeneous or stratified. The two dimensions – autonomous/dependent and open/closed – are not congruent, for it is possible for a peasant society as defined in the previous paragraph to be composed of 'open' villages. Thus in the Peruvian sierra an indian village may be composed of descent groups holding farm land under a communal form of tenure and yet supplying labour for and depending upon the neighbouring *hacienda.* In the open community, positions of wealth and power are open to all and there is a high rate of intergenerational mobility. In the closed community these social differences tend to be perpetuated from generation to generation, possibly being associated with, if not produced by, ethnic differences such as caste in Indian villages or mestizo/indian cleavages in Latin America.

However drably uniform the village may appear to the outside observer from the affluent West, marked internal differences in wealth and power exist. These are not accidental, for they have been achieved through conscious choice and action. Wealth and power are esteemed by the members of the community albeit often with ambivalence.

In the tribal society wealth is not achieved through the control of land, for this is held communally by village or descent groups, but through the control of labour. A farmer becomes rich by working hard and enjoying good health and by having sons who in their adolescent years produce more than they consume. He exploits them – though he is responsible for finding them wives and helping them to set up their own households. At a simple level, differences in wealth can to some extent be correlated with the life cycle. In the polygynous society the surplus which is produced can be invested in more wives – who produce more sons. It may also be invested in trade, but wealth does not usually enable one to operate a monopoly. The trader competes with scores of others and makes his profit largely from astute dealings and his ability to handle a large turnover.

In the peasant society the farmer is more likely to hold a fixed amount of land which passes to his heirs. As his family grows in size he can seek to augment his land, either by purchasing or renting from other members of the community or by begging for more from the dominant landowner. Here too surplus may be invested in commerce, the range of opportunities being greater and the possibilities for monopolistic control more than in the typical African tribal community.

In both types of society a number of redistributive mechanisms exist. The wealthy polygynist has a correspondingly large number of children, so that on his death their individual shares of his estate tend to be small. He cannot anticipate that all his children will achieve the same status as himself – that would be an impossibility. He hopes that one will perhaps emulate him, achieving success in turn by his own efforts. The rich peasant farmer, possessed of many acres, may well have numerous children among whom his land is eventually partitioned. In monogamous societies, with a high infant mortality, the patterns of land distribution can change dramatically in a very few decades.

It may well be that, at a given low level of technology, continued investment of the surplus to increase economic production is not possible – there is no more land available, trade cannot be expanded further. But whether or not such a position can be reached, mechanisms operate to translate economic wealth into political power, so that further accumulation is perhaps inhibited. In African tribal societies the wealthy farmer or trader takes a titled office, spending lavishly to ensure his election and thereafter relinquishing his economic activities. Tribute maintains him in relative affluence. But on his death his title does not pass directly to his sons. Again the fiestas of the patron saints of Latin American villages, or the feasts given by New Guinea 'big men', serve to enhance the political power and influence of the more successful men at the cost of considerable spending. Such power and influence may indeed provide a basis for further accumulation, but in the long run these mechanisms prevent the accumulation of wealth by a few from progressing to a point at which the structure of the community becomes radically altered.

Progressive wealth and power is neither unsought by, nor unwelcome to, its possessors; yet it is unplanned in our sense of that word. Lacking effective control over climate, disease and the fertility of his wives, the farmer cannot postulate the economic stages to success. Some of his success will depend on co-members of his community – they will support him with communal labour, vote him into office, provide opportunities for aggrandizement. His concern therefore is to nurture his personal relationships, with patrons as well as with social equals, so that he may exploit to the full any opportunity offered. These social skills may be much more fully developed than in an 'impersonal' modern urban community.

Attitudes towards wealth and its acquisition are ambivalent. One admires the man who, through his own efforts, reaches the top, yet wealth and power imply ranking – and if some are at the top, others must be at the bottom. George Foster (1965), in his thesis of 'the limited good', argues that in all peasant societies wealth and even happiness are seen as scarce resources, limited in supply, and that one man's gain is another's loss. He grossly overstates his case and has been justly criticized, yet there is a valuable element here. In a peasant community with a fixed amount of farmland (with no perceived opportunities for expansion outside the village), the acquisition of land by a wealthy man must make the seller poorer. In a vastly different context, the Tiv of central Nigeria, as Paul Bohannan (1957) describes them, believe that a man's power and influence derive from *tsav*, a witchcraft substance growing on his heart. It grows by feeding on his close kin on the male side, who weaken and may eventually die. Accused of such witchcraft the powerful man tries to deny over-complicity in the case at issue – he will not admit killing his brother or cousin – yet he will not deny the possession of *tsav*. While the weaker man envies, and in the Tiv case fears, his powerful relative, he nevertheless relies on him for security and support. If he is involved in a dispute with someone from another family, it will be upon the efforts of his powerful kinsman that his success in the litigation will rest. For in the tribal society, wealth and power bring benefits not only to the individual, so that he enjoys a relatively high standard of living, but also to the entire community which he represents.

In a closed or dependent society the outcomes may be different. Instead of being annulled or dissipated at death, wealth may perhaps be transmitted to heirs, thus creating a stratification in the community which had hitherto emphasized its egalitarian nature. The wealthy man, instead of becoming a genuine leader of this community, may in fact opt out of it – either physically by moving to the town, taking his wealth with him, or by joining the dominant sector, becoming one of the landowning group or closely associated with them. Such fears give rise to the trait of 'amoral familiarism' described by Edward Banfield (1958) – 'maximize the material, short-run advantage of the nuclear family; assume that all others do likewise'. Associated with this is a strong suspicion of others, leading to attempts to hide one's own success lest it become an object for public scorn. Leaders are imagined to use their positions for personal gain; and hence most men refuse such offices, and the cohesion of the community is weakened. Other writers about southern Italian villages confirm the dismal picture presented by Banfield but challenge his explanation: 'amoral familiarism is merely a pragmatic response to life in a hopelessly harsh and uncertain environment. It is the result of a stagnant society not the cause of its stagnation' (Peabody, 1970, p. 385).

Thus at one extreme we have the example of the African chief, resplendent in his robes, flaunting his affluence and being praised by his followers; at the other extreme villagers who refuse to strive overtly for success or to assume leadership roles for fear of the scorn and enmity of their neighbours. A fundamental cause of this variance lies, I believe, in the roles ascribed by the community to its successful members – in becoming leaders or in leaving and betraying the community. But in both cases the attitudes generated can be exacerbated: in southern Italy the extreme poverty of the villages described, poverty which is known by the villagers to be unduly harsh, accounts for the high level of mutual distress; in the Tiv case, a smallpox epidemic raised to an intolerable level the mutual suspicions which in more normal times could be coped with through the existing mechanisms (Bowen, 1964).

Many of the points raised above in the discussion of individual achievement are pertinent in describing the communities from which the shanty-town dwellers have emigrated. In looking at the different dimensions along which cohesion may be measured I seek firstly to show that life in the village may engender attitudes towards self-help and co-operation, later relevant in the urban situation, and secondly to distinguish between those village communities which seem to retain a strong hold over their emigrant members and those which lose them entirely.

The village community is by definition small, and relatively isolated and self-contained. Its members are bound together by multiple cross-cutting relationships. Innovative behaviour is inhibited, for the individual dare not risk the pursuit of some privately valued goal which would alienate him from his community. (It is through migration that the individual can perhaps indulge in his idiosyncrasies.)

Villages vary in the degree to which they are socially homogeneous. At one extreme is the African tribal community all of whose members trace their descent from a common ancestor.

They are, almost literally, brothers. At one remove are those communities composed of a small number of such descent groups, each proud of it distinctive origin yet sharing a common culture with its neighbours in their adjacent compounds. At the other extreme are the heterogeneous communities. For instance one could site the Indian villages containing members of a small number of castes rigidly segregated in their interpersonal behaviour by rules of pollution yet economically bound together by the *jajmani* ties of clientship. Or the Spanish American villages with mestizo and indian members in which physical differences have become blurred with centuries of intermarriage yet a social segregation, amounting to covert hostility, exists as the mestizo continually seek to emphasize their allegiance to the dominant Spanish culture while the indian remains loyal to his own traditions – if only because he has been given little opportunity to do otherwise.

In the homogeneous community one would anticipate finding a fairly high level of co-operative activity – in house building and in farmwork. But one must distinguish here between that which is truly reciprocal and that which reinforces the social ranking in the community. Thus in the former case A will help B with his harvest on one day; on the next B aids A; or, A calls on his kin to help him build his house, accepting tacitly an obligation to provide similar assistance when requested. An example of status-reinforcing activity is the work party called by a powerful or wealthy man (both the Yoruba of Nigeria and the indians of the Peruvian sierra seem to have an identical institution (Alberti and Mayer, 1971). The host calls upon all those with any ties of obligation or dependence to do a day's work on his farm. In return he provides music and a feast. He needs a capital outlay, and it is often argued that his expenditure may be little different from what he would otherwise have paid in wages – and hence the contract is reciprocal. Yet the host is advantaged in getting his work done at the optimal period. For instance all his maize is planted immediately the rains begin and not gradually over the following weeks.

The annual village feast may be evaluated to the degree to which the entire population is involved, each member contributing according to his ability. Conversely the feast may be seen as providing economic advantage to one group – the wealthy and powerful – or amusement for another – the poor. In either case the feast is viewed to some extent as symbolizing village unity and identity. For the village is competing with neighbouring communities, perhaps for land and now, in many parts, for new social services – a primary school or dispensary. The village is, in the dependent situation, in conflict with the state. Much of what it seeks is obtainable only from the state, through the mediation of a hierarchy of bureaucrats. The search for patrons within this hierarchy blends with feelings of repugnancy against dependency, perhaps stimulating efforts towards self-help. The belief, in the wealthier of the two Peruvian villages cited earlier, that government did little to help the village is not as paradoxical as may first appear.

The solidarity of the village community against the outside world coexists with an internal competition for power and wealth. The form taken by the latter determines the degree to which the former is reinforced or vitiated. The striving for achievement is individual, yet groupings of a more or less permanent nature may be discerned. In the tribal village the most significant divisions may be those based on descent or age. Descent groups may be envisaged as competing for land or for wives, yet if one becomes excessively large it subdivides and the genealogies are reinterpreted; the overall structure of the community is maintained. Age-grade members follow each other through a sequence of public duties – as labourers, warriors, decision-makers and elders. Alternatively the basis of village political activity may be factions, led by rival candidates for leadership. The leaders are usually wealthy men, their followers are bound to them by a variety of ties – kin or economic – reflecting ascribed obligations or a hope that allegiance will yield rewards. In each of the above instances the perceived grouping cuts across socio-economic strata. Factions and descent groups each contain a due proportion of rich and poor. A very different situation emerges when rich and poor, perhaps in the guise of ethnic affiliation, differences of origin, caste, religion, unite independently to oppose each other. Earlier remarks on leadership should be reiterated here. A distinction is made between those leaders probably achieving office as a consequence of their economic success, who are seen as protecting and benefiting the entire community, and those who appear to use office for their personal advancement – either in reinforcing their position (and that of their heirs) in the higher strata of the community or in leaving it altogether.

In the preceding pages I have sought to indicate the variety in the structures of the communities from which the urban migrants have come, partly in order to demonstrate that a universal 'peasant mentality' does not exist and should not be expected. Yet in addition to the common traits admitted at the outset – those of ignorance and powerlessness – others have become apparent during this discussion; but these latter are not in accord with the cruder notions of 'peasant mentality'. A typical feature of the village community is the relatively high rate of intra- and inter-generational mobility. A man is poor in his youth and old age, affluent in middle age as his sons help him. The estates of the wealthy are fragmented among heirs. These societies are competitive as men seek goals which emphasize individual achievement. An inability to control the natural environment, and the events in the world outside the village, is moderated by the belief that success comes through the manipulation of interpersonal relationships. The migrant encounters a similar situation in the informal sector of the urban economy. How far we can say that internalized attitudes foster the successful exploitation of opportunities is difficult to assess. But the skills learnt in the rural area are certainly appropriate in the urban situation.

With some obvious exceptions, such as Indian caste villages, these rural communities tend not to be rigidly stratified. Both social mobility and the nature of political groupings based on descent or factions prevent this. But at the same time these communities are now dependent ones, exploited by the state, the urban groups. The villager therefore uses not a single model to account for social inequality but two or more. One model is appropriate to the description of the entire society, stressing the conflict between urban and rural populations, government and masses, oligarchy and peasant; the other is appropriate to the local community. For the peasants who spend most of their working hours on the landowner's estate, the latter model may stress the same relationships of dependence and conflict; but for the villager from the open community the two models will be essentialy different (cf. Strickon, 1967).

The village with a strong sense of its cohesion and solidarity, engendered by belief in the homogeneity of its population, by an egalitarian structure fostered by intense reciprocal communal activity, is to be distinguished from one where all activity is looked upon with suspicion as being motivated by hope of individual, rather than community benefit. Migrants from the former may well see in the cities a situation in which collective action is inappropriate, but where it does appear feasible they will at least have the necessary skills to organize it. Much of this urban associational activity is, as we shall see later, based not upon urban residential area, but on membership of a community of origin. Yet not all migrants form such associations to an equal degree. In Africa, as I have indicated elsewhere (Lloyd, 1967, p. 204), some people, such as the Ibo, have very strongly developed associations based hierarchically on village district and province of origin, whereas others, the Hausa for instance, have none. One of the prime determinants here would seem to be the nature of Igbo village society – the epitome of the African tribal community referred to in these pages, in contrast to the highly developed states of the Hausa. In a similar vein Bryan Roberts (1974) has contrasted the strength of these urban associations in Lima with their virtual absence in Guatemala – and in fact in most Latin American cities. Many of the villages of the Peruvian sierra are, in my terms, open and strongly cohesive, in contrast with those of Guatemala, which are stratified into mestizo and indians, in which the richer mestizo see wealth as a means to escape from village life, in which little co-operative effort is undertaken to improve the community and which, in sum, has little hold over the allegiance of their members.

## TRADITIONAL COMMUNITIES?

In this chapter, I have assumed in a conventional manner that the migrants have come from a 'traditional' background which contrasts markedly with the 'modern' environment of the town. The village structures described have been those which existed prior to recent development – the growth of manufacturing industry in the cities, the achievement of national independence. But most of the migration described has taken place in the last three decades – decades in which the villages themselves have undergone profound changes. In fact as 'push' factors these changes have often been as potent in stimulating emigration as the 'pull' of urban attractions.

The villages have been drawn further into the social and economic life of the modern state. Roads have been constructed, primary schools opened, a few villagers may have a transistor radio and see the occasional newspaper. One or two of the elderly men may even be returned migrants from the city. Most of the villages in the more backward areas of the state are far less isolated than in the past. Some, nearer to the capitals, have lost their isolation completely, for they now grow food crops for the city and their people move to and from the metropolis with increasing frequency. The effect of these changes is that goals hitherto unknown to the villagers now appear within their grasp. Conversely the poverty and insecurity of rural life, previously accepted as the natural order, is now contrasted adversely with the better life of the town – especially by the younger villagers, often school leavers, who form the majority of the migrants.

Such invidious comparisons are enhanced when near-by communities experience different rates of advance. Earlier in this chapter mention was made of a study of two villages in the Peruvian Andes, one of which has become comparatively wealthy from fruit-growing, the other – lacking the right conditions for this crop – exporting its labour. In a similar study of two villages in south India Scarlett Epstein (1962) has shown how in the low-lying one irrigation was introduced and sugar and rice grown, whereas the higher village was unable to benefit thus and its men took up work in the processing factories or sought irrigated land outside their village. But though in terms of cash incomes both benefited equally, the 'wet' village remained conservative and traditionally oriented, for the changes were largely effected within the existing structure of the society, while in the 'dry' village a process of change was set in motion which seemed to be self-perpetuating. Thus while the former village seemed stagnant, the latter was taking off into sustained growth.

As the questionnaire study of the Peruvian villages has shown, economic success is manifested in less fatalistic attitudes towards change and development. Much of the literature of the 1950s suggested that the traumatic experiences of the migrants would create strains leading to psychological disorders. An epidemiological survey in and around Abeokuta, a large Yoruba town in Nigeria, showed however that those who had moved into the town were relatively healthy but that the incidence of symptoms of maladjustment was higher in the villages – though it was not clear whether this was the direct effect of village life or because those individuals least able to cope with the world gravitated to the villages (Leighton *et al.*, 1963). Studies infer that mental breakdown among students often occurs when they fail to achieve exceedingly high aspirations and not because of any great disparity between their new status and that of their youth and parental home.

As economic activities in the rural area become increasingly differentiated we can no longer presume consensus in the attitudes of the emigrants. The goals, value and knowledge of the son of the wealthy trader will not be those of the landless labourer's child. Again, as patterns of inequality alter – with the rich perhaps becoming more firmly entrenched, new categories of people achieving wealth and power – so will the strains of these changes affect beliefs. In many areas the 'green revolution' in agriculture has benefited families most unequally. The new opportunities are seized by the rich and powerful, who have the financial capital to invest in improved techniques and the power and influence to control co-operatives and credit associations to their own advantage. Traditional relationships whereby the rich man provided security for his poorer dependants – as in the *jajmani* system of Indian caste villages – are ruptured in favour of cash contracts. The big farmer hires labour when he needs it, when he does not, the labourer goes hungry.

Some measures of land reform destroy the communal holding of land, and agricultural experts believe that only through individual consolidated family holdings can output be increased. Other reforms attempt to break the pattern of small peasant holdings in favour of large state or co-operative farms on which the peasant becomes a wage labourer – if indeed he is lucky enough to be hired at all.

The political climate which has facilitated such measures of land reform and redistribution implies too the weakening of the rural oligarchy of big landowners where these existed. Peasants are conventionally portrayed as passive – and to a large extent they have been, as they have been unable to see a successful outcome to their protests; and the local rebellions which have occurred have been quickly quelled, reports of them rarely reaching the city newspapers, let alone the history books. Today, with their adversaries apparently weakened, the peasants are encouraged to press their claims with renewed vigour and to seize land. Their spontaneous activity is eulogized by city politicians anxious to make capital for their own parties and their policies. Operating in a reverse direction are those movements led and largely manned by the city intellectuals who, in the style of Che Guevara, hope to fan the embers of peasant discontent into the flames of national revolution.

Thus many migrants to the city come not from sleepy rural backwaters but from areas which have been engaged in tense political activity. But while radical city intellectuals are prone to interpret these movements as part of a grand revolutionary process which will ultimately overthrow the government, or capitalism itself, we must remember that the views of the peasants themselves are very different. Few are committed revolutionaries. Most see as their objectives the winning of a little more land, the easing of burdensome exactions of tax, rent and tribute. Where large private estates have been converted into state or co-operative farms, peasants are apt to complain that exploitation and domination by the state and its technicians is no better than by the erstwhile landowner – and at least they understood the rules of the game in opposing the latter, whereas the workings of the new bureaucracies are unfathomable. Tensions are created, too, when established local leaders find themselves displaced by other categories of men, favoured by the new regime.

Today the concept of a universal peasant mentality is perhaps a straw man, though I suspect that it lingers much more tenaciously in popular belief than in scholarly literature. However, the purpose of this chapter has been less to demolish the concept than to find something to put in its place.

Clearly, when the migrant arrives in the city he views his new environment through eyes trained in the rural area. His initial responses will depend on this rurally derived interpretation of his situation. Certainly in a matter of weeks he will learn new concepts, gain new information. But his earlier decisions will already have set him along certain paths which subsequently condition later choices open to him. For example in depending substantially upon his close kin on arrival he will find it difficult to break away from them later, repudiating debts incurred. The problem which faces us here is to decide how far attitudes learnt in the rural area continue to affect the interpretation of urban situations, and the decisions consequently taken. To what degree are they internalized – or were they but expressions of the realities of rural life?

Accepting that these attitudes *are* important, a further problem faces us. The migrants come from such varied environments. One can easily accept differences between African tribal villages and those of caste-structured India or the Latin American *hacienda*; but one must also be prepared for differences in village structure and the attitudes generated to be found in neighbouring communities consequent upon uneven patterns of recent development. Again all migrants do not have the same status in their natal communities – some are from rich, others from poor families. Finally, in an attempt to magnify the contrast between the 'traditional' environment of the village and that of the 'modern' city, we are apt to overlook the economic changes and perhaps political ferment which have occurred in the rural area in the more recent decades. Furthermore, while for the sake of emphasis I have focused here upon the village community, it must be remembered that many migrants come from the provincial towns and are already partially exposed to new values and a mediating environment.

Thus were we to take a group of migrants now living in a shanty town and watch them face a common situation, we should expect them each to interpret it differently. Is there a common factor which is sufficiently significant to help us predict their behaviour? Or can we but accept that their view of the world is an important but unmeasurable variable?

However, even if one is led to sympathize with those sociologists who hold that attitudes are not a useful field of study, either because the relationship between attitude and behaviour is dubious or because the attitudes cannot be ascertained at a generalized rather than purely individual level, it is still important that we should look at the rural background of the migrants. For this is an important variable in assessing the continuing link between the migrant and his home community and thus in understanding his decisions in the town. Should he for instance invest in a house in the village or in the city, or send his savings home in any other form? That such rural–urban links are important is now commonplace. Less attention has been paid to discovering why some individuals, some ethnic groups, retain a much closer, or different kind of relationship, than others.

# 5 The Migratory Process

Who emigrates to the cities, and from what areas do they come? The quick and simple answer is that migration involves most categories of people, rich and poor, educated and illiterate, and that they come from all parts of the state, its advanced and its backward regions, and even in some cases from beyond the national frontiers.

An abundance of statistical data exists on the migratory flow, most of it culled from censuses. From one country to another the pattern is surprisingly uniform and this has led to attempts to explain the discrepancies between sets of nationally aggregated figures. Yet much of this effort seems to be unproductive. The differences can be accounted for in terms of geographic environment – the proportion of the country which is rich or poor, the number and location of provincial cities – and in terms of the chronology of national economic development. Such reasoning tells us little about the process of migration.

Analysts are concerned to measure the magnitude of the migratory flow – its rate. On one hand they describe the composition of the urban population – how many are immigrant and from what regions do they come? On the other hand they calculate the rate of depopulation of the rural area. These two sets of figures are not necessarily congruent, for in a country where the majority of the population live in backward areas, migrants from these may predominate in the town, yet the few more advanced areas may be sending a higher proportion of their people to the city. The rate of migration from different areas not only changes as they become drawn more closely into the national economy but it also fluctuates with economic and political changes. For instance a boom in a major industry such as oil can lead to greater migration. So too can a change of government, as when a rigid dictatorship yields to a more liberal regime, promising greater opportunities and a relaxation of restrictions.

The same analysts measure too the incidence of migration – what category of persons are more likely to move? Here more detailed surveys are usually required, for while census data may give the overall level of education of the migrant population of the city it cannot usually tell whether each individual rural area is sending a disproportionately high number of literates. Only a village survey which records absentees can do this.

The third theme of the analyst is the route by which the migrant reaches the city. Does he, as early theories of migration allege, leave by steps or stages, first from his village to a near-by town, then to a provincial centre and only ultimately, after several years, arrive in the capital? Or does he go straight from his rural home to the city, called there by relatives whose social network forms a chain linking the two areas? Here especially, as I shall argue later, attempts to prove the primacy of one mode over the other seem to ignore the time dimension. Step migration gives way to chain migration – but, at any given period, adjacent areas or even neighbouring villages will be at different stages of the process.

Some of the most comprehensive and illuminating presentation of migration statistics have been provided by Caldwell (1969) in his analysis of movements into Ghanaian towns and by Balan *et al.* (1973) in their description of Monterrey, an industrial city in northern Mexico. Their detailed findings largely corroborate those presented for other parts of the third world. I use them extensively later in this chapter.

In attempting to interpret differences in rate, incidence and paths of migration, 'push' and 'pull' factors have been identified. The former operate to expel the migrant from the rural area – poverty and lack of opportunity resulting from a stagnant agriculture and/or shortage of land arising from increasing population or land reforms .The town 'pulls' people by promising wage employment and by its apparent glamour. The 'city lights' may not provide a permanent attraction, especially for the shanty-town dweller who gazes on them from afar, but in many a rural area social manhood is achieved not only through the traditional ceremonies of initiation but also through a brief period of work in the city. The 'push–pull' approach has been attacked however, not because the factors cited are irrelevant but because it suggests a dichotomy between unrelated factors. But both land shortage and city employment are the produce of a particular mode of economic development.

Economists have sought to explain migration rates in terms of the difference between urban and rural incomes. The former are certainly higher, on average, because most skilled and white-collar employment is located in the city. Minimum wages may be higher too, but it is more difficult here to correlate these with village incomes, setting the high cost of foodstuff and services in the city against the provision of these within the rural household. Modifying the crude differential which might be calculated is the estimation of employment prospects: the migrant may see his urban income as being three times as high as that in the rural area, yet he anticipates being unemployed for half the year and so his gain will be not three times his present income but only half as much again. Calculations of this order, however, tend to ignore both the migrant's estimate of his long-run chances of success in the town and a range of purely social factors. Even if a government were to legislate equal minimum wages in town and country, the cityward migration would continue – though perhaps not at the same rate.

## THE DECISION TO EMIGRATE

For some scholars the study of migration can safely ignore the individual migrant and his motivations. His course of action is predetermined by the factors of development and he is swept along by forces far beyond his control. The reasons which he gives for his actions are rationalizations made after the event, prompted by the dominant ideology. Questionnaire responses from migrants already well settled in the city show overwhelmingly that they came to find work– or, a poor second, to get education for themselves or their children. These are certainly not very illuminating data. Yet ignoring the decision-making of the migrant not only impoverishes our understanding of the migration process, it also deprives us of an image of a vital element in the life experience of the migrant which will affect his own perception of the urban environment and of his activities therein.

Rather than ask the shanty-town dweller why he left his village, we should base ourselves in the village and examine the antecedent situations of those who leave. But I know of no detailed study of this kind. Indeed it has many difficulties – one does not know in advance who will leave and when. Again, the 'decision' is not easily isolated. From his early youth the villager becomes aware of a wide range of possible goals and of means of achieving them. He estimates opportunities both in his own community and beyond it. His departure is caused by precipitating factors – he leaves school and needs to find work. This factor can be predicted in advance, but others cannot – a family quarrel or an accusation of witchcraft. (Such precipitating factors are not, of course, causes of the migration – they occurred long before migration emerged as a mode of solution and were then resolved by other means.)

Migration studies sometimes tend to assume that the villager is presented with a single choice – to emigrate or stay. Yet he has in fact a number of options available and his choice between them will in consequence determine future courses open to him. Yet few studies have attempted to delineate these options. Good examples are the Salisburys' (1972) description of the migration of Siane from the New Guinea highlands to Port Moresby (see below, pp. 155) and Garbett's analysis of the circular migration of the Korekore of Rhodesia. Both authors, being social anthropologists, give full weight to the economic factors but emphasize the manner in which each individual is enmeshed in a network of personal relationships which are involved both in the formulation of his goals and in creating opportunities and constraints in their achievement.

For instance a Korekore man has the option of working on near-by European farms or of travelling to Salisbury to earn cash. The young migrant has however usually paid only part of the bride-wealth to his father-in-law. Were he to take his wife with him, the father-in-law would demand that the payment be completed. In working near-by the migrant is able to visit his wife in his village, and fulfil obligations to his father-in-law such as bringing gifts and working on his land. In so doing he maintains close contact with his village kin and, incidentally, with co-villagers working on the European farms. In fact he tends to return to the same or neighbouring farms on each short-term migratory trip. In contrast the man who goes to Salisbury seems to lose contact both with his village and with his co-villagers in the city. He becomes a long-term migrant. He is far more ready to exploit new opportunities in the city and tends to have a more varied career (Garbett, 1976).

Let us look briefly at the way in which the potential migrant is likely to make his decision. Like others in his community he aspires to a better life. To a large extent this is expressed in material terms – more food to eat, an improved house and so on. Prestige too is important and this may, as suggested above, be gained from visits beyond the bounds of the community, especially to the city. He may see this better life as being achieved within the village. In this case he will contemplate either one or more seasonal migrations, leaving the village for a few months when agricultural activity is at its lowest to make a quick cash gain working as an unskilled labourer. From the poor arid zone of West Africa thousands of such men move south each dry season to work on farms and in towns in the wealthier areas. Or he may plan to spend one or two years away on one or more occasions; he becomes a 'target worker' – a man who sets out to earn enough to marry, to buy a bicycle or sewing machine before returning – or a circular migrant. In each case the returning migrant easily slips back into his traditional roles. One study of a Senegalese village reports that a very extensive periodic emigration of young men has done little to change village life. That the village is now beginning to change is in fact due not to migration but to quite unrelated government policies of development (Nolan, 1975).

Alternatively the villager may feel that his home community has so little to offer him that he must leave, at least for the greater part of his working life. This disparity between the perceived situation at home and the anticipated rewards elsewhere is relative. In the poorest areas unable to grow agricultural produce for export – and hence to yield a cash income to buy imported consumption goods – almost everybody may aspire to leave. In slightly more favoured areas certain categories – families without land rights, junior children unable to inherit much from their parents – may be especially disadvantaged. But equally the educated and the skilled may see their local community unable to satisfy their aspirations. The secondary-school leaver observes that few posts exist locally which require his level of education (and though local boys may be favoured for these few posts, the opportunities for promotion are poor). The successful craftsman or trader sees an expansion of his activities to be possible only in a larger, wealthier community. The educated youth sets off from his village knowing that the whole of his working life will be spent in urban areas. The illiterate emigrates tentatively to try his luck – if successful he will stay on in the city, if he fails to establish himself he will return perhaps to try again later or in some other area, becoming, by default rather than by design, the circular migrant.

In the more remote community the illiterate villager's perception of the city may verge on fantasy. Returned migrants will bring a breath of realism, though to boost their own self-esteem they may over-glamourize their tales. At the other extreme are those who have frequently visited the city, perhaps being sent to relatives during school holidays before their permanent move there. For each individual, his choices must be made against this background knowledge of the opportunities available, the urban situation. Possible goals are evaluated in terms of resources available. Few migrants leave home with large financial assets. Few too have technical skills relevant to urban occupations. Some have a literary education. Urban employers may be known to demand a primary-school leaving certificate as a sign of general competence and the illiterate may thus be deterred from going to the city. Yet in the city the illiterate, willing to undertake the most menial jobs, tends to remain unemployed for a much shorter period than the well-educated youth who does not deign to take a job below his qualifications but who remains in the city because so few opportunities exist elsewhere. A resource of similar significance is the possession of friends and relatives in the place to which one emigrates, for these will initially accommodate one and help one to get established. Such contacts will probably determine where one goes; for while a number of towns may seem equally likely to provide the migrant – and especially one with little education – with employment, he will choose that in which he will be welcomed by kinsmen.

Against the benefits expected from emigration the villager must estimate the costs. Will he be able to take his wife and children with him? If they remain in the village will they, with the periodic help of other male kin, be able to work his farm, so that his income in the town is pure gain? On the other hand will he lose his land rights through sustained absence, will his status in his village be diminished – or will he be able to return after decades and automatically assume the role of respected elder? The respective costs and benefits vary not only as between individuals of different social position in their community but also with age.

Viewing the migration process as the produce of men's decisions and actions – rather than that of blind forces – we may with profit stand back and look at the emergent pattern, reiterating our opening questions.

## MIGRATION PATTERNS

The shanty-town dwellers do in fact come from all areas. They leave the poorest regions because there are so few opportunities to gain a living from agriculture. At first such people may migrate seasonally or as target workers. But as knowledge of the city increases so will more men spend larger periods there. In most cases the successful migrant who returns to his village upon his retirement does little to transform its economy. He builds a decent house and with hired labour cultivates his land. He may open a small shop. At best he may be prepared to innovate new agricultural techniques. Thus cocoa growing was introduced from Lagos to the interior of western Nigeria by returning farm labourers. The area which becomes wealthier through the efforts of returning migrants, through government development policies, or as a result of a favoured environment – climate, soils, local market for crops – provides opportunities for its sons which the poor area does not; in the former one can aspire to become a rich farmer, a wealthy trader. But this same process tends to result too in more schools, in greater contact with the city, and so again the number of school-leavers exceeds the jobs locally available. Aspirations rise and are incapable of local satisfaction. Thus, in their survey of Monterrey, Balan *et al.* found that two fifths of migrants came from zones of high socio-economic status and the same proportion from zones of low status. In fact the proportion of migrants from the more affluent areas increased slightly between the 1930s and mid-1960s (1973, p. 66).

Distance is an obvious and important factor. Towns recruit more of their migrants from the near-by hinterland than from the remote areas because the journey is so much more simple and less costly. Again the nearer areas are likely to have experienced an earlier and faster rate of economic development, their people having greater urban contacts. But the distance which men have travelled to Johannesburg – from Zambia, Malawi and Mozambique – indicates that mileage itself is not a great obstacle.

Migration is selective not only between but within communities; each individual is not equally likely to migrate. In Africa and Asia men predominate in emigration – their wives follow them to set up home in the town. Educated women of course go to the towns to work, for their opportunities in the rural area tend to be fewer than those of the men. Unhappy wives abscond to the city. But in general the town provides women with few avenues for paid employment. In Latin America , however, the relatively large white or mestizo upper and middle classes employ living-in female domestic servants (in Africa and Asia men do such tasks). Some of these girls come to the city and stay with kin who help them to find work. Others are recruited in the rural area by their employers. These girls are mostly young, in their early teens, and they then either marry or become pregnant and are dismissed.

Male migrants too are predominantly young. Some accompany their parents to the city and thus do not journey of their own volition. School leaving is a break in one's life which disposes one to emigrate. But for both school-leavers and illiterates their bachelorhood in their late teens and early twenties is the obvious period in which to emigrate. One's kin will receive a single migrant – they will not tolerate an entire family, utterly dependent on them. The uncertainty and insecurity of the first few years in town are best tackled alone. As one grows older so do one's family responsibilities and involvements increase and constrain one's movements. Again, an older man with few resources who moves to the city is disadvantaged in competition for employment with younger men.

Education conveys information about the world beyond the local community. It instills (or attempts to do so) new values. It raises aspiration levels and provides a qualification which is a *sine qua non* for many forms of well-paid employment. Thus school-leavers emigrate. In surveys in rural Ghana it is seen that two thirds of the illiterates stayed in their village, having neither migrated in the past nor intended to do so; but only two fifths of those with a complete primary education were content to remain at home (Caldwell, 1969, p. 61). Similar results were found in Monterrey, though Balan *et al.* feel that, in recent decades, education has become a less significant selective factor, indicating not that school-leavers are more willing to remain at home but that the non-schooled are now leaving to a similar degree (1973, p. 146). Caldwell's Ghanaian survey suggests that there is more emigration from wealthier rural homes, but he believes that this may be a consequence of better education. He does however find a greater tendency to emigrate among junior sons in large families – the elder sons are constrained to remain at home to perpetuate their father's status (1969, pp. 72–5). Balan *et al.* see more migration among those who have relations in the city. Finally Balan *et al.* believe, though they have no data to prove this point, that the migrants are – all other factors being constant – more adventurous and capable of initiative than those whom they leave behind (1973, p. 167).

The picture of the individual immigrant to the city which emerges from our brief discussion is of a young man, often better equipped than his peers, who consciously decides to move to satisfy his aspirations. This is vastly different from one which portrays him as subject to uncontrollable economic forces, tossed by these waves like a piece of flotsam on to the shores of the city.

Sufficient has been said in the previous pages to suggest that the patterns of migration vary not only between communities but also over time. Any argument that either step or chain migration provides the correct model is clearly misconceived. Apart from anything else, the step model can be applicable only in those states which have a number of intermediate centres of employment – large provincial capitals, mining camps etc. Many states do not – Senegal for example. And as we have seen, in most of the countries considered here the national capital has grown with disproportionate speed while other towns have remained relatively stagnant. (It could be argued here that these towns, though not growing, nevertheless send their own sons to the capital, recruiting replacements from their own rural hinterland. But most of the evidence contradicts this. Some villagers do indeed go to near-by towns, but many move and go direct to the capital.)

A hypothetical example might clarify this point. Imagine a small, remote and backward community. Its first emigrants go to the near-by towns or perhaps mine to earn cash. They return after a few months to continue their traditional mode of life. A pattern of circular or seasonal migrations is established. Some of these migrants, instead of returning home, venture further afield, abetted by those whom they have met who themselves have wider experience. Eventually some of them reach the capital. Of these a few will succeed and reports of their good fortune will percolate back to the village. Eventually they will return, on visits and ultimately to settle. These men have experienced step migration. But they will encourage the youths of the later generation to come directly to the city. Gradually the links between city and village intensify as visits are made and as the household economies of urban and rural families become intermeshing. As the new arrivals to the city become established so do they encourage their kin to follow them and the chain movement increases by geometric progression. Simultaneously – perhaps as a result of the migratory flow, perhaps independent of it – the village develops. Tarred roads reach it, schools are built, new crops are encouraged. This too promotes emigration. In a few decades a village, lying say fifty miles from the city, is transformed from an isolated community into an outer suburb. Within any state some rural areas have already reached this position while others in the remotest corners are just beginning the process. Again, within a relatively backward area we may find a village already has a well-developed chain linking it to the capital, consequent upon the success of its early emigrants, and the present rate of emigration is high. The migrants from the neighbouring community were less successful, the chain has developed but feebly and the rate of emigration is low.

Countless variations can be made in this rather simple model. My point is to demonstrate that nationally aggregated figures which show gross rates of migration, the relative degrees of step and chain migration and the like tend to inhibit the understanding of a relatively uniform dynamic process the progressive stages of which have been reached by different areas and communities to very different degrees.

## A CASE STUDY

As one attempts to analyse the generalities in the urbanization process and to stress the dominant variables which seem likely to account for observer differences, so one tends to lose sight of the individual, the shanty-town resident whose actions and activities constitute the process. Case histories can illuminate an analysis – they are not a substitute for it. Mangin's account of the life of Blas and his wife Carmen (a composite of more than one life history) illustrates many of the themes of this and subsequent chapters (1970, pp. 47–54).

Blas's father was a Quechua-speaking Indian who worked on a *hacienda* in the Peruvian sierra. He migrated to a coastal sugar plantation, initially to earn money to pay for a religious festival, but he stayed, brought his wife to be with him and by her had seven children. Blas, the eldest, was Spanish-speaking but unschooled, and with the lack of employment on the plantation he was obliged at the age of eighteen to seek work outside. He travelled with a close friend to Lima, a city he had already visited and admired for its gay life. The two youths lodged first with an uncle, and though he could accommodate them only for a few nights – having but three rooms in a slum alley for a household of nine – other migrants from Blas's father's village were largely responsible for orienting the youths to city life.

Blas quickly found a job as a waiter in a small boarding house used by students and managed to save a little money. He impregnated Carmen, a maid from a near-by house, and they rented a two-roomed mud house in a most squalid complex of such shanties on a vacant building lot. Carman had come to Lima at the age of fourteen to work as a domestic for a dentist who had promised to educate her, but who rarely allowed her outside the house. After three years she left and worked in a number of houses where she received a small wage, much of which she sent to her mother.

Through the help of one of the students in the boarding house, Blas obtained a better job as a restaurant waiter. Although this was a relatively good job for a youth of Blas's background, the arrival of a second child, together with a rent increase, left him with little spare cash. Yet Carmen felt that she lived and ate better with Blas than she had in the homes of her employers. The filth of the slum settlement and the continual gossip among the neighbours inclined Blas to think of moving. Information that the landlord planned to clear his lot to build a cinema precipitated Blas into joining, at the invitation of a co-worker in the restaurant, a group of fifty families planning a land invasion. Most of these families were from the same region of the sierra and had been recruited, as had Blas, as co-workers or co-villagers.

Mangin describes vividly the preparation for the invasion, the secrecy entailed, and the letter to the wife of the president stressing their poverty and their political support. With minimal intervention by the police the invasion was successful. Blas and Carmen secured a plot of land fifteen by thirty metres and quickly enlarged the single one-room matting shelter to three rooms. Then with occasional help from friends he began the slow process of building his brick house, working mainly in the evenings and on Sundays. He hired a mason to help construct the walls – only to find later that the work was badly done and that the walls could not support the roof. Blas rectified the mistakes and roofed his home so that, one day, he might add a second storey. With an expensive cedar door the couple felt like genuine home-owners and talked of getting properly married.

Blas continued to work in the restaurant, though Carmen had never visited it – nor had she seen Lima's principal plaza. She, with the elder of her five children, tended a little shop in the front room of the house. A television set, powered by electricity from a private generator in the neighbourhood, helped to attract customers. The income from Blas's job and the shop made the couple relatively prosperous and they were not unhappy with their lot. Were they to have had a sudden windfall they would have invested further in their house and in their children's education. The older children all attended school and there seemed to be strong parental pressure and anxiety that they should do well and get professional jobs. The children spoke a little Quechua in the home, but Spanish with their peers; the parents had no strong interest in their children's fluency in the indian vernacular.

Carmen and Blas grumbled about the lack of basic services in their *barriada*, about the dust from the unpaved roads and the poor transport facilities. Blas was a member of the *barriada* committee which was pressing for these services as well as administering the allocation of new plots to immigrants. One of the main concerns of the committee was to improve the image of the community in the world beyond, negating the epithets of violence and crime bestowed by the Limanean middle classes and emphasizing instead the law-abiding nature of the community and advertising its communal attempts at self-improvement.

Blas and Carmen are typical, if slightly better off than the average *barriada* residents. In stressing their achievements one tends to gloss over their poverty – poverty, that is, in comparison with urban dwellers in wealthier nations. Their incomes permitted only the most meagre furnishing of their home and few, if any, leisure activities. Both worked very long hours either in home or restaurant; the journey to the latter by an overcrowded bus was exhausting and time-consuming. Carmen probably cooked on a small kerosene stove (Lima newspapers with tragic regularity report the burning of matting homes in overcrowded *barriadas* and the deaths of small children). Yet Blas and Carmen felt that they had successfully coped with the transition to urban life. They lived better than could have been possible for them in the rural areas and over the years their style of life in the town had improved. These changes were the result of their own efforts – in invading land, in building their house and in their continued attempts through the *barriada* association to upgrade their settlement. They had (probably unrealistically) high aspirations for their children.

Blas and Carmen presumably had their quarrels. Blas perhaps was occasionally unfaithful to his wife. Another observer might have seized upon these events to illustrate the social disorganization of shanty-town life, attributing them to the material poverty experienced. But to emphasize these characteristics at the expense of the feelings of hope and achievement of the *barriada* residents is so one-sided as to merit the designation distortion.

Yet the success of Blas and his family and the failure of so many others are apparently divided by little more than luck. Blas was lucky in getting the job in the restaurant, lucky in keeping it for so long (a tiff with his employers or the closure of the restaurant would have terminated it), lucky in that he and his family enjoyed good health (almost certainly uninsured, medical bills would have exhausted his savings, and forced him to sell furniture or the door of his house and necessitated the withdrawal of his older children from school to seek casual employment). Equally one must not ignore completely the personality characteristics – hard work and sobriety and the ability to get along with others, both co-workers and patrons – which enabled Blas to exploit the opportunities opened for him.

## ARRIVAL IN THE CITY

Early migration literature was heavily influenced by the rural–urban dichotomy, paralleling that between 'traditional' and 'modern'. The differences in culture and styles of life in the migrants' rural community and in the city were overstressed. In addition the migrant was seen as impelled towards the city by those uncontrollable economic forces. Other accounts tell of boys who ran away from home, arriving in the city's motor park penniless and friendless, quickly cheated and exploited by the delinquents of the inner-city slum. Such tales make good reading but hardly accord with the image given by recent surveys. Again much of the research of the 1950s and 1960s was directed towards the explanation of psychological problems experienced by the migrant consequent upon his supposedly traumatic move from village to city.

Today much more attention is focused upon links in the chain between village and city. The Monterrey survey found that two thirds of the migrants to that city had visited it prior to their eventual emigration (half of those who arrived before 1940 had made such visits, three quarters of the arrivals in the early 1960s (Balan *et al.*, 1973, p. 154)). Similarly in Caldwell's survey in Ghana, two thirds of potential migrants knew about city life from visits and one third of established migrants had made a prior visit; the remainder learned from returned migrants (1969, p. 121). Browning suggests that in most of the large cities of the third world two thirds of the migrants have friends or relatives living there (Balan *et al.*, 1973, p. 159 fn). It is these with whom the migrant lodges upon arrival. The story of Blas seems typical.

In Ghana over half of the city migrants stayed with close kin or village members on arrival (Caldwell, 1969, p. 130); in

Monterrey, too, similar proportions were discovered (Balan *et al.*, 1973, p. 162). These figures are certainly high when one considers that some migrants have no close relatives in the city, others come on transfer with a commercial firm, police or army and have accommodation found for them; the better-educated have schoolmates or can afford hotel accommodation. The hosts feed and lodge the new arrival until he can establish his own abode – often a period of weeks rather than days. In return the guest helps with the domestic chores – in fact younger migrants are often used as domestic servants by hosts who then become delinquent in their duties to advance their guest's career.

Fewer migrants report that their hosts find work for them; but the questions which provoke such responses are often ambiguous. Few hosts are in a position to offer a job to the new arrival – their efforts are directed towards introducing him to likely employers and advising him how to go about finding work. The migrant may well believe, ultimately, that he has succeeded by his own efforts. The hosts undoubtedly feel an obligation to help. In the Indian factory studied by Sheth (1968) kin and caste ties dominated recruitment patterns. Recently the trade union of a Lima car assembly plant, in presenting its annual claim for increased wages, bonuses and benefits, petitioned that vacancies should be reserved for relatives of existing staff. Hostility against the Igbo in Northern Nigeria was fuelled by beliefs (not altogether unwarranted) that clerks or artisans in authority would write to their natal villages for a youth to come to fill a vacancy.

Such dependence upon close kin already established in the city seems so obvious as to require little explanation or elaboration. The migrant arriving with little money and few skills has no viable alternative. Were this but a passing phase in the migrant's career one would give it little emphasis. In fact it deserves considerable stress. For this mode of reception not only helps the migrant to make the adjustment to city life, producing, as the surveys indicate, a much lower rate of psychological stress than the pessimists had feared. It tends to encapsulate him in a small community within the city from which it is increasingly difficult to become detached; for each decision or action limits subsequent choices. The generosity of the host creates debts which must be repaid, either directly or in helping subsequent migrants. The new arrival is introduced to others from his village, perhaps at a formal meeting, and these members constitute a major part of his social network.

The distinction already described (above, pp. 90–92) between the Red and School Xhosa of East London is the product of a peculiar situation – some villages had accepted Christianity, others had not. This distinction, too, may have been overdrawn. But Mayer's argument that everyday urban behaviour tends to reinforce the distinction does seem to have wider application and in every city one may watch the individual immigrant become more or less clearly attached to his ethnic community.

With growing land shortage in the rural area, with rising standards there of education, with the increases of skilled employment in the cities, the proportion of circular migrants falls, that of permanent migrants (or strictly those who will spend most of their working lives in the city) increases. Those who come tentatively to the city stay on when they find themselves in stable employment and balance those who had higher aspirations but in failure and frustration have returned to the village. The married migrant tends to travel alone; and most of the young migrants are unmarried. Both categories seek to set up their homes in the city, having their wives and children permanently with them, albeit making arrangements perhaps that close relatives in the village should look after their land or that children should be exchanged to take advantage of specific school facilities: a child is sent to stay with relatives in the village and attend a good local primary school – discipline may be better than in the local city school – while a village boy comes to the city for secondary education.

### *Intra-city movement*

The unskilled immigrant relying largely on menial and casual labour for his income needs to live near the city centre, to the loci of commercial and industrial activity. He needs to be able to seize quickly the opportunities of which he learns from his network of kin and friends. But once he becomes established in some comparatively steady form of employment his needs change. He seeks a more salubrious area in which to settle with his young family. Inner-city rents tend to be high and so he looks to the margins, where they will be lower even though off-set perhaps by costs of transport to work. With the saving made he aspires to build his own house – not only a long-term investment but also a most important form of security, for if he becomes unable to work through sickness or unemployment his family will at least have a roof over their heads. This house should, for the near-permanent migrant, be in the city. In coastal West Africa however men often prefer to build this house in their home community – a decision reflecting not only their strong desire to retire there (a feasible possibility given their continuing land rights and status in the descent group) but also the greater availability of alternative housing in the city.

Some descriptions of the peripheral squatter settlements surrounding Latin American cities seem to suggest that they are created by migrant hordes who camp upon arrival outside the cities' gates; that they were created through planned invasion clearly belies this. Their founders and most of their subsequent population have, as surveys indicate, already resided for several years within the city. Nevertheless these settlements can now receive directly the most recent migrants, though, for the reasons cited above, a dormitory suburb is not the best place in which to seek employment. West African cities such as Lagos and Accra lack such squatter settlements; yet they have had the same experience of immigrant growth. Here the peripheral land tends still to be held under customary forms of tenure, by indigenous descent groups. These groups, with little or no supervision by government, have sold plots to the successful migrants who have built houses ostensibly for themselves and their families. However, concepts of corporate property holding and traditional inheritance patterns deter the owner from sharing his house with his siblings – they may one day claim it as their family property. Instead he prefers to let his surplus rooms to tenants at a fairly moderate rent; he tends to be a more lenient landlord to tenants in distress. Such houses fulfil the needs of most indigent migrants. African cities too tend to be of recent creation and thus lack centres of decaying property. The immigrant communities tend to be peripheral to the city and the village–inner-city slum–peripheral squatter settlement pattern of movement is much less marked.

The choice of a residential area tends to reflect kin ties – relatives are clustered in the shanty towns even though their appearance to the external observer suggests complete heterogeneity. Pons (1969, pp. 70–71) for instance shows how the principal ethnic groups in Stanleyville are very markedly localized in a few areas. Scholars studying migrants to Lima from a particular village report that they are concentrated in very few localities – in the little shanty town in which I worked a third of the one hundred families came from a small village of 5,000 people in the high Andes. This degree of localization is not hard to understand – hosts will have more knowledge of available housing near-by and the recent arrival will probably prefer to be near his kin. Where the settlers actually control the allocation of vacant land within their claimed territory the tendency is to give it to kin of existing members.

The stated ideal in most third-world countries is that the migrant should eventually move into low-cost housing provided by public and private agencies. But outside Hong Kong, with its towering apartment blocks, this is not often realized. Despite much publicized schemes the number of such houses built tends to be extremely low, merely scratching the surface of the problem. The houses tend to be very small. They are inadequate for a large family (or for taking in tenants), stringent regulations prevent their use as stores or workshops and miniscule gardens inhibit horticulture. And even then their prices are within reach of only the most affluent of the poor. Families which, by pooling members' incomes, might be able to afford such houses cannot obtain loans, for their employment is insufficiently stable – a handicap of most jobs in the informal sector.

A solution would seem to be provided by those schemes, cited earlier, wherein the government lays out plots and provides basic services, leaving the individual to construct his house in his own time. But bureaucratic intransigence so often thwarts these. Portes gives two examples. In one such Santiago settlement the residents petitioned the government to ascertain just how much they would be expected to pay. It took several months for them to receive a reply. In the other some members of a Bogotá settlement scheme wrote to the authorities claiming that the latter were passing on to the settlers far higher costs for land and its development than they were in fact themselves paying to landowners and contractors (Portes and Walton, 1976, Chapter 3). And again, such schemes tend to be financially beyond the means of all but a small minority of the shanty-town population.

The attraction of building one's own house are many: one can add to and improve it as one has windfalls; one can use it as one wishes; it is one's security. Lack of legal title to the land may seem a strong deterrent, though a counter-argument suggests that the better the housing the less likely are the authorities to raze the area. One can be near one's kin – in the housing estate this would be unlikely (and one of the attractions of such settlement to the upwardly mobile is that one may avoid kin ties and responsibilities).

Latin American squatter settlements thus comprise those who have established themselves in the city and seek to build their own homes. They also include those who have been evicted from the inner city, for non-payment of rent or by a slum clearance scheme which has made no provisions for the displaced population. The latter arrive with their matting and with sheets of corrugated iron donated by friends to recommence their precarious existence. The existence of squatter settlements is due not simply to the achievement orientation of many of their inhabitants but to the complete absence of any alternative – neither government nor private landlords is providing housing on anything like the scale demanded by the migratory process.

*Family life*

Conventional Western expectations of daily family life within the shanty town are of disorganization, and deviance – of broken marriages, violence, alcoholism and crime. This image has been supported in large measure by the graphic descriptions of Oscar Lewis of slums in Puerto Rico and Mexico City. Yet social anthropologists who have lived more recently in shanty towns have given a very different picture: families are stable and law-abiding. In fact the negative characteristics seem to have been so little in evidence that these anthropologists have given us few descriptions of family life – they write of rather ordinary people who are however faced with situations not shared by the affluent members of their society. How may we explain these discrepant images?

Firstly the localities described may well be different. Oscar Lewis tended to pick long-established slum areas; the social anthropologists and social scientists have more often selected the newer settled areas. Oscar Lewis found that only 30 per cent of his Puerto Rican sample of shanty-town residents still lived with their first wives; Helen Safa (1974), working in the 1960s, in a settlement created in the late 1930s, found two thirds of the men with their original spouses. Four fifths of the families of Los Peloteros consisted of a nuclear family with or without other relative; only one fifth were of households headed by a woman and, of these, almost half the women were widowed, the remainder separated or divorced. (Similarly in a Limanean *barriada* formed in the late 1950s and censused soon afterwards, four fifths of the households consisted of nuclear families with or without other relatives.) Safa attributes the discrepancy between her data and that of Lewis in part to the age of the respective populations. Couples tend to stay together for the first twenty years of marriage. Then the age difference between spouses leads to widowhood, and the difficulties of unskilled old men in finding employment and the absence of property accumulated in previous years enhances the rate of marital breakdown.

The second locus of the discrepancy lies in the choice one makes between describing the ordinary families who form the majority of the population and describing the minority of deviant or problem families. Undoubtedly there are broken marriages and consequent financial hardship. There are prostitutes, though in all respects other than their calling they are often non-deviant, saving assiduously to be able to have a stable marriage and to educate their children. Alcoholism is present, for drinking in a local bar is often the only form of relaxation available – there are no gardens to engage surplus energy, and cinemas are distant and expensive. Yet would not a survey of respectable middle-class scholars also disclose 'problems' in a fifth of the households? Furthermore, as I shall argue later, the existence of such problems does not of itself constitute a denial of the established values in the society; members of a broken home do not deny marriage.

Thirdly, the presentation of family life in a third-world shanty town may, in emphasizing differences with that of the middle-class Western reader, assume implicitly or explicitly that the divergence is due to the poverty of slum residents. In fact the traits described may well be held in common with those of more affluent members of the society under study. Thus in Mexico and Puerto Rico the machismo of the shanty-town man is emphasized, though it seems to be part of Spanish culture. (In the Peruvian shanty town which I studied the recently immigrant sierra indians did not seem to exhibit this trait; studies of indian society report a more egalitarian relationship between spouses.)

Some features do of course predominate in the daily lives of the poor. They have to work hard; the day starts early and ends late as workplace is often far from shanty town and public transport is costly and inefficient. The search for a better job is always active; multiple occupations help to increase the family income. In the absence of gadgets and services housework is hard, and women in addition seek remunerative employment, though this is often scarce; much depends on whether domestic service is a male (as in Africa) or a female (as in Latin America) preserve.

With malnutrition and the insanitary conditions of most shanty-town houses, however houseproud or tidy the occupants try to be, the incidence of illness is high. Sickness is, in fact, one of the major impediments to individual mobility out of the shanty town, for it causes reduced earnings and the erosion of savings. In the 1950s it was common for Western observers to assume a high degree of mental instability among recent immigrants as a result of the trauma of sudden movement to very unfamiliar surroundings. Surveys of urban populations did describe the maladjusted and thus, apparently, the hypothesis was validated. Later studies have however provided a contrary picture. Mangin (1960) argues that characteristics found among urban migrants – for instance an intense preoccupation with health and emphasis on envy – were similarly prevalent in the rural populations from which the migrants had come. In the very comprehensive psychiatric survey carried out among families living in and around Abeokuta, Nigeria, cited above (p. 107), it was found that in general they had less psychiatric disorder than an urban and rural population previously studied in north-east USA. In this and other studies the evidence that migrants suffer more mental illness is ambiguous; and even when it does appear that they display a greater incidence of maladjustment one cannot be sure that the social cultural difference between village and city is the main cause. Other factors – the propensity for the less stable to emigrate, the frustrations consequent upon over-ambitious hopes – could be responsible.

### *Ethnic Associations*

Just as it is now widely recognized that the city immigrant arrives to be received by kinsman and friends who steer him through the hazards of his new life, so too is it stressed that the migrant retains close ties with his community of origin. He has one foot in the town but keeps the other firmly in his village. For this reason, terms such as proletarian, which implies a sole commitment to urban wage labour, are, it is argued, inapplicable. The ethnic communities into which the migrant becomes encapsulated are seen to be not only incongruent with class formation but also an inhibition to its development. However, these ties with co-villagers and the village itself may take a variety of forms – and each may be developed to a differing degree.

Firstly members of a rural community resident in the city may interact closely with each other, yet their individual and collective links with the village itself may be minimal. The debts incurred by the migrant upon his arrival are subsequently repaid to his hosts and new debts incurred. An intricate pattern of mutual assistance develops encompassing perhaps not only life's crises – unemployment and sickness – but also mundane everyday situations – the borrowing of food and utensils. Such associations are by their nature informal and tax the resources of the investigator to the full. A close watch must be kept on movements over days or weeks to ascertain whether given individuals interact more with kin and co-villagers or with neighbours. But the importance of such associations in providing social security for the shanty-town dweller has been widely stressed; so too has their role in helping him to adapt to urban life while at the same time fostering the retention of many village modes of behaviour – a 'residual ruralism' as some authors describe it.

Under certain conditions the overt solidarity of these associations may be enhanced. Where a migrant group is clearly distinct from its host population, its separate recognition by others will enhance its own self-identity. Thus in the coastal cities of West Africa migrants from the Muslim north, with their distinctive robes, are least assimilated into the urban mass. Again a consciousness of identity may be fostered when government treats ethnic communities as the discrete units comprising the city, using their elders or leaders as representatives. Thus an urban council may be composed of such men. In Northern Rhodesia, as Epstein (1958) described, government and the mining companies tried to sustain a system of tribal elders in the face of a growing demand for a trade union to bargain between workers and management. In some Nigerian towns it was the practice for social welfare officers to hand over a homeless and delinquent child found sleeping in the market or lorry park to the head of its village community. He was expected to find the parents or close kin of the child and return it to a proper home – only if he failed did the welfare department re-assume responsibility. Again, ethnic consciousness may be raised by aspirants to leadership who tactically choose to emphasize not universal criteria, hoping thus to win votes from all ethnic groups, but the special interests of their own group, anticipating that they will win the support of the entire group, without antagonizing too greatly the other uncommitted voters needed to ensure an overall majority.

In some instances an ethnic community may be held together by economic interests. Members of a single village may have a city monopoly of certain trades. Thus the newspaper vendors in Dakar come from one remote village, and strive to preserve their business for their own members. Men from one Peruvian sierra village are engaged in itinerant fruit and vegetable selling in Lima's affluent suburbs. On a different plane, the Hausa of Ibadan in southern Nigeria control both the export of kola nuts to the north and the import of live cattle to the city. Resident in a peripheral settlement, they adhere to the Tijaniya movement to distinguish themselves from the orthodox Yoruba Muslims. The intensity of their religious fervour unites a community whose economic position seems most precarious – the Yoruba themselves are noted traders and could easily assume the middleman role. These Hausa have, of course, a myriad of commercial links with their homeland; but they come, individually, from widely separated towns and within the Ibadan community there are no significant divisions based upon town of origin nor associations fostering links to any one town (Cohen, 1969).

However it would be unusual if migrants in the city were to have no ties at all with the rural area. As we have seen, most of them have spent their childhood there and, in coming to the city at an early age, leave behind parents and siblings. Affective ties remain strong. Most of the migrants hope to be able to send money home – for the education of junior relatives or for the care of parents in their old age. The frequency of visits home is conditioned by the length and cost of the journey – and also by the expectation that one should arrive laden with gifts. Often, and especially in Africa, it is felt that marriages should be celebrated in the home community, especially when, as so often happens, both spouses are its members. And ultimately most people hope to die in their villages, aspiring to retire there in old age or, should they end their life in the city, expecting that their bodies should be carried home for burial.

Emigration from the rural areas has been stimulated more by the stagnation of agriculture, and its consequent failure to offer men an opportunity for a substantial cash income, than by the loss of land through overpopulation, intensified capitalist development or land reform. Most, though not all, migrants retain rights over their farm land. A man who plans to spend but a limited period in the city may arrange for kinsmen to assist his wife to cultivate most of his farm, thus almost maintaining its production. With absence for larger periods, a man may be able to lease his land, leaving a brother in charge, or he may leave livestock in the care of his brother. Where rights amounting to ownership are held not by the individual but by the descent group or village community, a migrant may return in old age and claim, from land not currently used, a plot on which to commence farming. Such rights to land maintain the shantytown dweller's hopes to retire to his home community and provid him with a sense of security in that he may return if he fails to succeed in the city.

Many migrants have returned to their rural homes, to farm on a small scale, to open little shops and perhaps play an active leadership role in community affairs. But the near-universal response of recently immigrant city dwellers that they expect to return cannot be taken too seriously. In their old age they will find their own children, upon whom they have become dependent, resident in the city. Relatively few rural homes will be able to match the level of services – electric light, water, health facilities – enjoyed in the city. Most areas will not be able to offer suitable opportunities for continued work, through being insufficiently involved in the cash economy. Despite their statements and their dreams it seems likely that the majority of the migrants will end their lives in the cities. Ties between individual migrants and their families remaining in the rural area and between migrants in the city sharing the same home community are reinforced when a formal association develops in the city with the aim of improving the home community. Such associations have been widely reported in Africa, though in Latin America they would seem to be strong only in Peru; literature on India is silent on this issue. An essential ingredient for the formation of those improvement associations, as they are sometimes termed in Africa, would seem to be a rural community capable of collective action – one united perhaps by ties of descent rather than rigidly stratified by caste. In a desire to develop the village its leaders seek from their urban compatriots not only money – for they alone have a substantial cash income – but also their good offices in advising how things might be done, who must be manipulated. Those in clerical posts are expected to use whatever influence they might have. The villages thus vie with each other to have the new main road pass close by, to have a good feeder road, a primary school and dispensary. For reasons of sentiment the town dweller is pleased to accede to these demands – he may even have helped to stimulate them. Those active in such associations improve their reputation at home and are more likely to be offered leadership roles there, better opportunities for entrepreneurial activities. They may also improve their standing in the city, being recognized as leaders by city authorities, politicians and the like. The patronage thus enjoyed may bring them individual benefit. In fact the interests of the village's city-based leaders may even conflict with those at home, leading not to fruitful co-operation but to divided efforts and frustration.

Such improvement associations may exist at all levels, from the smallest village through the district to the province. Perhaps somewhat uniquely, among the Igbo of Nigeria these associations have been structured in a hierarchical pyramid, leading to the Igbo State Union. Educated and wealthy men who were prominent in the higher levels were nevertheless active members of their own village associations – for most came from the villages. Elsewhere, in Peru for example, a sharp dichotomy exists. Most indian sierra communities would seem to have an association in Lima, though its formal organization is often very weak, the intensity of ties with the village notwithstanding. These associations easily escape the notice of those not concerned with a particular community. At the other extreme are the provincial clubs, located in substantial mansions in the affluant suburbs, to which belong those who have found success in the city; in fact to be admitted is a mark of one's success. Though their efforts are ostensibly directed towards the home areas, it is alleged that most of the money collected is in fact spent within the town on the members themselves. These clubs are to be equated with other elite voluntary associations – rotary clubs or masonic lodges.

The discussion thus far has presumed that all migrants from a given community are equally involved in the interaction between village members in the city and between city residents and the home community. In many cases, and especially in Africa, this tends to be so. The very poor have an obvious interest in maintaining these ties. In the absence of state provision here lies their only form of social security – help from near-by relatives, a reintegration into their home community. Their contributions will be small, but they will tend to be assiduous in the fulfilment of their obligations. Their demands are satisfied by their wealthier compatriots, yet these may well feel that the success of the less fortunate is an impediment to their own advancement. But if they see their future as lying within their home community – as in retirement – they will be anxious to assume leadership roles, or at least not to earn the disparagement of their co-villagers. Again, though the poor attach themselves to their compatriots, they cannot afford a visit home very often. The rich migrant has his own car and maintains much more frequent and closer links within his village; he may build an imposing house there, a monument to his success and a symbol of his intention to return. In theory there exists, of course, a possibility that one breaks free of one's ethnic community and joins others who have done likewise – the collectivity of those not oriented towards a birthplace. In much of Africa this is difficult, for every man is identified with a local community and his efforts on its behalf are signalled with approbation not only by its members but by society at large. In Peru it is much easier, for it is only the migrants from indigenous indian communities who are so intensely tied to their home areas. The large mestizo population does not identify itself in this way to anything like the same degree and it is this category that the aspiring indian hopes to enter.

In Africa all ethnic groups in the cities do not organize themselves in the same manner. We have remarked already on the high level of Igbo organization, linking city and village as well as uniting immigrants to the city. The Hausa have a complex organization within the city but few ties collectively to their towns of origin. The most important factor here would seem to be the social structure of the home community. As indicated in the previous chapter, in a community which is solidly united by ties of descent the rights and status of individual members are preserved throughout their period of absence, and their allegiance is thus retained. The community is capable of collective action – and the absentee members find themselves playing an integral part. Such a relationship is modified by distance – it is more difficult to maintain a pattern of visiting when many hundreds of miles intervene; by national boundaries – one cannot lobby for one's village in the capital of a neighbouring state; by rural poverty – one is less likely to contemplate retirement to a village still within a subsistence economy and having no modern technological or social amenities.

The same basic factors would seem to operate in Latin America too. In the 1960s Mangin (1967, 1970) and other social anthropologists began to describe the village associations among sierran migrants in Lima, and these seemed strongly reminiscent of those reported during the two previous decades from Africa. However, these seem not to be a common phenomenon of Latin American shanty towns, as Roberts (1974) points out in his comparison between Peru and Guatemala. The associations described are typical of indigenous indian communities – not those dominated by mestizo populations. Moreover, as Lomnitz's graphic and detailed description (1975) of a little shanty town within the heart of Mexico City shows, an intense network of relationships, focusing upon self-help and based to a large extent upon community of origin, may be a dominant feature of the social structure of the urban community.

The lesson of these studies is that the ties of the immigrant to his co-villagers and to his home community not only needs to be stressed but also needs to be examined closely so that these differences in the nature of the relationships, their intensity and the differential involvement of persons of high and low socio-economic status, is fully explored. We must distinguish clearly between the personal links which bind the migrant to his family in the rural area, and those which unite co-villagers in the city; and between associational activities which serve to develop the home area and those which are for the benefit of the city immigrants themselves.

# 6 Urban Employment

The migrant comes to the city seeking work; yet the city provides insufficient jobs. The comparatively striking growth of the manufacturing sector, in terms of its output, is not matched by the increase in wage-earning opportunities, for most of the new industries are capital- rather than labour-intensive. The increase in employment may tend to match the natural increase in the total population, but it falls behind the increase in the size of the cities consequent upon both natural increase and immigration. Again the number of new jobs created each year in the formal sector is considerably lower than the population of school-leavers – with or without their certifications of successful course completion. Contrary to some economic theories, the continued immigration does not depress wages to a point that the flow diminishes, for as we have seen other factors impel the migrant from the rural area. However, the increasing poverty of those not in the wage-earning sector may, in time, affect the migration rate.

## TWO SECTORS?

The sources of wage employment are easily defined. With the increased provision of social services – education and health – with growing armies and police forces, the state bureaucracies rapidly grow. They are concentrated in the capitals, where over half of the more senior officials work. Manufacturing industry, as already mentioned, also tends to be located in the capitals, especially when these are also seaports. Largely controlled by international companies, it is geared towards the production of import-substitutes – consumer goods for the new wealthy classes, such as food and drink preparations, car assembly, and to some extent goods for the poor – cheap textiles and clothing, plastic household ware. The firms in this sector are run substantially on Western lines. Wages are good and a skilled worker may earn three to five times the national minimum enjoyed by the majority of the employed labour force. In many, though not all, of such firms, the wages form a small proportion of the cost of the product and the management can afford to be generous. It is anxious moreover to retain its skilled workers who may otherwise be seduced by newly establishing companies who prefer to poach rather than train their own employees. Fringe benefits are favourable. Workers enjoy a high degree of employment security. In consequence labour turnover is low. To a large extent these benfits have been grasped and expanded by well-organized and militant trade unions.

The existence of this cadre of skilled workers – sometimes referred to as a 'labour aristocracy' – tends to divert attention from the majority who are employed at minimum wage levels. Construction companies employ as many men as manufacturers and are notorious for hiring daily or weekly labour. Public services too engage thousands of unskilled workers, as dustmen, gardeners in the parks, and the like. Here the worker is likely to enjoy more security, though no better a wage.

But wage employment of this type, in what is now commonly called 'the formal sector', is enjoyed by only half of the city's working population. The other half, in the 'informal sector', have seized employment opportunities created both by the growth of an affluent middle class and by the poor masses in providing goods and services to meet their needs. It has done this largely without government backing, indeed often in the face of official intransigence.

In the informal sector enterprises are small – usually a man working on his own or with family members, apprentices or a few (and usually very poorly paid) wage employees. Production is labour-intensive and the product of the worker is low compared with that of the factory worker. Work is usually irregular and insecure. The informal is also an unenumerated sector; for while copious statistical data exists on the numbers and modes of employment in the larger enterprises – usually those with more than five (as in Peru) or ten (as in Nigeria) employees – very little is known of the numbers, say, of artisans or domestic servants. For long, governments, abetted by their economic advisers, have looked upon this sector as unproductive, to be ignored in the hope that it might wither away. Institutions for the provision of credit to aspiring entrepreneurs have not been created. Official recognition has more often taken the form of harassment. Thus, as King (1977) reports, labour officers in Nairobi sought to punish artisans with apprentices on the grounds that the latter were being used as unpaid labour. Street hawkers have been the prime target. Not only are they so apparently unproductive – ten vendors in a small area selling such a quantity of identical goods as could easily be managed by one of them – but in the city centres they constitute a nuisance to the middle-class public. Attempts are thus made to reduce their numbers by licences, to force them into limited market sites (where most of their customers would not find them) or more simply to ban them, though such attempts are rarely successful for long.

While formal and informal sectors look so different, they are nevertheless highly interdependent. The growth of the latter is a result of the development of the former. To a small extent the informal sector produces not directly for its clientele or customers, but for industry in the formal sector. A factory management may see an advantage in having certain components made not within its own premises but by a number of independent artisans. In Nairobi, as King describes, the firms assembling and marketing bicycles fit front guards and carriers made locally, for these are much more satisfactory for local needs than the imported equivalent. Small fashionable boutiques put out work to tailors and seamstresses working at home rather than set up a small factory with the official paperwork relating to employment and tax that this would entail. The artisans themselves often prefer such arrangements, for not only do they preserve their independence but the evasion of tax and social security insurance payments results in a slightly higher immediate remuneration.

Most of those in the informal sector produce directly for a

clientele both rich and poor. The building and furnishing of middle-class private houses is largely in the hands of such artisans. Many too are engaged in the repair of cars and the electric gadgetry of the home. They charge less than the supplying companies and give the satisfaction of personal service. Their reputation and success depends on their skill and personal contacts. Others are traders, hawking fresh vegetables, fish and meat from door to door in the richer suburbs. Finally the domestic servants – cooks, stewards and butlers, gardeners, drivers – abound on a scale paralleled in Victorian England; even a modestly paid clerk may afford a maid. These employees not only liberate their employers from the domestic chores but they enable them to be more fully employed – the wife may go out to work too, the husband may have an office job by day and work in a private business or in lecturing in the evening. In such cases both spouses need a car – but the employment of a driver enables them to manage with one and so frees them to spend elsewhere.

The other part of the informal sector exists to serve the poor. Here too artisans produce cheaply, not the high-quality goods desired by the rich, but substitutes for the already low-priced mass-produced goods – sandals, for instance, made from discarded tyres, furniture from waste packing cases or substandard planks, innumerable metal goods made from empty drums and cans or scrap metal from cars. Services too are provided: one woman launders for her neighbours so that they are free to take up full-time employment. Even the simplest domestic equipment needs occasional repair, and the poor household, lacking a basic tool kit of hammer, spanners and nails, must call upon a professional for the most ordinary of tasks. Petty trading is one of the most numerous occupations, partly because it requires a minimum of both skill and capital. The hawker and the small shopkeeper in the shanty town are not often able to sell at prices below the suburban supermarket; but they will sell in small quantities and give credit to regular customers. They are patronized by those of the poor who will not enter the bigger shops either from shyness or from fear of insult and ridicule of their rural dress or speech. With workplace so far from the shanty town men buy their midday meal from vendors of cooked food who, better than local restaurants, can anticipate tastes and provide minimal quantities at a price which gives them a small return on their limited outlay.

Finally there are those defined by the affluent classes as criminals – an element which to some writers seems to characterize the informal sector, but which in fact forms a very small part of it. Some do live by thieving, perhaps in addition to another occupation. There *are* prostitutes. Such people usually find their occupations better served by residence in inner-city slums than in the peripheral shanty towns. And, of course, many engaged in 'honest' occupations indulge in practices of dubious legality, like the artisan who obtains his metal scrap by night from a factory waste tip.

Literature on the third world is bedevilled by the Western concepts of unemployment and underemployment. Attempts to measure the former are difficult – censuses and large surveys give ambiguous data. Labour exchanges exist in most capitals, but in many cities few workers apply, seeing this as a waste of time and effort; and correspondingly, firms do not report vacancies, preferring to fill them either through the services and recommendations of their other employees, or through daily selection from the group perpetually found waiting at the factory gate. Estimates of increased unemployment which start by subtracting the numbers of newly recognized wage-earning jobs from the number of school-leavers, presuming these to be searching for such jobs, tends to grossly overstate the problem in ignoring the opportunities created in the informal sector. In fact most surveys suggest that the migrant to the city who is prepared to undertake menial work finds employment within a few weeks of his arrival. It is those with higher educational qualifications who refuse to do such work for fear that it will cost them a subsequent opportunity to accept a post commensurate with their abilities, or will reduce their esteem in the sight of their kin and friends, who sometimes remain jobless for months or even years. Again, in passing through the capital cities one does not notice large numbers of idle people. In fact, the concept of unemployment was developed in nineteenth-century England, not in London, a city with an informal sector as predominant as that of any third-world city today, but in the towns of Lancashire and Yorkshire where the sudden closure of mine or mill could suddenly deprive hundreds of a livelihood without any immediate alternative employment. An unemployment rate of 10–15 per cent may be common in the third-world city, but this represents to a considerable extent a rapid flow of some people between jobs, rather than a large number of men and women without income for long periods. The problem, as several writers have stressed, is not unemployment but poverty.

Poverty however is seen as the consequence of underemployment, but this is an even trickier concept. To the Western observer most of those in the informal sector are underemployed, such as the tailor who is sewing for only four hours a day, even though he seeks contracts to engage him for double that time, or the petty trader with his minute turnover. (Officially fully employed is the messenger who sits idly in the office corridor for most of the day save when told to fetch a file or a cup of tea.) But to measure such underemployment one must either use a highly subjective criterion – how much does the man *want* to work? – or postulate a given technological standard – how much *could* he produce in a day? In every society people are underemployed in the sense that with improved tools their output would be higher. Nevertheless such methodological quibbles must not blind us to the fact that the major cause of poverty in the shanty towns is that too many people are chasing too few opportunities. The situation is ameliorated by the fact that the opportunities are shared so that few are completely without the means of self-support.

In this chapter I have emphasized the degree to which the so-called formal and informal sectors are interdependent: the artisans of the latter use raw materials produced by the former; domestic service by the poor serves the wealthy; artisans and traders provide goods for the poor commensurate with the low wages received by so many in the formal sector. This interpenetration exists too at the personal level – one cannot clearly locate a man in one or other sector. For many men have more than one occupation – factory work by day, taxi driving by night, for example. As a later section describes, men currently working as wage earners in the formal sector aspire to set up as self-employed artisans. Family members, even husband and wife, may work in different sectors – he perhaps as a junior clerk, she selling cooked food for labourers at a building site.

The designation of the informal sector, so long ignored by scholarly economists as well as government planners, has served to pose new questions: Can its productivity, admittedly low in comparison with the formal sector, be raised to a level significant for economic development? What is the social significance of the sector in providing a livelihood for such a high proportion of the unskilled city immigrants? Should one plan for its growth or its obsolescence?

## CAREER ROUTES

Given the pattern of employment opportunities outlined above, how does the individual migrant chart his course? What constitutes a successful career? As we have seen, the migrant comes to the city with meagre resources – some formal literacy perhaps, little or no capital, and few skills relevant to urban occupations.

For wage employment a complete primary education is increasingly being sought by employers as a necessary qualification. For clerical posts it is an obvious necessity; but the middle-class household looking for a garden boy, or the factory manager hiring unskilled labour are taking the prized certificate as evidence of a general level of ability, however remote formal schooling may seem to the needs of the job in question. In noting this tendency authors see the illiterate or semi-literate immigrant being restricted, to a degree much greater now than two decades ago, to the informal sector (here excluding domestic service).

Entry to the ranks of self-employed traders and artisans demands both capital and specific skills. Surveys and studies of individual entrepreneurs disclose, however, that it is possible to begin with a remarkedly small capital outlay. One study of Lagos shopkeepers showed that half were illiterate and started with an initial capital of less than £100 (cited in Lloyd, 1974, p. 77). A comparable study of hawkers in Hong Kong reported that the value of the present stock of over half the sample was below $300 (£25) (McGee, 1973). These are no mean sums considering the wage levels obtaining and they certainly constitute a hurdle which many find difficult to surmount. Yet one does not need to have been born into a family of modest means to be able to raise such a sum; men from the poorest homes have, by dint of hard work and saving, been able to accumulate sufficient to begin their operations.

Skills specific to one's chosen trade are less easily acquired. Of little general significance in the overall pattern is the training given in technical schools and colleges, for these have produced so few qualified men. Entry to courses demands, too, certain educational qualifications. Factories train their own recruits on the shop floor and many workers thus gain a little technical knowledge and manual skill which they hope to be able to employ when they begin to work on their own account. Thus a worker in a car assembly plant hopes to learn enough to enable him to be a mechanic; the employee of a textile factory thinks he will know something about the quality of different kinds of cloth to assist him in prospering as a trader in this commodity. But perhaps the most common form of skill acquisition, though the least studied, is through apprenticeship to a self-employed artisan. Among the Yoruba of southern Nigeria, as I have shown elsewhere (Lloyd, 1953), a system of apprenticeship in modern crafts (tailoring, goldsmithery, shoemaking, carpentry, etc.) and a guild organization developed, which clearly evolved from the traditional structure of descent-group-based crafts, though exhibiting many features typical of medieval Europe. Similar systems which have been reported elsewhere, as in the Kenyan case, do not have these indigenous roots but have developed in response to the needs of city life. The artisan takes on a young boy, perhaps a relative and usually someone recommended to him, and in return for a fee gives him board and lodging and imparts all his knowledge to him. The size of the fee tends to reflect the length of the training period and the consequent time that the boy will be usefully helping his master in production. Once trained, the youth will seek to work on his own. This again necessitates capital to buy tools. Many workers in the factories at Agege, Lagos, had in fact received craft training and were hoping to save £20–£50 to buy the minimal set of tools. (Others had learned to drive but needed money for the professional driver's licence.) Lacking his own tools the artisan must seek work as a journeyman for a more successful man. His wages will probably be extremely low – a barrier to saving but a disinclination to remain in dependence for longer than necessary.

Many men acquire their skill in a less formal manner, through working as a wage labourer. Thus a building labourer may pick up enough knowledge to be able to start his own business, the shop assistant to open his little stall. The point which must be emphasized here, too, is that the skills employed in the majority of occupations in the informal sector are relatively simple ones, capable of being acquired by most people either in the course of their employment, or through forms of apprenticeship which are easily entered.

Described in terms of a residual category, the informal sector is sometimes presented as one of poverty. It is forgotten that many wage earners in the formal sector are on minimum rates and that success in the informal sector can bring quite substantial rewards. One difficulty in looking at types of employment in terms of occupation or relationships of production is that in each category one finds a wide range of incomes. The discrepancy between the wages of a skilled worker and a street cleaner, though regularly employed by the municipality, have already been noted. Equally obvious is the difference, in the field of domestic service, between the conditions often enjoyed by the servant in the home of an expatriate executive – regular hours and time off, bonuses for overtime – and the young maid kept in virtual servitude in a lower-middle-class household. The term petty trader includes both the youth hawking a tray of dusters, biros or matches in the city car parks, and the holder of a prosperous market stall. One tailor may find it difficult to attract enough custom to occupy him for more than one day a week, while another, making similar garments, has three or four sewing machines, a bevy of apprentices and one or two journeymen and still cannot meet all his orders. Latin American writers frequently use the term 'marginal' to refer to all of the urban poor – a half to two thirds of the city population. However, Quijano (1972, 1974) has redefined the term to cover the lower half of this category, but he divides his marginal population into two: the marginal proletariat – wage earners with the lowest and most unstable incomes – and the marginal petite bourgeosie – the poorer trader, artisans and professionals. Such a distinction highlights the great differences in life styles between the two major categories of marginal and non-marginal. Furthermore it facilitates the recognition of divergent interests between moderately wealthy and poor within specific occupational categories, modifying the hallowed distinction between proletariat and petite bourgeoisie.

The figures given by Balan *et al.* in their study of Monterrey and which are abridged in Table 3 summarize this picture;

Table 3: Annual income range (in '000 pesos) of men aged 45–50 in Monterrey, Mexico, 1965

| | | First quartile | Median | Third quartile |
|---|---|---|---|---|
| Lower manual: | Small firm | 5.4 | 7.5 | 8.5 |
| | Large firm | 8.4 | 9.9 | 11.8 |
| Upper manual: | Small firm | 8.4 | 10.0 | 11.9 |
| | Large firm | 11.4 | 14.8 | 20.8 |
| | Self-employed | 9.4 | 16.2 | 21.8 |
| Non-manual: | Lower white-collar | 13.9 | 18.8 | 30.4 |
| | Small entrepreneur | 13.5 | 26.5 | 40.5 |
| | Middle white-collar | 22.5 | 36.3 | 55.5 |

Adapted from J. Balan *et al.* (1973, p, 235).

Over half the managers, entrepreneurs and professionals in the sample earned above 120,000 pesos a year.

In 1965, 1,000 pesos = £33 or $US 80. The statutory minimum annual wage was approximately 7,500 pesos.

other authors, while not providing such exact data, confirm it. The existence of minimum wage levels in the formal sector results in the lowest incomes being found in the informal sector; but the successful self-employed artisan or entrepreneur may earn considerably more than a factory wage employee of similar education and skill. (In discussions such as these it must be remembered that a statutory minimum wage is usually well below the sum necessary to maintain a family above the poverty line. In Nigeria the government raised the minimum wage in 1966 to a figure just half that deemed by a commission of inquiry to be the minimum necessary for a family with two children; it argued that it could not afford to pay more. Those in receipt of a minimum wage, and even those earning more but having larger families, thus live in a style seen to be quite inadequate by standards recognized in that country. They do however survive – they are, in Latin American terms, the marginals.)

The two major sectors provide different routes to success. In the formal sector the clerical employee can envisage himself on a career ladder. With promotion facilitated by the acquisition of additional educational qualifications gained through private study or intermittent periods of education, he can rise to quite high executive or even administrative posts. The semi-skilled worker can hope to improve his status to that of a skilled worker, but here his prospects end. He may be promoted to foreman, joining the ranks of supervisory staff; but his chances of receiving such training or education to make him a qualified engineer are minimal. For the unskilled worker the chances of betterment are slight. He may with a good employer enjoy security but his job is a dead end. In fact with increasing age he may become less employable.

Self-employment offers opportunity, though at greater risk and with very small chances of ultimate success. However, success is always more visible than failure and there is no dearth of local role-models who have made good. Independence and the apparent control of one's own destiny are valued both by the individual concerned and by his society. It is thus hardly surprising that this mode of employment is the aspiration of most men – at least in their dreams, for it may be difficult to realize such ambitions.

To find a simple career path for the average migrant through this myriad of occupational opportunities is well nigh impossible, and few have tried. Yet some indication of likely routes is beginning to emerge from the literature. We are here considering the immigrant with few resources – not the secondary school leaver who searches, perhaps for several months, for the expected teaching or clerical post.

On his arrival in the city the migrant wants work quickly – his kin will not maintain him for long. He accepts whatever work he finds, perhaps moving quickly from one job to another either of his own volition as he seeks higher rates of pay, or because the jobs themselves are so transient. He is looking for good employment, probably in the formal sector, because here the wages are better, the jobs more stable and secure. But ultimately he aspires to self-employment. His prime problem is when and how to move from formal employment to self-employment. An important factor is his success in the former. The higher and more secure his income, with its fringe benefits of insurance and pension, the less likely he is to be able to find a mode of self-employment which will yield him a commensurate income. For from his good wages or salary he will be saving relatively little and will not be gaining any high level of technical skill. The less successful wage earner will probably move earlier – his prospects in wage employment are bleaker, the income sought from self-employment much lower. Yet he must acquire the initial capital needed. With a few pounds saved he buys the tools needed and open shop, but with insufficient customers and a few bad debts he is back again in wage employment. King gives a graphic example of a Kenyan youth who hovered for years between wage and self-employment as his ventures into the latter failed before becoming ultimately successful.

Gachangiu, ultimately a self-employed maker of bicycle carriers, entered the labour force in 1958, at the age of seventeen, when he was successively employed by European settlers, first to feed hens, next as a garden boy. After a few months with each employer he worked briefly as a hotel cook. Then he spent a year apprenticed to an established village blacksmith. The minute income did not match his ambitions but he did not immediately seek alternative work. A younger brother was about to leave for further studies in England, and Gachangiu decided that he ought to have at least a primary schooling, so for six years he attended a village school, gaining his certificate. But this did not seem to qualify him for jobs any different from those which he had previously sought. He helped in a general store and then became an employee in another carrier-making enterprise in Nairobi. Anxious to be his own master, he set off with another employee and tried to set up his own business in a provincial town. The investment of his total savings of 200s. was insufficient to yield more than a most meagre income and he returned to take up unskilled wage employment in a fertilizer factory. Within days he was arrested and imprisoned for four months for non-payment of tax. Out of jail, he worked first on a building site, then on his step-mother's farm. Once again he returned to blacksmithing, working for his former employer in the village. Again, after but a few months, he tried another employer before moving to Nairobi, where he was able to rent the machinery needed to make carriers. After vicissitudes, in which he lost the use of the machines, he was eventually able to buy them and to become at the age of twenty-eight his own master. But he lived and slept at his place of work in a shelter three feet high and made of waste metal sheets. In ten years his ambitions had changed remarkably little. His story illustrates the hazards encountered – the risks of independent business activity, the unpredictable arrests and, in sum, the difficulties in accumulating sufficient capital to launch one into success. (King, 1977, pp. 114–18.)

A contrasting example from Guatemala City is provided by Roberts. Pepe grew up and completed his primary schooling in a provincial town. He learned to be a barber and also became an active member of a band, one of whose members eventually invited him in 1940 to the city. Here he found work as a barber and subsequently with his friend, established his own shop. One of his customers, a hospital nurse, got him a job as barber in a military base where he worked; here Pepe learned from his patron enough about his work to enable him to work as an unqualified nurse, giving injections. Pepe returned to private business until, in 1959, his original friend and helper found him the post of bus inspector with a company in which he now worked as an accountant. At the same time Pepe moved from the inner city to a shanty town. Here his wife tended a small shop. Upon his retirement from the bus company in 1962 he devoted his whole attention to his shop, arguing that he was at fifty-three years getting too old for the tiring work on the buses and that he needed to establish a little business with his own capital to maintain him in his old age (Roberts, 1973, pp. 141–2). In the terms of Balan *et al.* this final move of Pepe would be defined as downward mobility, but examples such as this merely indicate the danger in hierarchically arranging all occupations in terms of skill level or current income.

In general the less well-educated are likely to move into self-employment sooner than those better-educated who are more successful in getting good wage employment. As we shall see below an early start also facilitates success in trade or artisanship. The older a man becomes, the less likely is he to start a flourishing business – his hopes, as illustrated by those of Pepe, are to provide himself with a moderate income, commensurate with his needs in his retirement.

The rapid movement from one job to another, as the recent arrival searches for work which is both congenial and remunerative, or the recurrent periods of unemployment experienced by construction labourers, both tend to give an impression of considerable instability in shanty-town dwellers' employment. This in itself is not a false picture. But it must be balanced by one which stresses the occupational stability of those who do become established in the city. Thus of the Hong Kong hawkers studied by McGee, nearly three quarters had been engaged in this activity for more than ten years – and many of these had been operating from the same sites for long periods. Similarly Bienefeld (1974) reports that, in his example of workers in Dar es Salaam, Tanzania, half of the wage earners but two thirds of the self-employed had been in their current jobs for more than three years. Though striking, such findings are hardly surprising, for self-employment involves such an investment of capital, skills and personal relationships that sudden changes of occupation are hardly feasible. These surveys tend to over-emphasize those who have successfully remained in self-employment. They fail to catch those who, through failure, have reverted to wage employment or returned in frustration to the rural area. Balan *et al.* give examples of the former in discussing downward mobility – a grocery-store owner who became an unskilled labourer, a taxi driver who became a policeman. The Salisburys (1972) describe the shame felt by such individuals and the strategies open to them to cope with their failure.

The Sianne man who is successful in private business in Port Moresby, New Guinea, earns more than he could possibly do in returning to his village to grow coffee. So he focuses upon an urban career. Much of his success often depends on the custom of newly arrived immigrants and he cultivates these relationships, taking care that his generosity does not outmatch the returns. If he aspires to enter the local political arena on his return to his village he must amass capital; so he turns to taxi owning. But this is a most risky enterprise. In failure, a return to the village is out of the question, as it would mean accepting too low an income. He probably does not own a private house so he cannot become a landlord. To take an unskilled urban job would lose him prestige among other immigrants. He may seek an off-beat occupation which confers high prestige – one such man became a professional boxer; or he may turn to illegal activities which, though not prestigious, can yield high returns. But in all these options the degree of risk is high and the likelihood is that these men will fail, castigated as unable to adapt to urban life.

Surveys also show that self-employment tends to predominate among older men. One explanation offered is that entry to this sector was easier a decade or two ago – now there is much more intense competition. But Balan *et al.* (1973, p. 220) argue that such figures indicate that the number of persons entering the sector is constant, but when several drop out the older men predominate in the survey samples. Nevertheless, statistics apart, self-employment is seen by most both as an avenue to success and as a suitable mode of work in one's later years.

Moser (1977) has described the men and women selling in a retail food market in Bogotá. She emphasizes the widely different scale of operations – one third had a gross turnover of under 200 pesos per week, one sixth a turnover of over 800 pesos. These differences reflect the manner in which the sellers entered the occupation. Elderly women begin trading when they lack other means of support, they have little capital and with declining health grow steadily poorer; 'they come to the market to die'. Younger women with families come when, widowed or abandoned by husbands or obliged by pregnancy to leave domestic service, they are forced into seeking their own livelihood. They view their trading as a long-term commitment and tend to have medium-sized stalls. Their family commitments however inhibit their expansion. Older men enter the market when unable to find wage employment or when they seek a quiet occupation for their retirement. Their scale of operation depends on the capital which they can invest – they hope neither for much expansion, nor for alternative employment. Younger men who enter the market see it as a career. They aggregate savings from friends and relatives, and in their early years, with few family commitments, can accumulate capital. They aspire to rise to wholesale selling, though their chances are meagre. The variety of goods sold in this food market is great, ranging from highly perishable luxury fruits to the staple root crops. Each trader must choose what he will sell and so adopts strategies to maximize gains (as do the younger men) or to minimize the possibility of loss (as the older stall holders do).

## THE CRITERIA FOR SUCCESS

As I have indicated above two routes to success exist in the urban sphere: one through wage employment, the other through self-employment. In the former an educational qualification is usually a necessary prerequisite, and, in the clerical as opposed to manual occupations, advancement may be tied closely to the acquisition of certificates of higher learning. Educational qualifications enable the youth from the underprivileged home – the remote village, the dependent town, the landless family, perhaps of slave origin – to enter the newly emergent upper classes of his society. Education becomes a substitute for patronage until the competition for career posts between those equally qualified grows to such a level that friends in high places again determine one's success. Educational success nevertheless demands hard work and concentration; and the provision of school fees, so that one can take up opportunities offered, may still require the support of a wide circle of kin, friends and patrons.

In the spheres of self-employment formal qualifications tend to be eschewed, and the prosperous self-made artisan or trader will scorn the unemployed school leaver with his 'useless' certificates. He will stress instead the necessity of hard work and the importance of seeking patronage. These two qualities are seen not as alternatives to success but as being equally necessary. By hard work alone one's progress is minimal. Major leaps forward are possible through the mediation of others, but one must work hard to take advantage of the opportunities offered.

Craft occupations and the minor professions are highly competitive. Scores of men offer a similar range of products – a range often limited by the availability of cheap mass-produced manufactured goods. Business may be highly seasonal, with but a few weeks of hectic activity at major religious festivals or harvest periods. It may fluctuate as wage increases and inflation determine the cash available for non-essential goods. To gain customers one must try to build up a regular clientele; to retain them one must supply a product of better quality and lower price than one's competitors. Skill and hard work are obvious criteria for success in such a field and it is these qualities which are most often cited when men attempt to explain the good fortune of others. Ultimately one reaches a psychological determinant – some men are more achievement-oriented than others.

However, the mode of the achievement of success lies principally through the acquisition and accumulation of capital. A minimum is needed to establish one's trade. With further reinvestment in better machines, in the hiring of extra labour, one improves or increases one's product. Savings or investment in alternative enterprises cushions one against those spells of recession which drive the less fortunate out of business.

As we have seen, the capital necessary to establish an enterprise is often very small. A young man may be given such a sum by his parents, or he may save it from his wages. In the latter case he is better placed if he has few dependants to support. The same applies in the years of early accumulation. Several studies have demonstrated that those who start young are more successful. Not only does a young man have a smaller family to feed, but his wife, not yet fully occupied with the care of several children, may even be able to assist him in his trade, or contribute her own earnings to the family pool. Choices may have to be made between having a larger family and restricting its size, between reinvesting profits in the business or building a better house and paying school fees for one's children. As the children grow older they may be able to help in the business, the increased numbers involved acting as an insurance against the sickness or absence of any one member. Conversely the artisan will probably prefer to see his children concentrate on their school activities, so that they obtain good wage employment from which they can later move into self-employment, rather than being forced by illiteracy into the latter in the most disadvantageous circumstances.

Skill and hard work lead to the accumulation of profits. Business acumen and the prevailing pattern of values guide the allocation of profits towards reinvestment or consumption. Perenially besetting all the poor are the crises of sickness, unemployment and legal disputes which can, overnight, erode one's savings. By virtue of their employment, few men are covered by forms of state social security or insurance. Ultimately security lies with relatives and friends, but these contribute their support when one's own savings have been almost exhausted and one is on the verge of destitution. Unlike insurance schemes they do not distribute the burdens equally upon all members. Among the poor of the shanty town sickness is clearly more prevalent than among the wealthy – poor diets and insanitary conditions facilitate the spread of disease and the development of body malfunctions. Unemployment, through loss of job or a business recession, is common. Discrimination against the poor leads to gaol sentences in cases where the middle-class person might well go unpunished or merely be fined. Little wonder that the shanty-town dweller sees life as a game of snakes and ladders with moments of good fortune alternating with disasters which send one back many moves. It does seem a matter of luck that some people have more of the good fortune and so approach the top, while others are continually being relegated to the bottom. But unlike in the children's game, in which each throw of the dice gives one the same chance of landing at the foot of a ladder or the head of a snake, in real life successes and failures tend to be cumulative.

The analogy has its limits: life is not a game. Bad luck – the loss of a job, illness, imprisonment – is likely to reduce a family to starvation level. Bereft of an income, lacking the cushioning afforded by social security payments, and with help from kin and neighbours given but grudgingly, daily life becomes a struggle for survival. Many men cannot cope and turn to drink, abandoning their families. Yet the family, with its multiple incomes, remains the prime means of support – wives and older children are, it is hoped, earning when husbands are not. If men appear cheerful and optimistic, as so many of them do in such periods of adversity, it is because they realize that self-pity is dysfunctional to success. They must struggle to stay alive, struggle to make minimal progress; but all around them experience the same tribulations.

In a fascinating study of Spanish American rural migrants to Denver, Colorado, Hanson and Simmons (1969) recorded the progress of their subjects over a long period. They first subdivided them into two groups according to their initial socio-economic status and then further divided each group – the initially high socio-economically into thrivers and stumblers, the socio-economically low into strugglers and losers. These terms are self-explanatory. The allocation of the migrants to these categories is shown to be mainly a function of the stability of employment gained and the incidence of misfortunes.

To revert again to criteria for success: a vital resource is an established network of personal contacts. Such is obviously necessary as one seeks for wage employment and needs information about opportunities available and personal introductions to enhance one's likelihood of success. The artisan or trader tries to build up a regular clientele, both through his personality and through relationships established in other spheres – through extended kinship, membership of voluntary associations and the like. In many cases, unable to supply a better product than his competitors, he relies most heavily on these personal contacts. Equally he depends on his suppliers – the tailor relies upon those who will supply him with cloth at a competitive price, the food seller in the market hopes that his wholesaler will regularly bring him produce of good quality, at reasonable prices. In taking on a new apprentice the craftsman may measure his advantage not only in terms of increased labour input but also in terms of the new personal relationships with the boy's family and the opportunities which they may yield.

For all workers there exist two ways to a better standard of living – the improvement of personal status *vis-à-vis* one's fellows, and the collective improvement of the work conditions of all those similarly employed. Thus the wage earner can seek promotion, or he may through his trade union try to gain a larger slice of the cake for his peers. As we have already seen, aspirations of promotion are virtually limited to the clerical realm. For the manual worker there are few opportunities save in the progression from semi-skilled to skilled status; beyond that point the route is almost completely closed. Strongly organized trade unions tend to exist in the large internationally controlled companies and the public services. Smaller firms, often managed by oriental or indigenous businessmen, try either to prohibit union activity entirely (by sacking activists) or to develop a very patriarchal form of domination. To the extent that they can threaten the national economy by halting transport and communications, or damaging vital export industries, the former unions can be politically powerful. It is the 'labour aristocracy' which is so organized; and it alleged that their demands are framed in terms of their own self-interest – that they try to maintain a substantial differential between their own wages and the incomes of the majority of the poor, rather than espouse the collective interests of all workers. This claim seems justified. However, the issues involved in strike action by these unions often transcend their specific wage claims to involve such criticism of government as to win wide popular support. Again, the self-employed realize that a successful wage claim by the factory employees will enable them to raise their own prices and profits. The speed with which food prices in the market rise after a wage increase reflects such opportunism on the part of the sellers rather than any change in the supply or demand of their product.

Union activity is correspondingly weak among the least skilled workers and those such as casual labourers in sporadic employment. And it is these, rather than the 'labour aristocrats', who predominate in the shanty towns. They are much more likely to subscribe to the values of the self-employed among whom they live and many of whom they seek to emulate.

For the self-employed artisan or trader, forms of co-operative activity are minimal. Market sellers may try to fix prices, but the agreed price will probably differ little from that reached under free market conditions; they have no sanctions to use against those who undercut. Craftsmen suffer a similar disability. Collectively they may gather to protest and their demonstrations may sway public opinion; but means of coercion are non-existent. Their actions are directed not against their customers but against the government, which imposes rules and restrictions and suppliers to control the flow of goods. Thus hawkers protest against the reduction of licences or the closure to them of certain streets; taxi drivers go on strike in protest against police harassment. The public are slightly inconvenienced, but it is the demonstrators who, lacking any strike fund, suffer most. Again the larger businessmen tend to control the trade associations and their interests are often incongruent with those of the small man; but the protests of the latter are muted when they rely substantially on the patronage of the former and on their wholesale suppliers. Furthermore, they are unlikely to seek to destroy those whom they aspire to join.

For the self-employed man, therefore, betterment lies in accumulating capital and expanding his business. This may be achieved in two ways – by increasing the scale of his enterprise and by a proliferation of activities or moving into new spheres. The successful craftsman may engage more of his family members in his business, buy a few additional machines, take on apprentices and hire journeymen. The trader opens shops or stalls in other localities. Ultimately the size of the business may warrant its incorporation into the formal sector. But many men lack the management abilities which make such expansion possible. Rather than try to control a larger staff they will encourage their dependants to set up on their own, helping them with advice and perhaps loans. In return they receive not only gratitude but the advantages of a widened personal network of indebted individuals who in supplying information and sharing contacts provide a greater security and stability for their own business.

Where lack of technical or managerial skills inhibits the growth of an enterprise – as when a mechanic with a small workshop is unable to convert his business into a full-scale garage – capital accumulated may be directed towards other enterprises similar in scale. The mechanic starts a taxi service, for example. Alternatively a move is made towards a higher level of activity. Thus the successful Bogotá food retailers hoped to become wholesalers. The Nigerian bicycle repairer aspires to sell cycles, the tailor to be a cloth merchant; for the trader always seem to be richer than the craftsman whom he supplies. While the skills which the former possesses are not beyond the abilities of the latter, the greater capital involvement and the degree of risk in holding stock yields a substantially higher return.

Thus in the sphere of work the dominant ethic among the shanty-town dwellers is likely to be that of an entrepreneurial petite bourgeoisie rather than that of a true proletariat – a stress on individual hard work and initiative, on the establishment of a personal network as a major resource rather than on collective bargaining and activity.

# 7 Residential Communities

Social anthropologists, notwithstanding their predilection for the holistic study of the residential community, have, in their research in the cities, tended to focus upon the ethnic community – the migrants from a single rural area. They have in consequence stressed the continuing relationships between co-villagers which persist in the town and the ties maintained with the home area. Economists see the migrant as a worker, rightly viewing his role in the production process as the prime determinant of his poverty. Marxists too write as if man's relationships in work were the only ones worthy of consideration. Few scholars have tried to describe the residential community within the shanty town.

To the untrained eye the endless sprawl of hovels up hillsides or across swamp land suggests an absence of identifiable residential communities. Add to this the perceived heterogeneity of the population, and the fact that most of the men and many of the women are away at work for long hours, and the image of the dormitory suburb, similar to that of the middle-class areas of Western cities, comes readily to mind. Yet those outsiders who have lived and researched in such areas often report strong feelings of corporate identity and well-developed local organizations. They are, of course, more likely to report such a situation when they do find it than focus upon its absence when they do not; but their descriptions suggest a fairly widespread phenomenon.

That ties of reciprocal help should bind neighbours in the shanty towns is to be expected. Here certainly there is a contrast with the domestic independence found in more affluent suburbs. But the bonds are often much stronger than this. The residential community in the shanty town may seem very like a village –

not, as is often argued, because its people still betray their rural origins, but because it is a small and largely self-contained unit with a stable membership, having its own mode of social stratification, competing with neighbouring units in its relationships with the outside world.

Nevertheless the variety in the structure of these residential communities must not be overlooked: some are like little villages; others, at the opposite end of the continuum, are like staging posts of impermanent newly arriving migrants. Not only do censuses of income and occupation and length of residence reveal substantial differences between individual shanty-town settlements but they themselves develop a local reputation – some are happy or progressive places, others depressing. Migrants are variously attracted to them both, influencing and being influenced by the dominant ethos. Economic conditions are not a sole determinant here; Clinard and Abbott describe two slum areas in Kampala with similar characteristics of income and education. One had a high crime rate, the other a low one. The latter was a more integrated community and had less ethnic heterogeneity, with more friends being made within the ethnic unit; people participated more in local associations; family relationships were more stable; there was less movement out of the community; in all people felt it was a good place in which to live (1973, pp. 143ff.).

The image of ethnic heterogeneity masks the nuclei of close relatives. The existence of the latter should not surprise us. We have seen how the newly arrived migrant relies upon his close kinsmen to find him accommodation. They are likely to recommend a near-by site not only to retain affective links but also because their knowledge of opportunities is territorially restricted. When a site has been settled illegally and the founding members still control the allocation of vacant land, it is most likely that they will favour their own kin, their affines and their close friends – who will in turn seek to introduce their own kin and friends. When husbands and wives, or friends, come from different areas this network of family relationships may embrace an increasing range of ethnic units.

I have already noted that, in the small shanty town which I

studied in Lima, one third of the people came from one small sierra village. Susan Lobo found an even more striking clustering in another part of the city:

> The clustering of *paisanos* from the environs of Huirahuacho in Apurimac is typical in a number of features of *paisano* clusters. Once the logic of organization within such a grouping becomes evident, one finds a marked contrast with the 'chaotic' nature of squatter settlements so often implied or assumed in the literature. The Huirahuacho *paisano* cluster in Carongo includes eighty-four households and approximately five hundred and forty individuals. In the centre of the cluster, there is an open space measuring approximately thirty by forty feet. Here is located a spigot where most of the households living in the cluster obtain their water, and near which clothes are washed. The spigot is the focal point of much daytime activity. The open space is also often used as a semi-secluded area in which children play and adults sit and talk; secular and religious activities and fiestas often take place here. In many respects, open areas within a *paisano* cluster serve functions similar to those of the traditional central *plaza* in many highland villages and small towns. As is common in many of the *paisano* clusters, the houses within the Huirahuacho cluster face inward toward the open area, creating a somewhat insular pattern, due to the narrow, often meandering, passageways that lead into or through the area. The arrangement of passageways discourages intrusion into the area by those who do not live there or have immediate business there. Within this cluster there are also located four small house-front stores, one small restaurant that also sells beer, a shoe repair shop, a tailor shop, and a variable number of pushcarts from which prepared food is sold. (Lobo, 1976, pp. 115–16)

The bonds existing in these communities at the time of settlement are subsequently further strengthened by those of neighbourliness, of drinking groups, of co-godparenthood, marriage of children etc. People became linked to each other not by single stranded relationships but by multiplex ones. Lomnitz (1975) describes how a woman in the Mexican shanty town which she studied contemplated throwing her alcoholic husband out of the house but then changed her mind, for his drinking companions were her own brothers.

Often, in the early days of the community, the first settlers of a site or those who planned its invasion, constitute its governing committee, allocating the remaining land, seeking official recognition and legal title to the land, agitating for basic services. They provide a focus of identity for the community. If the settlement prospers it may be eventually incorporated into the local government structure of the city. Alternatively, as in Peru, these local committees may be given formal recognition in being incorporated into the state community development organization. In Tanzania and Zambia the shanty-town settlements are controlled and led by the local branch of the dominant political party. In these processes of incorporation the original leaders may well be displaced in favour of other men more acceptable to the national government and its agents. Nevertheless the settlement remains a recognized political unit responsible for some aspects of its own administration. However, in other situations where outside political recognition is not bestowed upon the settlement, its committee of leaders, having accomplished its original aims in creating the community, slowly lose its authority. The reasons for this are discussed below.

Few other types of formal association seem to develop within the shanty town through indigenous efforts. The youths may have a football club. The local primary school, though state-controlled, may have a largely autonomous parents' committee. But other formal associations are stimulated by outside agencies. Churches, charitable bodies and a host of voluntary associations, largely managed by the middle classes, seek to bring welfare and services to the poor. Their efforts seem particularly pronounced in Latin America – owing perhaps to the proximity of the United States, the dominance of the Catholic Church and the size of the local middle and upper classes. One study of their operation in Peru is graphically titled *From Invaders to Invaded* (Rodriguez, *et al.*, 1973). The activities of these bodies are determined by locality – they seek to provide clinics, nurseries, sewing and cookery classes for housewives in a given area, not to members of a particular ethnic group. It is argued that they actually encourage communities to vie with each other to obtain the benefits offered, rather than to organize cooperatively to pressure the government for improved services to the shanty-town poor. Furthermore, it is alleged they act as purveyors of middle-class values and that they foster among the poor the belief that they are incapable of organizing themselves through laziness, corruption and suchlike and that they are thus dependent upon external assistance. Radicals see in these activities a strong deterrent to class-based action by the poor. Opinions among the poor themselves tend to be divided: aspirants to upward social mobility tend to welcome the activity of these associations in assisting them to achieve middle-class life styles and values and to establish contacts with more influential persons; others see their schemes as irrelevant to the life and work of the poor and view their agents as well-meaning meddlers.

The strength of relationships within a given residential community can be assessed only in comparison with those links outside it. Most of these have already been mentioned. Close relatives may be widely scattered across the city; members of one's ethnic community too are scattered, even though local concentrations may be observed. Public transport between shanty towns tends to be poor and costly, inhibiting the frequent visiting that might otherwise take place. Except in those cases in which an employer provides housing for his employees – a comparatively rare phenomenon in the modern city and in any case beyond the scope of this book – the latter tend to be widely dispersed. Residential relationships do not coincide with those between workmates. Furthermore, the shanty towns contain a higher proportion of those in self-employment or in irregular and low-paid employment. The well-paid government factory employees tend to live in the housing estates. It is the latter who are most strongly recognized in trade unions; the former are but peripheral members of the unions, if they are members at all, and do not seek their individual betterment through such corporate activity.

People may leave their shanty towns to go to church, though the studies of local communities do not usually describe any pronounced religious activity; the migrants appear comparatively areligious. They attend hospitals and clinics in the city.

The young people go to dances and cinemas. They shop not in the middle-class supermarkets but predominantly in the larger open markets situated in poor areas of the city where they expect to find variety and low prices. Small shopkeeping is a feature of the shanty town itself, enabling local residents to buy minute quantities often on credit. Thus while the residents of the shanty towns move about the city, availing themselves of some of its services, they are both too poor and too busy to participate to any great degree.

The picture that has been building up is one of a shanty-town community whose members are bound together by a dense network of multiple relationships, while their relationships to individuals and institutions beyond the limits of the residential community are weak, tenuous and instrumental. The cohesion and sense of identity fostered may be further enhanced. For instance the community may have clear territorial limits. Sometimes a few adjacent blocks in a very large agglomeration may possess a designated identity yet their boundaries may have little social relevance. In other cases the shanty town is located on an undeveloped site within a middle-class suburb. In the latter case the knowledge of the hostility of the affluent neighbours and the suspicions (often well founded) of their attempts to procure the eradication of the eyesore in their midst enhances the cohesion of the shanty-town residents. Again, individual residents may have experienced ostracism on the part of more fortunate relatives who seem loath to visit them.

Finally, identity is created by the stability of the population. An image of impermanence is created by the decrepit appearance of many of the shanty town's dwellings – though this appearance is more often the consequence of their being half completed than of decay. Again, since shanty towns do differ so much in their affluence, their reputation and their amenities, it seems reasonable to suppose that the migrant will move from one to another as he succeeds or fails in establishing himself in the city. Such after all is the pattern set by the upper working classes and middle classes of cities in the industrialized world living in estates and suburbs with vast areas of uniformly designed and priced flats and houses. But in the shanty town such movements seem to be minimal. Little data exists, but MacEwen (1974) describes an Argentinian shanty town from which only twenty-eight families in a total of nearly 250 moved out within a four-year period – and eighteen of these returned to the rural area. Thus intra-city movements affected only one per cent of the households each year.

The shanty-town house, built with the labour of family and friends over a long period of years, is designed to suit the whims and needs of its occupants. Legal title to the land may be lacking. Its construction does not meet official standards – ridiculous though these may be in the local situation. The market value of the house is thus low. Its owners cannot realize a substantial sum to use as the down payment on a house in a newly developed estate. Nor are potential buyers easy to find – complete strangers are unlikely to seek entry into the cohesive little community. Again, by the time that the owners of the shanty-town house are ready to move, they have probably produced a large family. The desirable little bungalow in the suburbs may be within their means – but it will not accommodate all the children. Should the parents decide to leave their grown children in the shanty-town house, moving out themselves, they will not be realizing the capital already invested and necessary to buy or build their new abode. The more likely pattern is for adult children to move out to establish their own homes – first perhaps in rented accommodation until they, like their parents, move to a shanty town to start their own building. If one is accumulating capital at a steady rate one may of course start building a second, and then a third house – for oneself, for one's children or as an investment. But for the vast majority this is but a dream; with small and sudden windfalls they can but make some slight improvement in their existing home. And so the residents remain, year after year, becoming increasingly confined to their local community as sickness and age inhibit travel on crowded buses. Yet some of them have been economically successful, as their houses demonstrate – the community embraces persons widely differing in wealth and life style.

Consider for example the range of incomes reported by Whiteford (1974) in a small shanty town in Popayan, a provincial city of Colombia. Here over a third of the household heads earned less than $10 monthly while 10 per cent earned between $30 and $40 and 6 per cent earned more than this. A similar divergence occurs in the total incomes of households, with nearly a fifth receiving less than $10 monthly and a little more than a fifth receiving over $40. Whiteford's figures also demonstrate the wide range of incomes within particular occupations. Thus those in small-scale commerce earned between almost nothing and $50–$75 monthly, with a mean of nearly $20. Those in government service fell within the same range, but with a mean of nearly $35, while those employed in industry earned between $20 and $100, with a mean of $40. In Laquian's shanty town in Manila in the Philippines, the range of incomes seems a little less marked, 30 per cent of the residents earning below P100 a month and 10 per cent receiving above P200 (1969, p. 286). It seems likely, on the basis of these and similar figures, that the mean income in the upper quartile of the residential population of the shanty town is between three and eight times that of the lower quartile. Even if we take the lower range it is nevertheless a most striking one – and one which we would not expect to find in a more affluent suburban area.

These differences in income, both individual and household, are reflected in housing and life styles. At one extreme the house is constructed of garnered waste materials – packing cases, corrugated-iron sheets, matting and sacks; at the other extreme a well-constructed brick or cement-block house, glazed windows and imposing front doors. Within the former one finds a simple bed, a crudely made chair and table, but in the latter plastic upholstered furniture and a number of gas or electric items – cooker, refrigerator, iron, television.

Typical, in many ways, of the relatively prosperous shanty-town resident is Don Francisco, who figures repeatedly in Safa's (1974) account of Los Peloteros, in the Puerto Rican capital, San Juan. Don Francisco had lived in a number of places in the capital before he moved, in 1940, with his young bride to Los Peloteros, where he remained for the next twenty-three years.

In his early life he worked in a variety of carpentry and construction jobs, but in 1957 he was able to establish his own business and became a successful small entrepreneur. He was in fact so successful that he was able to buy a house in an urbanization and he had hoped to retire to a small country estate with a two-acre citrus farm, but death intervened. Through his wealth and success he was one of the most active of the informal leaders of Los Peloteros, a much admired man who constituted a role model for other residents. He gave all his eight children a good education; his eldest, a daughter, was a trained typist who studied at evening classes to be a Spanish teacher, hoping one day to emigrate to the United States.

Don Francisco attributed his success to his own hard work and abstinence. He admits that he was once a free spender and poor; but he joined the Seventh Day Adventist Church and abjured such vices as drinking, lotteries, parties and women. As Safa writes, Don Francisco accepted poverty: 'there has always been poverty and there always will be poverty ... anyone who has to work for a living is poor... This does not mean that the poor man must accept his low station in life as they did previously' (1974, pp. 34–5). He warned his neighbours against attempting to rise too quickly; success lay through slow and steady saving. His religion sanctioned poverty, but his church was active in relief projects. His daughter too felt that the opportunities for success are there for those who can grasp them – she acknowledged her own debt to the support given to her by her family. Politically Don Francisco was conservative, a supporter of the Populist party and staunchly anti-communist.

Don Francisco was perhaps as atypical a resident of Los Peloteros as an unemployed drunk. But his career is one that most would hope to emulate; and it is as important to focus upon such men as upon the least able, society's 'problem cases'.

This range between extremes of poverty and relative affluence may be attributed to various causes besides individual personality. Firstly the life cycle: the poorest are often the very young, still looking for stable employment, or the aged, too senile for regular and demanding labour. The affluent households are often those with adult children who contribute substantially to the domestic budget. Again, as we have already seen, while some residents come to the shanty town having accumulated a little capital with which to start building a house (but with too little and without good enough prospects of future income to use it as a down payment on a house in an estate), others arrived with almost nothing, evicted by a landlord for non-payment of rent or as a consequence of inner-city slum clearance. These latter were admitted to the settlement on the basis of their relationship with existing residents and their good repute, not because of any prediction of their future prosperity. Finally, as described above, the few residents who do prosper in the city often remain within their shanty town rather than move elsewhere. And so the settlement increases in heterogeneity with respect to wealth, occupation and place of origin.

House building is the concern of individual families. Neighbours will help each other with the more demanding tasks and with expertise, but there are few reports of any more large-scale co-operative activity. However residents do have shared interests in the provision of services and the acquisition of legal title to the land. Title is an important issue to those who have squatted upon or invaded the area settled; most are probably rather vague about the locus of ownership. They are uncertain too about the steps which government might take to assert its own authority. Fears of eradication may for a few months deter the squatters from investing time, labour and saving in a permanent house; but the longer they remain and the better the quality of their housing, the more difficult it becomes to dislodge them in any precipitate move. The need for a title recedes except for those with the better houses who may wish one day to sell them.

Piped water and electricity are eagerly sought by all the residents of a newly founded shanty town, for apart from the convenience these services are apt to be cheaper than alternatives – a water rate for stand-pipes costs less than water supplied by a tanker lorry which fills a forty-gallon drum at one's door. Other improvements are certainly desired by all residents. For instance all would vote that the road through the settlement should be tarmaced to lay the dust raised by passing lorries and cars; but while the richer residents might be prepared to contribute towards this in order to protect their furnishings, the poor see it as a luxury which they can ill afford. The collective action which the settlement achieved in its early days in establishing its squatters rights and in getting basic services tends to weaken as the years pass and as residents place different values on the suggested improvements.

In consequence some of the more affluent residents of the shanty town grow disgruntled at its lack of achievements. They aspire to move to a better area but, as we have seen, they are often trapped. In their frustration they withdraw from active participation in the community, concerning themselves only with their own wellbeing. They eschew the rules of leadership which, in their economic success, are seen as their due. Other affluent residents however seem less concerned with the more material signs of success. For them a higher value is placed on the esteem which they enjoy in the community, demonstrated by the deference paid to them, the invitations to become a godparent or to attend parties. They are in effect seeking recognition within the local community, not in the wider world outside, though as local leaders they do attract the attention of outside agencies. The poor, conversely, may simply lack the resources to participate in communal activities. They have no spare cash. Their time is fully occupied in looking for work or in trying to maintain a plurality of occupations. Yet their security depends heavily on the goodwill of their neighbours, and their wholehearted support in these activities is a valued form of insurance.

Many writers have commented upon the relative lack of communal activity within the shanty town. The high level reached at a period of invasion and struggle for title and basic services subsequently declines. Is this a demonstration of apathy, as the culture-of-poverty theories would suggest? It is not clear how these critics measure an optimal level of activity – they merely infer that the shanty-town residents could have done so much more; and here again one detects a covert assumption – in such a situation middle-class persons would have done much more. However, comparison with middle-class activity is hardly fair. Pressure groups sustained by these classes rarely involve many persons, whereas in the idealized activity expected of the shanty town everybody is expected to contribute in time and money. Again, the middle-class leaders of pressure groups have readier access to municipal officials than have those of the shanty town.

In his study of settlement of the poor in Guatemala, Roberts (1973) attributes their inability to organize to a lack of knowledge which actors have of each other. They come from very different social backgrounds in villages and provincial towns, localities often separated from each other by hundreds of miles and by wide cultural variations. They have little knowledge of the type of jobs done by others and are slow to develop role expectations. Residence in the shanty town is recent and perhaps transient. These factors inhibit the development of trust between individuals – a trust which does exist between middle-class persons because they have relatively clear images of the identity of others even though personal interaction may be infrequent: one trusts the local bank manager to be treasurer of the club because one 'knows' that he will behave honestly. While the factors cited by Roberts do seem plausible in accounting for a lack of organizational activity, they nevertheless seem to ignore the dense network of the interrelationships which may develop within the shanty town and which ought to supply the missing ingredient – trust. MacEwen attributed this lack of trust to status competition between neighbours:

> the processes of differentiation and movement among the poor, while scarcely discernible to the outsider, were of crucial importance to the people involved. As far as residential relationships were concerned, the intense status competition that was produced by limited mobility and the stress on manifestation of appropriate status-symbols produced a strain towards conflict and tension within the neighbourhood rather than one of solidarity. . . In short, 'mobility' produced a strain towards individualization of the poor, placing them in competition with one another, and thus depriving them of a basis for collective leadership and consciousness. (1974, pp. 222–3)

In many studies of community action it is reported that shanty-town leaders are distrusted, that they are seen to use their position to enhance their own interests. Such popular allegations are supported by credible stories of men who absconded with funds, or who invested them in some venture in the hope of making a quick profit before repayment fell due; of development schemes which either brought lucrative contracts to the shanty-town leaders or placed the water pipes, the little square or some other service closest to their own houses. In the little community one's public and private persona are more difficult to separate. But we must leave the issues of leadership until the following chapter, when we shall consider the relationships between the shanty town and the state and the city. We return now to our earlier theme – the aspirations of members of the shanty-town community.

## ASPIRATIONS

Let us assess, at this point, the goals sought by the poor and the routes by which they are seen to be achieved. Firstly, many men aspire to return to the rural area of their birth; and even if this seems to the observer to be a pipe-dream, it nevertheless determines the actor's current activities. The rural area represents a secure refuge should he fail in town – there he will be able to farm and maintain himself, albeit at a level no higher than if he had never emigrated. If successful in the city he may invest his savings in land or a small business to ensure a leisured and comfortable retirement. In either case he depends upon the goodwill of those in the village who control the allocation of scarce resources. He must maintain his reputation by visits and gift-giving and by his activity in his urban ethnic association; a man who ostracizes his co-migrants in the city can expect few favours on his return to the village.

Secondly the migrant seeks employment in the city. As I have outlined above, the man with few resources probably starts in irregular wage employment, combined perhaps with odd jobs either on his own account or for an artisan. Regular wage employment will give him the security that he seeks; but such jobs rarely offer any significant avenues for advancement. His hope is to save so that he can set up in business on his own, though the chances of success are slight – many fail to accumulate enough capital, others make false starts and are driven back into wage employment. In this activity the shanty-town dweller depends upon a network of relatives and friends who may provide information about job opportunities and upon patrons – those with relationships beyond his own sphere – who can make valuable introductions and place lucrative contracts in his way.

Most men arriving in the city have passed the age of primary schooling and manual work for long hours inhibits any desire for private study. These men admit that there is a definite ceiling upon their possible attainments in the formal sector of the economy – and only a lucky break will bring in the informal sector. But for their children these constraints are not seen to operate – for them, as the story of Blas and Carmen suggests, the way is wide open. After 'to seek employment', 'the education of one's children' is cited as one of the major reasons for emigration to the city. However, in West Africa, I have met parents who send their children home to the village, to lodge with relatives and attend a long-established primary school, hoping thereby that the young will not be contaminated by city life; but this option is not available in most parts of the third world, where the rural areas are deprived of all but the most inadequate primary schools.

Education is valued as a route for mobility for two reasons. It is an alternative to established routes and is thus espoused by the underprivileged in traditional society – the poor who are not eligible for high political offices, those from dependent villages who cannot aspire to posts in the capitals, those from communities raided for slaves in the past. Though those in the privileged sectors may be better able to afford education and have like advantages in access to it, they may yet see it as a threat to their own system of values and so are surpassed by the enthusiasm of the underprivileged. Again, education is seen as an impersonal mode of advancement: with the necessary certificates one will gain a commensurate job and income; one is not reliant upon influential patrons – at least not until the supply of school leavers vastly exceeds the jobs available and the certificate is but a licence to join the queues of applicants. Education thus appeals to the newly arrived migrant who is without patrons. Finally, of course, education is a *sine qua non* for most jobs in the formal sector.

Education demands sacrifices from parents. Secondary-school fees may be high, especially where many of the places available are for boarders. In Nigeria for instance a year's fees almost equals the annual minimum wage. Primary schooling may be free, but parents are expected to buy books, equipment, uniforms and so on. Lastly the cost of education must include what the youth might otherwise have earned, or contributed by his labour to the domestic enterprise on farm or in workshop.

While all parents seem equally adamant that their children should receive a good education, their efforts in this direction are conditioned by their own backgrounds. Thus in our Nigerian study we found that educated parents said that they would help their children with homework; they would discuss their children's progress with teachers; with rudimentary knowledge of the school system – having themselves passed through a few stages – they could steer their children into better schools. Illiterate parents on the other hand spoke of flogging children who played truant or, more positively, of always ensuring that their children had their dinner money or such fees. A similar contrast in attitudes is cited by Balan *et al.* in their Monterrey study. Here sons from mobile and non-mobile families are compared. In the former families the value of education is stressed; in the latter it is imposed as an obligation. In the former it was assumed that children would study and that the parents would make financial sacrifices; in the latter, children were expected to help their parents even at the risk of jeopardizing their own careers (1973, pp. 259–60). One factor which distinguished mobile from non-mobile families was the existence in the former of relationships with persons of higher socio-economic status.

Many shanty towns have, as a consequence of policies of universal primary education, their own local schools; yet these are often inferior in quality to those in the more affluent suburbs. As MacEwen (1974) reports of her Argentinian shanty town, many parents send their children to these better schools, thus both further denigrating the local school and also setting themselves apart from their community, withdrawing from one area of activity which could act as a focus of its interests and cohesion.

Another major goal of the shanty-town dweller is the ownership of his own house. First and foremost this is a mode of ensuring security – with irregular wage unemployment or the fluctuating and uncertain income from self-employment, eviction for non-payment of rent is an ever-present hazard. But the house is also a status symbol – and in communities where income cannot be readily guessed from occupation it becomes a prime sign of success. A man such as Blas with a comfortable house for his family has 'made it'; the internal stratification of the shanty town is evidenced in its housing. Yet the house competes with one's business and with education, for disposable savings. In a Lima shanty town, I gained the impression that the university students came from the more modest houses. It was not possible to assess accurately the wealth of each home but it seemed that families from fairly humble rural backgrounds were depriving themselves so that their children could pursue their studies. Conversely other families, perhaps because they saw themselves as downwardly mobile (or for other reasons felt that they should occupy a higher status in society), were clearly investing heavily in their houses and their furnishing, while their children made indifferent educational progress. Similarly in a longitudinal study of Irish migrants to Newburyport, Massachusetts, in the mid and late nineteenth century, Thernstrom found that in those families where the head had become owner of his home, his children tended not to rise above his status; upwardly mobile children came from non-owning families. Social mobility was not a cumulative process (1975, p. 157).

When one asks the shanty-town resident to account for the success of himself and his neighbours the answers, as the example of Don Francisco illustrates, tend to be in terms of hard work, patronage and luck. Hard work and patronage may seem, to us, to be antithetical qualities; to others they are both equally necessary. Hard work on its own is not enough to raise oneself much higher – one's savings do not materially affect one's income. The great leap into a job of a higher rank is furthered by the help of others – though one must work hard to get the benefits from opportunities offered. Luck and good fortune provide these opportunities. They equally safeguard one from the pitfalls of sickness, legal troubles and such disasters. Hard work is a highly individual quality; yet one is not working in isolation. As we have seen, one needs a network of peers to provide information in getting jobs or contracts, to assure security when one is in trouble. One needs too the assistance of others in dealing with the wider world beyond the confines of the shanty town. Again, help in finding work is important. But in many other spheres, too, the rural migrant faces the complexity of an intransigent bureaucracy: to get an appointment in a hospital needs many introductions; to renew a driving licence takes several days of queuing at successive offices. In West Africa it is useful to have friends with 'long legs', who will pilot one's application through the appropriate channels. In some South American states the simplest application for a permit or licence must be typed in formal language on special legal paper which can be purchased in but few stationery shops. The 'public letter writer' of the African provincial town or village may be losing his clientele as the youths acquire basic literacy; but at a higher level there still exists a role to be played either by professional middlemen and brokers or by amateurs who are prepared to use their influence on behalf of their friends.

The image created by the hopes and aspirations of the shanty-town dweller is one that we would recognize as and term 'petit bourgeois'. Mangin so characterized the attitudes he found in Lima in the early 1960s:

The dominant ideology of most of the active *barriada* people appeared to be very similar to the beliefs of the operator of a small business in nineteenth-century England or the United States. These can be summed up in the familiar and accepted maxims: work hard, save money, trust only family members (and them not too much), outwit the state, vote conservatively if possible, but always in your own economic self-interest, educate your children for their future and as old age insurance for yourself. (1967, pp. 84–5)

Numerous other scholars have quoted this passage with approval, accepting its validity in areas studied by them. In a slightly different context Mangin has argued that the poor of the shanty town have more in common, culturally, with the middle classes of their own state than they have with the poor of other nations. The notion of a sub-culture of poverty universally shared by the poor, has for Mangin, little empirical validity. The shanty-town poor are marginal to the middle classes in that they aspire to their style of life even though, as yet, they cannot share it.

Yet some aspects of middle-class ideology do not appear to be shared by the poor. Key characteristics often cited are long-term planning, saving and deferred gratification. In contrast the poor are apt to spend lavishly for the present, to engage only in short-term investment. Observations of behaviour would seem to support this distinction. But let us consider the occupational milieu in which these values are located. The middle-class man is typically in white-collar employment, placed on a narrow ladder of advancement through a bureaucratic hierarchy; that is, he does not expect to change jobs, he enjoys considerable security and can expect regular minimal promotion; transfer to a higher rank is achieved by merit – by outstanding performance in one's job, by passing examinations. In such a situation one certainly can plan far ahead. The milieu of the poor is almost the exact reverse; there is no clear path of advancement –self-improvement lies in seizing extraneous opportunities; to learn of these and to be able to exploit them one relies on a wide circle of friends and helpers. The poor cannot enter into long-term commitments because they have so little security of income and cannot foresee their position ten or twenty years ahead. In this sense they cannot plan – they must always maintain themselves in a state of readiness to grasp the passing opportunity. The careful maintenance of one's personal network is essential. Thus the poor perhaps tend to over-emphasize the importance and efficacy of patronage, just as the middle classes stress the impersonality of factors assuring success – ignoring the countless contrary examples available to them in which personal issues have undoubtedly been critical. Again, the poor do in fact invest – their expenditure on housing and education testifies to this – through, as we have seen, they use their savings on the immediate improvement of the home, rather than in commitment to long-term mortgage repayments; ignorance of the educational system deters planning, though not fantasies. Savings clubs are widely reported. Of common occurrence, being reported from West Africa, Peru and the Philippines, is the type where a group of friends contribute, weekly or monthly, a like sum, each member in turn taking the entire collection. This avoids the danger of a dishonest absconding banker, if not that of the member who takes an early turn in receiving the collection and then drops out. Such savings are widely used for house improvement or for the purchase of productive equipment.

The very maintenance of personal relationships may necessitate expenditure which the middle classes may describe as wasteful or deleterious. Thus expenditure on household furnishings may raise family prestige and have an indirect pay-off. Lomnitz (1974) describes how, in a shanty town in Mexico City, small groups of poor men gather regularly to drink; in so doing, incomes are equalized and the bonds of mutual loyalty and affection so created serve to enhance the social security provided for these men by their peers. As she writes, it is not a question of whether these men can afford to drink but whether they can afford not to. Nevertheless, while such drinking is functional in maintaining a minimal level of security, it does prevent saving for other purposes. But for the very poor, security is the prime requirement.

In some spheres the behaviour of the poor seems clearly different from that of the middle classes – in family structure, for instance, where the matri-centred households of the Caribbean are contrasted with the normal middle-class pattern. Either, it is argued, these discrepant patterns are highly valued by the poor – in which case they are renouncing middle-class norms; or they are seen by the poor and middle classes alike as deviant. Hyman Rodman has found a way out of this dilemma in his concept of the lower-class value stretch.

> By the value stretch I mean that the lower-class person, without abandoning the general values of the society, develops an alternative set of values. Without abandoning the values of marriage and legitimate childbirth, he stretches these values so that non-legal union and legally illegitimate children are also desirable. The result is that the members of the lower class, in many areas, have a wider range of values than others within the society. They share the general values of the society with members of other classes, but in addition, they have stretched these values, or developed alternative values, which help them to adjust to their deprived circumstances. (1963, p. 209)

The poor may not always act like members of the middle classes. They may not condemn those practices which differ – they may even confer approval. But this need not constitute a conscious rejection of the dominant values of their society, or the creation of a counter, alternative ideology.

Viewing the shanty towns with fear and guilt, middle-class Western observers have been anxious to measure the degree of tension and frustration experienced by the poor in an effort to gauge their revolutionary potential. Typical survey questions such as 'What would you like to be?' produce answers which range from fantasy – though indicative of the esteem in which top occupations are held – to realistic assessments of one's probable achievements in coming years. Variants of the 'Are you satisfied with your life/achievements?' question seem vacuous in the extreme, since it is unclear whether the respondent is comparing his present position with that of his peers in the city, with those left behind in the village, or with an internalized standard. Again a stated improvement in recent years may be relative to one's peers, or absolute in terms of rising living standards. It seems too much to expect an answer of a few words to express something as complex as a subjectively experienced satisfaction in the totality of one's activities. How often does the expression of satisfaction merely imply making the best of a bad job, an inability to see an alternative route which would bring happiness?

However, the surveys, whatever their value, do indicate a high level of satisfaction and the researchers report their results confident that these are not belied by other evidence; that is, people do seem content. Yet the patent differences in living styles between the shanty-town poor and the middle-class whom they daily observe, and those between their actual position and their aspirations, must, it would seem to an outside observer, lead to frustration of some kind. Two factors seem important here – the concepts held of equality and of failure.

The liberal Westerner believes that man was born free – subsequent inequalities are attributed to the social system. Many Africans, however, would begin by stressing the natural inequality among men – they are born with individual differences in aptitude and personality. In some measure this is their 'fate', though this need not imply an absolute predestination. Such views are consistent with an open tribal society in which high political office or success as a wealth trader was open to all, and not restricted to a few with an ascribed birth right or inherited wealth. Thus the modern civil servant or businessman is applauded for his educational or entrepreneurial success. To the Yoruba, a man who has risen by his own efforts has 'suffered a lot' in youthful deprivations and deserves the rewards now enjoyed. Nationalist ideologies too sanction the replacement of expatriates in the bureaucratic hierarchies by local citizens.

Such views would not be necessarily shared by people from the lower strata of a caste-like society. Any belief in the inevitability of inequality is countered by an experience of oppression and dependency: the poor are not happy with their lot – they would like to be better off if only they could see how they achieve this. The middle-class stereotype of the Andean indian is of a sullen, taciturn, resentful individual. Though this may well describe the indians' behaviour towards the dominant groups in his society, it need not characterize his relationships with his peers.

To a middle-class white-collar employee, failure lies in the non-attainment of a position which one thought one should have been able to achieve or which one had considered to be one's due. The concept must coexist with a clearly defined goal. In this sense the self-employed entrepreneur does not fail. He may hope to be rich, but he usually lacks any clear image of how he will succeed. Opportunities are unspecifiable; the pitfalls along the way unpredictable. Inasmuch as he is not as well off as he would have hoped, he explains that the right combination of factors has yet to occur. Waiting, like Mr Micawber, for somthing to turn up does not necessarily imply apathy, rather, it demands intense activity so that one is ready to seize opportunities as they arise.

Western analysts have tended to present explanations of failure as a dichotomy between individual and structural factors: either the individual attributes his lack of success to personal failings, or he blames the society in which he lives. Obviously the latter mode of explanation, in implying opposition to dominant groups or an image of an alternative form of society, is threatening to the existing system. However, the responses most frequently recorded are of explanations in individual terms – people fail because they are lazy or have bad luck. To some extent they may be internalizing the epithets bestowed on them by the middle classes. Yet their comments do largely reflect the reality of their own lives. Accepting the structure of society as unproblematic, differential degrees of success can be attributed to personal factors. But to ask 'Why should I be poorer than him?' is a different question, and one on a different level of analysis from 'Why should we all be poor?' The individual explanation derives perhaps from one's ego-oriented cognitive map, the structural explanation from the externalized analytical map. The two are not dichotomous but complementary: to stress individual factors in explaining failure does not deny the existence of structural factors – it may merely obscure them.

Thus explanations of failure in individual terms may coexist with an image of a relationship of conflict between rich and poor. The poor see themselves as oppressed by 'the government', the 'oligarchy'. A feature of such images, as Quijano (1972) has stressed, is the diffuse nature of the opponent perceived by the poor. They cannot see exactly who is exploiting them. This seems understandable given the foreign control of much business, or the indirect nature of most of the taxation of the urban poor. (The peasant visiting the city may see the potatoes which he sold for 1p. a kilo sold retail for ten times that sum – and he justly feels exploited by middlemen or state buying agencies; but the wage earner knows little of the distribution of his firm's profits or the duty paid on his beer.) Furthermore, opposition is muted by the admiration of those in high positions who have risen by their own efforts, and by the existence of bonds of patronage with such people. Thus the African may denigrate his government while applauding a co-villager who has achieved high office in it. In describing the attitudes of people in a Colombian shanty town, Whiteford notes that while they condemn the oligarchy for idle and luxurious living, they speak in glowing terms of those with whom they have been involved – the landowners who subdivided their land, doctors and dentists, their employers. It is, writes Whiteford, as if they were saying, 'oligarchs are exploitive people, and we would be very much better off without them. Nevertheless, I have never met one whom I did not like and admire' (1974, pp. 170–71).

Such ambivalence, product of the growing discrepancy in the living styles between rich and poor, coupled with individual aspirations to middle-class status and beliefs in the possibility of such mobility, underlies the political activity of the shanty town, to which I now turn.

# 8 Political Consciousness and Participation

The outbreaks of urban violence in the black suburbs of Harlem and Watts in the 1960s encouraged in the middle class of the third world fears of even worse rioting in the shanty towns of their cities. The affluent of these cities were sitting on a powder keg. Their own poor were experiencing, as they saw the situation, much more extreme forms of deprivation. To them, violence seemed the most logical outcome. In the event there were very few outbreaks in the shanty towns; and in fact the urban guerrilla movements which did develop during the decade in some cities were recruited predominantly from among discontented intellectuals, clerical workers and the skilled manual workers – not from the very poor. Research carried out within the shanty towns showed, as we have already noted, an achievement-oriented population largely satisfied with its success in establishing itself in urban life, essentially law-abiding and, for much of the time, politically conservative.

Other Western viewpoints stressed the social disorganization believed to exist in the shanty towns. This 'culture-of-poverty' theme suggested that the population would be politically apathetic yet prone to outbreaks of unstructured violence – aggression being one of the correlates of poverty. Here again research workers in the field found a substantial degree of social cohesion in many of the shanty towns studied, and demonstrated a lively and constructive political activity which, in its local scale, perhaps gave an appearance from afar of quiescence but was certainly not symptomatic of apathy.

These same themes find a lively expression in radical literature which explores the revolutionary potential of the various underprivileged groups in society. Which groups – the peasants, of various levels of wealth, the urban 'labour aristocracy' of skilled and well-paid workers or the lumpenproletariat of very poor and irregularly employed – will form the spearhead of movements aiming at the overthrow of the existing ruling groups? Maoists, lauding the example of China, put their faith in the peasantry; orthodox Marxists in the skilled workers powerfully organized in trade unions; Frantz Fanon and his followers look to the lumpenproletariat. Each of these schools of thought seems to seek a pattern of revolution, applicable universally without regard to the variety of local conditions.

In the Western concepts of liberal democracy, political participation is seen as a positive value, a mark of political maturity. Participation enhances the likelihood of political stability. It is furthermore the duty of every citizen. Therefore levels of participation should be raised in the third-world countries. It is argued that urbanization facilitates and encourages participation, but this comparison between urban and rural life seems of dubious validity. The villager may have little awareness of national issues, but he is usually concerned with affairs within the local community; and participation in meetings, and in voting, is usually high – whether at the behest of the landlord or from community spirit. National issues may impinge more directly upon the daily life of the shanty-town dweller, but government and its policies may still seem very remote from daily needs. Economic development in the poorer nations tends to produce greater inequalities, though perhaps with a limited absolute improvement for many people. Though rising living standards may indirectly lead to greater political participation they may also threaten, rather than enhance, political stability. The urban poor of today's third-world cities enjoy much greater exposure to the mass media than did their peers in the industrializing nineteenth-century Western world – an exposure which both reduces their ignorance of the world about them and also channels the dominant ideologies into their homes.

The governments of the third-world nations do not entirely share this western view of the value of political participation. Feeling, as they so often do, relatively insecure, they appear loath to countenance too many demands, too varied an array of solutions to their countries' problems. Their attitudes towards the poor of the shanty towns has ranged from limited encouragement to blatant repression. Where political power is held firmly by a single party or by the military, programmes of self-help may be encouraged, as in Kenya or Peru. These contribute to local community development while allowing national finances to be directed exclusively towards major industrial projects or prestige schemes which bring more benefits to skilled and clerical workers than to the very poor. But a danger lurks in that the very success of the local projects encourages the poor to make greater and more unacceptable demands. Government must be seen to be firmly in control of the political process – not vainly trying to master a runaway vehicle; it stresses mobilization from below while continuing to constrain that mobilization very firmly from the top. In contrast, where rival political parties contend for power, each will tend to argue that social benefits flow not from local action but from the beneficence of the government; political support will receive its later rewards. An attitude of dependence upon government is thus encouraged. In studies of shanty towns both sets of attitudes have been reported – a belief in the efficacy of local self-help and the more apathetic dependence on government. In part the difference undoubtedly reflects the ability of the community to organize itself; but in a substantial measure too it represents variants in the dominant ideology of the nation.

A major difficulty in assessing the degree of political participation in any population lies in the definition of that term. One broad and readily acceptable formulation runs 'activity by private citizens designed to influence government decision making' (Huntington and Nelson, 1976, p. 4). This stresses activity rather than attitudes, private citizens rather than professional politicians, government decisions and not those of non-public authorities such as private companies and attempted influence rather than successful coercion. Forms of activity covered embrace, positively, lobbying and voting and, negatively, the numerous modes of protest from the peaceful demonstration to more violent measures. But such a definition is behaviouristic and excludes all cognitive aspects – the knowledge of government processes, attitudes concerning the legitimacy of governments, beliefs relating to the concern which government has for the poor. All of these contribute to a latent disposition to act and surely cannot be ignored. Inactivity can coexist with widespread hostility to government – a hostility that merely awaits mobilization.

Again, discrepant estimates of political participation often stem from too exclusive a concern with either state or local activity. At one extreme, it is argued that the shanty towns seem to have little impact on policy making at the national level; yet community political activity may be likely. In contrast, participation in national politics may exceed that in local matters.

It seems best therefore to examine political consciousness and activity from the two viewpoints – that of the local community and that of the state, a view from the bottom upwards contrasting with that downwards from the top. In doing this we shall be contrasting the activity generated by the poor themselves with the mobilization by the political leaders of the state. But in distinguishing between the two viewpoints we must not neglect the continual interaction between the two levels. National ideologies which variously stress self-help and dependence have already been cited. So too has the possibility that successful efforts at self-help lead to a heightened political consciousness and greater demands. Again, as Portes has pointed out, the poor may be completely inactive and yet still constitute an influence on a government whose leaders (and the affluent groups in general) see the poverty of the shanty towns as a continual threat or challenge to themselves, their policies designed to thwart the lurking dangers (Portes and Walton, 1976).

## POLITICS FROM BELOW

'In my study of four *poblaciones* in Santiago, 90 per cent of the household visited had radios and 30 per cent had television sets; installment payments on these and other appliances seemed to play a far more important role in the hierarchy of the families' preoccupations than the social structure of which they were a part' (Portes and Walton, 1976, p. 91). These shanty towns seem to have been rather more prosperous than most, yet the emphasis on immediate needs has been stressed by many writers. With irregular employment and income, whether as wage earners or in self-employment, and in the absence of most forms of insurance save the assistance of kin and neighbours, the problem not only of paying for luxuries but also of finding school fees and even of assuring meals for the coming days, are bound to be uppermost in most peoples' minds. In focusing upon such situations we are looking at what I have termed the individual's ego-oriented cognitive map. Perhaps he does not often externalize himself from his society, looking at it from the outside; but if he does, we shall not find out unless we ask specifically. For most of his overt activity *is* concerned with his immediate needs.

As we have seen in the previous chapter the individual shanty-town dweller tends to see his success in terms of individual achievement, his failures in his bad luck. Many of his needs he sees as unique to himself. It is by his own efforts that he must assuage them. Most of these needs are furthermore apolitical: he needs money to eat or to enjoy a modest style of life and this is to be gained by working harder, finding more customers or getting a better job. He is content to work within the perceived structure of his society.

Some needs are shared equally by neighbours – all seek better services, the provision of water, electricity, sewerage, local schools and clinics, tarred roads and drains, legal title to land. These common needs may be met by collective action – indeed collective support is often expressed by the donor agency as a prerequisite. Since these services are territorially located, the local community is the unit of activity. What can it achieve?

Individuals from the affluent middle classes often expect the poor to replicate the forms of activity to which they are accustomed – forms in which unemployed housewives and retired persons, anxious to find a meaningful occupation, having a variety of professional skills and a knowledge of bureaucratic machinery, lobby and organize to achieve their specific goals. But the poor of the shanty town lack most of these resources.

With workplaces often far from home, a man rises early and returns well into the evening. To increase earnings many have multiple occupations. Many wives are employed, they too being absent from the home for long hours. The weekends are occupied either in income producing or in domestic chores – shopping, cleaning the house. The population is young – there are few retired persons, especially when the prevailing desire is to return to the rural area. Very few people can afford the time to engage in collective activity. Money may be collected for specific improvements – a levy to pay for the installation of piped water or the construction of a new classroom – but the community is not able to pay for a permanent staff. Those who are active in community affairs usually pay from their own pockets whatever they spend on such tasks. Immediately after their invasion of land the leaders of a squatter settlement may have an income from the allocation of vacant plots demarcated by them. The established leader may receive gifts as a reward for his brokerage between patrons and clients. But many would-be-activists are deterred by the high costs and small return of local participation.

Levels of information tend to be low. The recent immigrant to the city does not know what bodies are responsible for different activities. Peattie describes at length how she and the leaders of La Laja (described above, pp. 16–17), a Venezuelan shanty town in which she lived, tried to investigate and to stall the building of a sewer pipe emptying into the lake where people regularly bathed and washed clothes. She lists three major barriers to communication for the people at the bottom to 'competent authorities' at the top. She was able to help in surmounting each barrier.

It should be clear from the foregoing that one of the first difficulties experienced by 'the people' in their wish to complain was their lack of knowledge of whom to complain to. In fact, the people of the barrio wasted a good deal of time complaining in general – into the air, as it were – or complaining to the wrong people: the sanitary engineer, the representative of the Ministry of Health, the state representative of the water and sewer agency, the governor of the state. Even when it became known – largely as a result of my somewhat more sophisticated investigative activities – that the appropriate agency was the Corporación de Guayana, the people in the barrio had no idea as to which part of the agency they should address themselves.

I made some attempts to explain to other residents of La Laja the organizational structure of the development agency, but I do not believe that I was able to convey to any one of them a clear image of the division of functions that exists between the planners and engineers, or between the central office in Caracas and the local offices on the site. The last was particularly difficult for La Laja to comprehend; that a person sitting behind a desk in a CVG office, which they could not see, had only the most limited powers of decision and often was not even adequately informed of plans for the area, made in Caracas, was something which they had no adequate basis for understanding.

Secondly Peattie herself had time and money to spend on the enterprise which most residents had not, with the result that most delegations consisted not of the community leaders but persons of secondary importance.

Finally, I was of unique usefulness to La Laja in being a person with some roots in the barrio who was, at the same time, clearly a member of the *gente buena*, a 'Doctora', a person of upper-class level. When the head of the development agency was expressing – to the head of the consulting American group – his well-founded objections to what I had done, one of the things he said was that he could not understand how an educated woman, a 'Doctora', could have behaved so. Partly this was a feeling that I should have come to him personally and shown personal trust; partly it was a conception of my role – which I did not share – as an agent of CVG in dealing with 'the people'. Part of this was, I believe, a feeling that I was somehow on the wrong side of a class line. A class system like that of Venezuela, formed in a pre-industrial economy, is reflected in the structure of politics and administration. To put it most simply, the administrators are superior not only in power and position but also in social class to those whom they administer, and their feeling about the social class difference is such to suggest notions of caste. (Peattie, 1968, pp. 86–7)

In this and similar cases the company concerned seemed only too anxious to quell a protest against its proposed plans. But even where the bureaucrats are ostensibly helpful and their task is to promote development, an impasse is reached because the petitioners of the shanty town do not understand the formal rules operated within the bureaucracy and its own desire to retain control of the process. The shanty-town leaders fail to produce the necessary files or forms and plans, and are denigrated by the officials as lacking in drive or enthusiasm.

The educated African elite comes, in many states, from the same rural areas that provide the migrants to the shanty towns. The latter often have in consequence, in their personal networks of kin and co-villagers, men of influence to whom they can turn for help. This situation is much less likely in Latin America, though here, as in Africa and elsewhere too, contacts with such patrons may be made through urban employment – one perhaps has a kinsman who works as a domestic in the household of a well-placed civil servant.

The success with which these meagre resources are deployed rests on two further factors – the cohesion of the community and the efficacy of its leadership. The former has already been discussed, in part, in the previous chapter. It is easier to get people to work together in the small community than in a larger one. Ethnic heterogeneity may result in a lack of trust between members, though this should be obviated by long co-residence and an intensification of relationships as families seek friends and godparents from among their neighbours. External threats – the fear of eradication of the shanty town – also brings members closer. Ross (1973) suggests that in the Mathare valley settlement of Nairobi, Kenya, police raids against illicit brewing (a major source of income for many residents) fulfil a similar function. A belief that the rest of the neighbouring society looks upon the shanty town with disparagement is another unifying factor – absent of course where no such inferiority is imagined. Perhaps the strongest deterrent to collective action lies in the wide range of socio-economic status in the settlement. Services sought collectively ought to benefit all households equally; provision of electricity does so – subsequently the richer pay more as they use more. But many improvements sought after the initial needs of water and power have been met, while welcomed by all residents, fall low in the priority of the poorer residents.

These same issues recur in the assessment of the efficacy of local leaders. Several factors are operative in the bestowal of leadership status upon one or more residents. They may hold positions of seniority according to traditional criteria – they are aged, of long residence in the city or the community, perhaps being a founder member of the latter. Like Don Francisco they may have been successful in attaining a higher socio-economic status, either through wage employment or entrepreneurship. They have contacts outside the community. They are charismatic figures able to galvanize the community into action. Ross describes Kiboro, the highly successful chairman of a Mathare valley settlement in Nairobi:

> His abilities as a leader and organizer are extraordinary, and he is responsible for almost all of the important decisions the village committees make. He chairs all meetings whenever he is present, talks more than anyone else, and continually oversees the work of others in the village. Of tremendous importance to his success as leader is the wide range of contacts he has with politicians, administrators and businessmen in Nairobi and Kiambu. When problems arise that he is not able to solve, he knows whom to go to for assistance, and how to approach him. His contacts have been tremendously important in gaining informal promises from the government that the community will not be bulldozed, in getting school fees remitted for many villagers [i.e. residents] and in obtaining government encouragement for many village development projects. (1973, pp. 171–2)

Kiboro became chairman of the community council in the early 1960s, soon after it had been formed to counter government moves to evict the settlers. He seems to have held office without competition from rival leaders until the end of the decade, when he was imprisoned. Ross feels that the organizational success of this community rested in part, though not exclusively, on the personality of its leader.

Leaders have such varied personal characteristics that classification of them present difficulty. However, one can distinguish between the local ward boss and the upwardly mobile benefactor such as Don Francisco.

> In the Mathare valley the village leaders are different from most other people. . . They are older, more likely to have lived in Nairobi for a long period of time, more likely to have lived in Mathare before the Emergency, and more likely to have spent some time in a detention camp during the Emergency. At the same time, they are less educated, less likely to be employed, and less likely to own land in the rural areas. They do have lower incomes than non-leaders in the community. (Ross, 1973, pp. 172–3)

Though Ross does not tell us explicitly, Kiboro probably shared these characteristics. While Kiboro's success derived from his control of the residents and his contacts outside the community, his continuing prestige in the community rested upon the retention of this brokerage role. He ensured that everything passed through him and that patrons and clients did not meet face to face or through the mediation of another. Yet while such men possess power they do not necessarily enjoy affluence nor are they aspiring to higher positions outside the community.

Accusations abound, in shanty towns, that the leaders are using their positions for self-aggrandizement. This is in keeping with a local ideology that all one's activities are oriented towards achievement, that friendships are not purely altruistic but will have potential pay-offs. The leader who is among the wealthier in his community is suspected of favouring those projects which will bring him personal benefit – services are sited close to his house, his street is tarred before others; or he is seen as exploiting his contacts with those outside the community more with a view to finding better employment for himself than to bringing the desired improvement to his community. Such fears threaten the leaders' control over the residents and, in the long run, his credibility with officialdom – he cannot rally the support required for successful co-operative effort. Without a following such a leader is usually ready to relinquish his role, alleging that his people have been ungrateful, while he continues his upward social mobility by other means; for community leadership was probably but one among many spheres of activity.

Both types of leader are essentially conservative – the benefactor is successfully manipulating the world which he knows, the ward boss is dependent upon a static array of forces. Neither openly challenges the legitimacy of the social system. Inasmuch as their prestige is evaluated by the benefits obtained for their communities their sphere of action is constrained. To become involved in national politics would probably be detrimental to their local role. (In African states local leaders elected to the national parliament were subsequently defeated at the poll when their constituencies appeared to have received few rewards for such support.)

Leaders frequently hold no formal office, and even if they do, they have few sanctions to employ against members of their community. On balance their success lies more in their manipulating patrons than in mobilizing or coercing the residents. Lobbying is their major activity – as it is for other members of the community with their individual requests. The right officials must be found and these inveigled into action with a mixture of blandishments and threats. The shanty-town dweller has few sanctions to wield. Faced with apparently intractable bureaucrats, they may seek publicity through the local press or radio in the hope that the recalcitrant ones will be identified and reprimanded. A threat of eradication is perhaps best met by a direct appeal to a political leader to intervene. He is rewarded with promises of votes if successful – or a transference of support if he fails. Peaceful demonstrations too may draw attention to the plight of the community.

Violence is generally eschewed, firstly out of fear that it will be met with extreme repression. A shanty town under threat of eradication – because it lacks title to its land, is an eyesore in an affluent suburb, is dangerously sited on hillside or swamp, or is merely insanitary – would be inviting its demise by too strong a protest. Secondly, violent action may destroy the patronage relationship carefully developed over previous years with officials and politicians. These men have been measuring their own power and prestige in terms of their following in the shanty towns and this is lost when they clearly have no control over their clients. Violence by a single community is most unlikely to bring the desired rewards. The level of political activity in any community is the outcome of a cost-benefit analysis of the alternative causes of action available. In most situations lobbying is cheapest and most effective.

The foregoing pages will have indicated some of the reasons for the apparent lack of uniformity in levels of political activity. While one shanty town obtains a wide range of services, its neighbour, with similar needs, gets few of them. To some extent success encourages further efforts, failure leads to apathy. But it is also argued that community activity is strongest in the initial years after foundation. If created by invasion the community has an initial core of leaders with proven success. The needs of the community are greatest at this period. As the services highest in the list of priorities are provided, so does unanimity as to the importance of others wane, and the unity of the community declines. With the passing of years the socio-economic levels represented broaden in their range. Education and affluence are often held to be factors correlated with increasing political participation; but in the context of the shanty town they are as likely to lead to a reduced interest in community welfare, a greater preoccupation with personal upward mobility. This does not mean that such people have a lower level of political consciousness – they probably do have a much better understanding of the political process and well-formulated attitudes towards it. But they are less likely to question the legitimacy of the social structure and they see few available channels for useful political activity open to them.

Diversity in levels of activity and a differential success rate tend to inhibit the collaboration between neighbouring shanty towns. When needs are expressed in highly specific terms it is less likely they will be shared by adjacent areas. One community seeks water – its neighbours already have it, but want electricity. Where all are equally in need a competitive spirit is likely to prevail. Government lacks both finance and technical ability to supply all needs in the short run. A few favoured areas will be successful owing either to the lobbying of their leaders or the whims of the political leaders in providing a showpiece of their policies. Where several large shanty towns demand a service its provision will probably demand an organization beyond the capability of the local community leaders. In Lima some of the older shanty towns have developed into municipalities with the full range of bureaucratic offices, almost as inaccessible to the mass of the people as the government agencies they replaced. Mass demonstrations which involve large numbers generally make few specific demands and result in no permanent organization. If a popular leader does emerge he is likely to be either repressed or co-opted into a government-inspired body for mobilizing the poor. It would be an unusual situation in which a government favoured the development of an autonomous movement among the population of the shanty towns.

Political demands can, of course, be articulated through organizations other than those based upon territorial units. The trade unions are an obvious example. But, as we have noted, union activity is strongest among skilled and clerical workers – and these categories of people are more likely to reside in the housing estates than in the shanty towns. The wage labourers in the latter areas, with their low incomes and irregular work, are either enrolled in the weaker unions or are peripheral members, taking little interest in union affairs and expecting little benefit from union bargaining. Associations of artisans, craftsmen and minor professionals tend to be poorly developed – there is little that they can bargain for except perhaps an increase in the number of licences; there are few means by which the leadership can control its following by sanctions.

The poor do indeed belong to ethnic associations but these are defined in terms of a rural community. In the city members are scattered. They may and frequently do put pressure on government to provide social services in the home area, but there is no basis on which they can make similar demands to benefit themselves in the city. These associations furthermore embrace a membership which often ranges from the very poor to the affluent. In such a group economic interests cannot be congruent. Yet though they are ineffective in obtaining collective benefits for their members they do form important channels whereby individuals may present their petitions. In our Nigerian survey (Lloyd, 1974) most poorly educated men said that they would represent their views through the mediation of a more influential person. (The better educated said that they would write to the newspapers.) The men so lobbied are likely to be from the petitioners' home area. They in turn contact the officials capable of initiating action. But here again the emphasis is on the representation of individual grievances, and their individual solution, even though the grievances may be commonly experienced. In most cases the petitioner sees himself, in fact, as competing with his fellows, using his superior contacts to achieve what they cannot do, rather than using his personal advantage for collective benefit.

It is conceivable that such ethnic associations may combine to form larger bodies, more efficacious in political articulation.

In Nigeria the Igbo State Union stood at the apex of a pyramid of province and village associations and served to emphasize the claims of the Igbo people to social and economic development to attain parity with the neighbouring Yoruba. The state union was of course led by educated men and very soon its leadership became fused with that of a political party – the National Council of Nigeria and the Cameroons.

In an article describing the political activity within a very poor shanty town in Bombay, Owen Lynch (1974) argues that the Dravida Munnetra Kazagham (DMK) is 'not an ethnic group with a para-political function, rather, it is a political group with para-ethnic functions'. The DMK appeals strongly to the Adi-Dravidas, an outcaste people from South India. Its ideology stresses concern for the poorer classes, has anti-Brahmin undertones and an emphasis on egalitarianism; it thus attracts the lower strata. It also teaches Tamil nationalism and thus helps to give a sense of identity to this urban migrant minority, an opportunity for them to enhance their claims in competition with other ethnic groups. The shanty-town poor are nevertheless cynical about the possibility that the party leadership will achieve much of practical benefit for them. Such political parties, at the local level, 'are symbolically caste neutral but structurally allow caste interests to be aggregated and expressed. By the same token they are class neutral but allow the class-based demands of an urban proletariat to be aggregated and expressed.'

Though popular opinion usually stresses the immutability of the caste hierarchy, the literature on India provides many examples of castes which have managed to rise in status. This has been achieved largely by Sanskritization – the adoption of the learning and ritual of higher caste groups and acceptance by them. But the individual member can benefit only through the elevation of his caste. The new opportunities thus created were not open to a mobile individual. In his monograph on the Jatavs, a leather-working outcaste community in Agra, India, Lynch (1969) shows how these people have exploited the new avenues of political activity in the independent state to enhance their status. In stressing the egalitarian ideologies espoused by the state, the Jatavs have managed to erode much of the caste discrimination from which they previously suffered.

## MOBILIZATION FROM ABOVE

In a discussion of communal politics we are poised between activity spontaneously generated by the poor and attempts to mobilize their support made by groups within the national elite. The communal parties are led by the educated and affluent whose personal interests seem often to transcend those of their following. Yet the sentiments which they articulate among the poor have not necessarily been latent ones. They have often found active expression in small ethnic unions. Political parties however tend to articulate demands which have not previously found overt expression.

The political leaders of the third-world nations are drawn mainly from the professions. They are educated and relatively wealthy men. Some have come from affluent homes, others (especially in Africa) have very humble origins. They compete among themselves for power and seek the support of the masses both as a means of attaining political office and of subsequently legitimizing their rule.

In the pre-independence periods rival leaders claimed to be

rightful heirs of the colonial power by virtue of their popular support. Recently, in Salisbury, Rhodesia, the nationalist political leaders, in returning to the capital or the larger provincial towns, have measured their popularity by the size of the welcoming crowds, the length of their triumphal motorcade. In Nigeria in the late 1940s the NCNC sought to establish a mass membership through the affiliation to the party of hundreds of small village and district ethnic associations. But beyond such indirect methods and the mass demonstration, little is done to mobilize support, for the necessary organizational base does not exist.

With the establishment of an elected legislature political leaders must seek support at the polls with promises of benefits to follow their success. A military government, however firmly entrenched through its control of physical forces and lack of internal dissension, nonetheless feels a need for overt popular support to establish its legitimacy, both in the sight of the outside world and of possible internal dissidents. Crudely put, it wants to be loved.

Parties and governments differ markedly, however, in the degree to which they seek to mobilize the poor. Handelman (1975) provides a useful classification which, although designed for Latin American data, seems universally applicable. With 'paternalism without mobilization', ties of patronage are formed between members of the ruling elite and subordinate individuals or small groups. Favours are rendered in return for support or acquiescence. The bond between landlord and peasant is imported into the urban scene. 'Government-directed co-optation' consists of granting certain benefits to the poor to assuage their demands without attempting to mobilize them. As an example Handelman cites the Peruvian military ruler Manuel Odria, who tacitly allowed the invasions of public land and creation of shanty towns as a means of reducing tension. The 'popular party' led by middle-class persons seeks to organize the masses. It has a class-oriented policy but tends to be pragmatic rather than have a coherent ideology. 'Basically populism does not mobilize the poor on an ongoing basis or raise their sense of political efficacy. Consequently, its migrant supporters are not truly politicized and may easily desert the movement.' The 'reformist political organization' seeks to establish an organized base and to provide an articulated programme for change. In most countries, however, such attempts have been relatively unsuccessful. In Latin America, Chile is the outstanding exception. In the final category, that of 'radical mobilization', the party seeks a radical change in the socio-economic system, usually in Marxist terms. Some small parties filled such a role in Chile in the early 1970s, though observers have noted that the shanty-town people were more interested in changes directly affecting their lives – houses or schools – and less in ideology or more distant changes. Much of the political mobilization here was carried out by university students. But, as elsewhere, such efforts to translate the limited demands of the poor into more general political issues serve only to alienate the poor through the destruction of such organzational activity as they had been able to generate spontaneously. Some writers have, in fact, argued that class-consciousness is neither a necessary prerequisite for the success of a radical party nor, in most cases, an essential ingredient in its success. It is the product of the subsequent attempts by the successful political leaders to change the structure of society and its dominant values.

The apparent lack of political consciousness and activity in the shanty towns is thus attributed to the failure of the political leaders to mobilize support through local organizations. In very few cases, Chile being a classic exception, has this been done. Various reasons are suggested.

The political leaders share, with others of similar socio-economic status, the guilt and fear with which the poor are regarded and are little less ignorant of the characteristics of shanty-town society. Their estimate of the needs of the poor rests more on their own predispositions than on the demands which the poor themselves might express. A party with but a rudimentary organization of its own may try to gain mass support through alliance with or control over a trade-union movement; but the shanty towns provide so few bases for such links. Even where a community council does formally exist it is questionable whether the leaders have much influence over their members. To be successful in mobilizing the shanty towns calls for massive efforts on the part of the party. Against such a need the party must set the possibility that, in making a direct appeal to the poor, it forfeits the long-established support of more affluent groups in the society. The investment required is furthermore risky. On many occasions massive support for a certain politician has been followed by an equally dramatic rejection. In Colombia in 1970 the ex-dictator Rojas Pinilla appealed directly to the poor, disillusioned by the Conservative–Liberal coalition which served to unite the oligarchy. His populist party was almost successful. Yet a few years later, with the dissolution of the coalition, Roja's party, now led by his daughter, won only a small fraction of the vote. Most studies suggest that the political support offered by the poor is essentially pragmatic; politicians who do not fulfil their promises are rejected. So too are those who seem unlikely to achieve power. A vote for a loser is a vote wasted. A patron without power or influence is of little use.

A different situation exists in those states, such as Tanzania, where a dominant party (perhaps the only party legally recognized) has a highly developed local organization. Here the village or ward council is often congruent with the local party branch and one asks how far this body exists to transmit upwards the demands of the poor, how far to receive instructions from above and to quell local discontent. In such situations a nationalist ideology attempts to obliterate social divisions of a class nature.

## LEGITIMACY AND OPPOSITION

Some studies have focused upon the levels of community organization within the shanty towns; others discuss the degree of political mobilization. Both are likely to stress the pragmatic demands made by the poor and the channels of patronage by which their goals might be achieved. The nature of the demands and the choice of channels imply an acceptance of the existing structure of society. This acceptance is buttressed by the expressions of satisfaction with urban life, of success in adapting to new environments and of hopes for further upward mobility. Yet in most of these studies one also finds statements reflecting the dissatisfaction or disillusion of the poor.

Thus Lynch (1974) reports that while his shanty-town dwellers were enthusiastic in their support for the DMK, only one man in his sample believed the promises of politicians seeking election. All of the remainder distrusted the politicians. Whiteford writes that the people of a Colombian shanty town 'feel life is a fight against a conscious conspiracy perpetrated against them by the "oligarchy" which wishes to maintain its power and can only do so by keeping the "common people" from ever really asserting themselves'; or, as one informant graphically expressed it, 'the rotating oligarchy which does nothing but eat, fornicate, and sleep while the people slave to suport them' (1974, p. 170). In our own Nigerian studies the better-educated stated that they felt that the government sought to benefit all classes, but the poorer tended to say that government 'helped its own people' to the exclusion of the masses.

Such expressions of hostility seem widespread, but they have been subjected to little detailed investigation. One reason perhaps is the diffuse nature of the statements. Conflict is seen between government or the oligarchy on one hand, the masses on the other. Little attempt is made to distinguish different interest groups within the dominant class. Again, though exploitation is clearly suggested, its mode is ill-defined. This is quite comprehensible; the peasant saw himself exploited by his landlord, the worker in the small factory by its owner. But the mode whereby the poor contribute to the salaries of the rich through direct and indirect taxes levied by the state is not easily understood, least of all by recent rural emigrants. They themselves pay little or nothing in direct tax. Nor can the poor possibly comprehend the decision-making process in the modern state. They have, in short, no easily visible points on which to focus their opposition.

This opposition is tempered by relationships existing between the poor and members of the dominant groups. In the African city the poor can often identify members of their own community in the higher civil service, often in fact close relatives. These latter they will readily approach for help. The rich, in turn, feel that their poor kin brings shame on their families and will in fact try to lift them from poverty. Whiteford balances his statements cited above with his informants' admissions that the oligarchs whom they had personally met were invariably very nice people. Again, among the dominant groups are not only those born into wealthy families but also men who have through study or entrepreneurial activity worked their way to the top. These men are lauded as exemplars of the ideals of upward social mobility. As the Yoruba of Nigeria would express it, 'they have suffered a lot and merit whatever high rewards they now enjoy'.

Further more, as Strickon (1967) has pointed out we operate not with a single model of society but several. In the Argentinian village which he studied, the people described the opposition between the oligarchy and the masses at a national level, thus using a conflict model, but relationships within the village were seen in terms of the interdependence of all categories of persons. The landlord occupied an ambiguous position as a member of the hated oligarchy on one hand and as a revered local patron on the other, but since he participated little in the life of the capital the villagers were rarely appraised of any incongruity.

With their limited vision of the world one cannot expect the poor of the shanty towns to have a clear image of an alternative structure of society. Little in their daily experience suggests new and more advantageous patterns of social relationships. They express their opposition to the existing society not in terms of its structural deficiency but of the corruption of individuals working within it. The African educated elite does not disburse its wealth, but in paying for expensive education for its children ensures its perpetration into succeeding generations; traditional society often had much more mobility. Changes of regime are advocated because of the maladministration of the incumbent rulers. Their successors ostentatiously clean the Augean stables – and usually enjoy (and perhaps stimulate) demonstrations of popular support for their actions. Yet while the poor are apparently satisfied, the dominant groups remain in power. A few scapegoats suffer, but the basic structure of the society remains largely unaffected.

Much of the Western literature on social stratification assumes that each individual operates with but a a single model of the structure of his society, though between individuals differences will exist. Some emphasize power, often money; some see classes in conflict, others as rungs on a ladder. I believe that each individual operates with several models. Some, as Strickon argues, are appropriate to specific situations – for instance national or local-level activities. The ego-oriented cognitive map, denoting goals and routes, tends to stress the petit bourgeois values of individual achievement. The externalized view of one's society, the view as from a mountain peak, may well emphasize the conflicts between rich and poor, ultimately imposing constraints upon one's goals and successes. Such maps are complementary; and it is our task to see how they co-exist. We should not, as is so often done, presume that when one scholar describes individual achievement, another class-consciousness, one must necessarily be misreporting reality. As in the Redfield–Lewis debate cited earlier, different questions produce different answers – a theme taken up in the next chapter.

The descriptions of the low levels, or local nature, of political activity in the shanty towns, interpreted as signifying the accepted legitimacy of the social structure, and political stability or quiescence, have tended to obscure a high degree of hostility and opposition in the political consciousness, ineffective because of its latency and diffuse focus. Expressed in terms of models, recent research has tended to emphasize those elements pertaining to the ego-oriented cognitive map. Radical scholars have, indeed, described the situations which they observe in Marxist terms, emphasizing the conflicts between different social categories, the contradictions inherent within the structure. What is lacking is the actor's own portrayal of this externalized structure. Between what groups and in what mode does *he* see conflict – if in fact this is the model used?

# 9 The Future

The past three decades have witnessed a universal process of development in the nations of the third world. A limited degree of industrialization has taken place, with capital-intensive manufacturing industry predominating. This has been located in the major cities, especially the national capitals. The attraction of these cities, together with concomitant developments in their rural hinterland – land reform or capitalization of agriculture, technological stagnation or rising population – have led to a massive flow of population towards them. But insufficient wage-earning jobs await them. The migrants remain poor. In the absence of state social security many create jobs by which they eke out a livelihood. Neither the state nor the private construction sector can adequately house the migrants, so they construct their own dwellings which reflect the squalor of their daily lives. These are the shanty towns which contrast so starkly with the modernity of the city centres and the affluence of the suburbs of the newly rich bureaucrats and entrepreneurs, and which invoke so much guilt and fear.

Yet in stressing the global uniformity of the process one tends to overlook the considerable diversity in the shanty towns. Their physical appearance is largely a function of the environment: the matting shelters neatly aligned across the desert slopes on the outskirts of Lima, contrast with the bamboo huts tightly packed along the swampy margins of a drainage canal in Calcutta. Culture too imposes its imprint though more strongly perhaps in styles of dress than of housing. While some shanty settlements occupy vacant lots near the centre of the cities, or even within the richer suburbs, others stretch for miles beyond the peripheries. Some are of recent creation, others have existed for several decades. Some house a higher proportion of the better-paid wage earners, others are inhabited by the very poor. The shanty town established through the invasion of private or state land – a typical Latin American pattern – contrasts with that in which the migrants themselves have purchased land from indigenous owners and built houses for their own occupancy and for renting – the West African pattern. The illegality of the former type of settlement has attracted attention, both as a demonstration of protest and in indicating a basic need of the settlers – a legal title which will give them security. Yet in the daily lives of these people, it is their poverty which dominates their activities, not legal issues.

These factors contribute to the diversity which has been reported by social anthropologists studying these shanty towns. For each scholar his own locality seems to possess a character very different from that of neighbouring settlements. In one the residents actively co-operate towards the acquisition of basic services, in another they are apathetic. One shanty town seems to exude hope, the other despair. The 'slums of hope' house those migrants who feel that they have successfully adapted to city life and still aspire to a better future for themselves and their children; to the 'slums of despair' gravitate those who cannot cope, who have lost the will to try. Inner-city slums, the decaying tenements in what were once good middle-class and upper-class residences, are typically slums of despair; yet these attract too the newly arrived migrant who seeks to be near the sources of employment. The peripheral shanty town, settled by those who have established themselves in the city and now seek to build their own homes, is a typical slum of hope; yet here too one may encounter the poor evicted through poverty from rented accommodation. Hope and despair refer not to localities or buildings but to people, and one of the characteristics of the shanty town is the diversity of its population, both ethnically and socio-economically.

These distinctions between 'hope' and 'despair' were rarely noted by outside observers in the 1960s. Typical, and indeed influential, was the description given by Lerner:

> The point that must be stressed in referring to this suffering mass of humanity displaced from the rural areas to the filthy peripheries

of the great cities is that few of them experience the 'transition' from agricultural to urban-industrial labour called for by the mechanism of development and the model of modernization. They are neither housed, nor trained, nor employed, nor serviced. They languish on the urban periphery without entering into any productive relationship with its industrial operators. These are the 'displaced persons', the DPs of the developmental process as it now typically occurs in most of the world, a human flotsam and jetsam that has been displaced from traditional agricultural life without being incorporated into modern industrial life. (1967, pp. 24–5)

Scholarly statements such as this fuelled the prophecies of imminent violence and communism. While recent research has tended to portray a very different image of the shanty town, its findings are too often restricted to costly monographs and academic journals. The popular image of the shanty town too often continues.

In this book I have been focusing upon the shanty town rather than the inner-city tenement slum or the housing estates developed by private or municipal authorities. I have deliberately stressed, and perhaps over-stressed, the attitudes of hope and achievement in an effort to counter-balance the existing popular conceptions. I have tended to emphasize positive rather than negative features. But, of course, between hope and despair there exists a continuum.

That 'hope' today exists in these shanty towns, is, I believe sufficiently demonstrated. The vital question is 'will it be realized?' What is the future of the shanty town? If the people fail to attain the goals to which they now aspire, will they become disillusioned and frustrated, sinking into despair?

The shanty towns are, for the most part, the creations of the past three decades. Such settlements did indeed exist prior to this time but they embraced a much smaller proportion of the population of the cities. Today often a quarter, or even a half, of a capital's population is in its shanty towns. This rate of growth has been accelerating. Even France had its *bidonvilles*, but the modern industrial state has the resources to cope with and overcome such a problem. The poor third-world nations are unable to do so.

We can sketch, hypothetically, the possible developments. Looking at the configuration of the city we may see the continuing growth of shanty towns, replicating the pattern of the past decades. Alternatively governments may take action to reduce the size of the shanty-town areas. Mere eradication of settlements (often to free land for high-class development) is no solution, for the displaced people merely build another shanty settlement in a less conspicuous area. Programmes to rehouse the population in low-cost dwellings have, in the past, had little effect – and seem unlikely to be successful in the future. Hong Kong is one country which has rehoused its immigrants in high-rise flats, but it is in a unique situation in being a relatively wealthy state and in lacking a rural area crying for development. In the majority of states governments pursue active policies for industrialization and profess the importance of rural development as a means of stemming the flow of migrants (though some forms of development would be more likely to increase it). Urban development has received a low priority – as if it were a problem which would hopefully go away. Government housing estates, though ostensibly for the poor, too often fall within the means only of the skilled worker or lesser bureaucrat. Architects are loath to reduce their standards. Finance corporations prefer to lend to the established wage earner for short periods rather than give long-term morgages at high risk, seeking a quick turnover for their money. Political leaders feel that they must reward the middle strata for their support. Self-help schemes seem to them to offer a welcome solution. State investment is minimal and involves little transference of wealth to the poor, who themselves provide their savings and labour. Tensions resulting from poor housing are removed and the poor are encouraged to become integrated into the dominant sectors of the society. Yet such schemes do nothing to resolve the problems of poverty – in fact, in encouraging investment in housing, savings are directed away from more productive uses. Again, such schemes perpetuate the pattern of low-density housing – one-storey houses predominate, rather than high-rise flats – with its high costs of services and transport. The city extends further outwards. Yet however much one feels that higher priority should be given to urban housing, particularly at the expense of certain lavish monuments to government prestige, the very scale of the problem is one which few governments can meet.

With, or more often without, government assistance the population of many a shanty town has over the years frequently improved its housing. Ramshackle huts are transformed into modest bungalows, streets are straightened, levelled and paved. In their style of life the residents differ little from those of a low-cost housing estate, but the regular uniformity of the latter contrasts markedly with the kaleidoscopic pattern of the former as houses reflect not only the differing wealth of their owners but also a range of personal idiosyncrasies. This image of self-improvement is one which governments and aid-giving agencies try to popularize, both to stimulate further activity and to excuse their own failure to invest in housing. Yet while some shanty towns do develop thus, others do not. A continual renovation of flimsy structures leads to little or no real improvement. Stagnation or decay is their prevailing characteristic.

Thus the shanty town as a physical entity may improve or deteriorate; new areas may be settled, old ones may be redeveloped as housing estates. But such changes may well obscure the movements of individual persons into and out of the shanty towns, up and down the social ladder. Were the migrants largely reliant upon rented accommodation, we should expect them to move to better or poorer areas as they prosper or fail. Similarly we should expect such movement if there were an open market in housing. But, as we have seen, the shanty-town house, constructed by its owner, is often difficult to sell. He is trapped within the settlement and must accept its future.

To predict which of these courses of development is the most likely is no easy task. The number of variables which we must take into account is large and their future values uncertain. In the previous chapter I have sketched the processes occurring within the shanty town, and these we might try to project into the future. The patterns of migration will alter and these will be reflected in the changing composition of each settlement. Some entrepreneurs will flourish – but will they develop into petty capitalists or will they quickly find the ceiling of their expansion? Will new entrants to the city economy find the same opportunities available to them as their predecessors? How far with the strengthening of ties between neighbours after long co-residence in the community be conditioned or vitiated by their differences in wealth? Will the political experience of the shanty-town dweller cumulate in increased tension and opposition or in greater aspirations and participation in a structure perceived as legitimate?

These trends within the shanty town do not moreover operate in a vacuum. They interact continually with developments at the national level – the state of the economy and of the political system. Events quite unconnected with the small community contribute to national prosperity or poverty, to an increase or decrease in the number of jobs available. Struggles for power between rival groups of political actors are manifest at the local level in increased repression of dissident voices or in more strenuous attempts to materialize the support of the poor.

The predictions that we make depend however on the models which we ourselves employ. The questions of sociologists fall within two broad categories – how do societies persist, and how do they change? Those focusing upon the former will perhaps seek to understand the degree to which the shanty-town population is integrated into the wider urban society. The shanty town and its people are seen as marginal. The presumption is that in a healthy society they will eventually become integrated – sharing the values of the dominant groups, becoming incorporated in the political process, making full use of urban societies. The fear exists that they will not become integrated – either at all, or at least quickly enough. And they will thus be as a festering sore a danger to the healthy body. Surveys conducted in this vein tend to show that the shanty-town dwellers certainly do accept the dominant values of their society and aspire to the style of life held by the strata above themselves.

An explanation of change lies in the concepts of conflict of interest between individuals and groups and of contradictions between structures. Western radical observers have thus sought to apply their models of social class to the situation in the third-world cities. Categories of persons are labelled as working or middle class, proletariat and lumpenproletariat, bourgeoisie and petite bourgeoisie. But as we have already seen it is with difficulty that such terms are exported to new situations. The strictly defined proletariat is but a small proportion of the working population – and its members often retain strong ties to the rural area, have little commitment to wage-earning employment (and may even have multiple employment). The very poor in the shanty town are not a lumpenproletariat if by this is designated people who reject the norms of their society. The petite bourgeoisie of self-employed artisans, small entrepreneurs, clerks and minor professionals is too wide a category to be of analytical use. A much more rigorous study is needed of the types of social relationship entered into in the various occupations cited – an evaluation, in other words, of the various modes of production. One needs, too, to ascertain how far the behaviour of men accords with the categorization advanced. Too often it seems to be inferred by scholars that a group defined as a proletariat will behave according to our own presuppositions, whatever they may be. In emphasizing the relationships deriving from the work situation, man's role as a member of a residential community is neglected. Finally, such labelling exercises give a static picture of man in his society. He is located solely according to his present economic status with reference neither to his previous position nor to any status to which he is aspiring.

These sterile exercises in labelling lead furthermore to a highly deterministic view of man. His behaviour is to be deduced from his economic status. He is subject to forces within society quite beyond his control, and perhaps his comprehension. As Lerner writes, he is flotsam and jetsam. The viewpoint adopted in this book, however, is that man's actions are to be understood with reference to his view of the world. Man is a strategist, continually making choices between alternative courses of action. He seeks to understand the world in order to control it, and in so doing he both enhances his understanding and changes the world. His understanding derives from the concepts and propositions which he has learned, his past and present experiences.

As observers we may bring to the situation a different set of concepts. Our experiences are unlike those of our actors. We have access to other sources of information. But the actor's view of his world should be an essential ingredient in our own picture. Our understanding and prediction of his actions will be much more sophisticated with this ingredient than without it. But the attempt to elucidate and then to describe the actor's view of a situation is, as we have seen in Chapter 3, a difficult task. Diachronically we can chronicle those experiences of the actor which are likely to influence his current attitudes and perceptions. The pattern of Chapters 4 to 8 reflects this process. As a heuristic device it has been postulated that man uses different maps for different situations – I have outlined an ego-oriented and an externalized map. Ideally these should be congruent. But each emphasizes different features of a world view, the ego-oriented map being more concerned with the achievement of immediate goals, the externalized map with the perception of constraints upon one's actions which are inherent in the structure of society.

The questions that one asks, as an observer, help us to fill in small parts of these different maps. A battery of related questions may supply considerable detail in some areas while leaving others blank. Field studies within shanty-town communities, where the researcher has been engaged in witnessing daily activities, have tended to yield reports stressing the aspirations of the people, their dependence on relationships of patronage. Far less attention has been paid to their expressions of hostility towards the existing structure of society, though this has been postulated by the armchair theorists. For some these attitudes of achievement-orientation and hostility are incompatible. Unless we are to believe that our actors are incredibly muddled, the discrepancy must indicate bias or misrepresentation on the part of the observer. Yet it would seem that these attributes *are* quite compatible, reflecting the emphasis upon ego-oriented and externalized maps respectively – the world as it is seen to be and within which one must operate and a world regarded as lacking legitimacy, a world to be changed.

In attempting to predict future developments in the shanty towns, it would seem profitable to focus upon three areas of change – the patterns of migration, the potential of the informal sector and the growth of political consciousness. But, as was noted above, while we try to assess what will happen within the shanty town, we cannot isolate the situation here from the events of the wider world.

It seems prudent to assume that, for the foreseeable future, the prevailing patterns of economic development will continue: the third-world nations will remain dependent on the industrial nations, notwithstanding continual bargaining to improve their individual terms of dependency. Economic growth will be achieved largely through capital-intensive industry and financed heavily by foreign capital. Though the poor nations certainly aspire (or so claim) to free themselves from this dependency, the chances of any major change seem slight, given the interests both within and without the poor nation which support the existing situation.

On the other hand, one cannot assume a stable political system. The above form of economic growth will certainly perpetuate and possibly increase the degrees of social inequality experienced. Tensions will rise which governments may try to alleviate through fairly radical structural reforms; but these may be difficult to carry to completion given the status of dependency. A left-wing government is then either violently overthrown as in Chile, or more gradually transformed as in Peru. Again, the military assumes power to 'restore stability', but as its popularity wanes it seeks to restore a civilian government. There is thus a continual flux between progressive and conservative policies, policies which alternately threaten or reinforce the ties of dependency. In most states it seems likely that little major change will occur. Yet there is always the chance that a peculiar set of circumstances will provide the opportunity for a successful revolution. What these circumstances are forms, of course, the basis of radical debate as dogma vies for supremacy with empirical analysis.

A most inconclusive debate rages about the desirability of cityward migration. On the one hand the cities are seen as the loci of rapid development; their populations become modernized; the growth of the cities is thus to be encouraged. The alternative view focuses upon the social problems of rapid growth and poverty; the costs of these far outweigh the economies of scale – and these too are said to vanish once a city exceeds a certain size. Politicians are less hesitant. They fear the growth of urban poverty and political radicalism or violence and tend therefore to seek measures to reduce the migratory flow. Their active efforts are directed towards the development of the rural areas and a relative apathy is shown to urban problems.

However, it seems highly doubtful that many of the proposed measures of rural development will stem emigration. It is assumed that men will not come to the city if the lowest incomes obtainable there fall below those of the poorer farmers; yet, as we have seen, the migrants seek not only immediate income but the promise of future opportunities and social mobility – and this the city will continue to offer. Many policies of rural development are aimed at the production of cheap food for the cities. Highly capitalized agriculture and the state buying of crops at fixed prices are advocated. But the former will drive men from the land (assuming that it is existing farmland, not frontier areas which are so developed) and the latter will impoverish the farmers and increase their sense of exploitation. Again, while rural development may raise the standards of living, it also leads to more and better schools and the continued emigration of the better-trained and the more achievement-oriented who still find that the rural area provides too few opportunities for their talents. Thus immediate attempts to control or reduce the migratory flow seem liable to failure.

Nevertheless a peak may soon be reached (if it has not already been reached in some communities). Either most young men leave the village for a few years, to return later; or so many leave permanently that there is little underemployment among the remaining population. But the number of people who have to remain on the land in order to feed the urban population will depend on the prevailing levels of agricultural technology.

Patterns of migration, too, will change. Most would-be migrants now have relatives or friends in the capitals and will expect these to receive them and help them to find work and accommodation. The relationships which develop from chain migration will be perpetuated. Yet it is equally likely that, with better information about job opportunities throughout the country, the less well-educated migrant will avoid the capital, seeking employment in a less competitive locality. The educated migrant however will see in the expanding city the best opportunities for his talents.

The characteristics of the shanty towns will thus slowly change. The immigrants will be better educated than those of previous decades. More of them will have a wider network of local kin. But as the earlier migrants marry and bear children, so will the proportion of second-generation migrants increase, at the expense of recent arrivals. Whether the second generation, schooled in the shanty towns or in neighbouring suburbs, will be better educated than the new immigrants will depend on the distribution of educational resources. In some countries rural education has rapidly developed in recent years, in others it has not.

Many writers have asserted that this change in the composition of the shanty town will be highly significant. It has been emphasized that the recent immigrant still maintains his rural ties, and these give him economic and emotional security. He assesses his urban achievements in relation to his status in the village, and congratulates himself on having established himself in the city. The city-born youth do not share these attributes. The shanty-town adolescents will compare their opportunities with those of their peers from the affluent suburbs. An increase in tension and violence is predicted. Again we, as observers, tend to see an analogy in the cities of the industrial nations. As yet few studies of second-generation migrants have been made. Cornelius in a study in Mexico City found that they had greater political knowledge and consciousness but that they participated less. They were not more dissatisfied nor did they negatively evaluate the existing society. They lacked the political experience of their parents in invading land, organizing ethnic and other associations. They tended to be less involved in co-operative activity and were more inclined to see mobility in terms of individual action (1975, pp. 65–7).

Loss of contact with the rural area does not necessarily mean, of course, a decline in ethnicity. Many situations will continue to exist in which a man feels that his personal advancement lies through the manipulation of compatriots; or in which the expression of a collective identity is seen as desirable to protect the status of all members against encroachment by others, perhaps by new waves of migrants from other areas. An emphasis on ethnicity is bound to detract from the consciousness of class and from class-based associational activity.

Our next area of prediction concerns the economic opportunities which the future migrant (and the second-generation migrant, too) will find in the city. Given the continuation of present patterns of national development, it seems certain that the large commercial enterprises, the state and para-state bureaucracies, will not be able to create jobs for more than a minority of migrants or of primary-school leavers. Most will have to be absorbed into the informal sector. This term, as we have seen, is a handy designation for an area of economic activity in which half of the cities' populations are now, in many states, engaged. Descriptively it implies small-scale labour-intensive activity, poverty and patronage; it lacks precision as an analytic tool, for it embraces several types of social relationship. The activities so embraced are not homogeneous, nor are they independent of the opposed formal sector – they are usually dependent upon it. The informal sector exists as a creation of capitalist production, carrying out tasks which the latter cannot or will not itself assume.

National plans for economic development have hitherto tended to ignore the informal sector, assuming that it produced nothing and therefore could not be a candidate for expansion. Indeed, its activities were frequently constrained by harassment – the control of licences for trading, the arguments that use of apprentices contravened labour codes. Recently, however, scholars have recognized the productive capacity of the informal sector, and, more tacitly, its role in easing tensions and maintaining political stability. Some schools of thought now actively advocate the development of the informal sector as a panacea for the perceived ills of the poorer nations. Policies stress several courses of action. Fewer restraints should be placed on activities, and, more positively, men should be assisted with credit. Large firms should sub-contract many of their processes to the small workshops and independent artisans (thus implying that the latter produces the goods more cheaply than the former – and perhaps that this in turn derives from low wages and incomes in the informal sector). Again, a progressive redistribution of income is suggested. The blow to the dominant groups is society is softened as, in a period of rising real incomes, their own incomes merely rise more slowly than those of the poor. (Whether the privileged groups in any third-world society are likely to be sufficiently altruistic or to feel sufficiently threatened to accept such a narrowing of income differentials is not assessed.) Such a measure would, by increasing the purchasing power of the poor, increase the market for cheap goods and services produced within the informal sector. The sector would also grow of course with the continuing development of manufacturing industry and growth of upper and middle strata.

Such measures in no way change the relationship between the informal and formal sectors. But it is hoped that, in raising absolute living standards for many and providing increased opportunities for upward mobility for a few, the 'contradictions of capitalism', which as radical writers suggest will bring societies to the brink of an inevitable collapse, will be avoided. The existence of the informal sector is predicated however on the working of long hours for low financial returns – and for many very low returns. Ameliorating some of its characteristics will do little to change the prevailing patterns of inequality. It is problematic, too, whether the increase of opportunities destined for a few would create a substantial group of small but relatively prosperous businessmen. The difficulties of capital accumulation, the lack of skills, the intense competition between producers, all combine to inhibit growth; the successful are as likely to invest savings not in further production but in their children's education. Again, it is agreed that if a large market is developed for any commodity produced by artisans, this will be seized by the formal sector and the artisans probably driven out of business rather than incorporated into the new enterprise. The political repercussions of the growth of a category of small entrepreneurs can be seen as threatening. They would challenge the dominance of the large companies or that of state enterprises in the national economy, and in so doing would weaken the solidarity of the national elite against its masses. It seems unlikely that any planned developments will substantially alter the pattern of opportunities available to those already within the informal sector.

For those about to enter the informal sector, the newly arrived migrants, the picture is similarly unpromising. Ease of entry has been stressed. An individual can succeed with very little resources of skill or capital. As the city grows so do more positions become available; more domestic servants are needed, more craftsmen. But in many spheres the best positions have already been allocated – the market stalls at the prime sites are taken, and will be reallocated by their holders to kin or to the highest bidder. Groups of migrants from a given area have combined to establish a quasi-monopoly over a certain activity; through their mutual co-operation they can successfully compete against a newcomer. The new migrant may of course be admitted into one of these groups, but, in general, he faces a much less open situation than did the migrants of two or three decades earlier. However, the very instability of enterprises in the informal sector creates niches for the newcomer. These may be few in number and restricted in scope, but they will contribute to the popular belief that with drive and initiative one can succeed in the city. Denied access to scarce jobs in the formal sector, unprotected by state social security, the migrant in the shanty town is obliged to find work of some kind. Often he is underemployed (in his own estimation as well as ours) yet he can dream about and plan the manner in which he might expand his activities and set out upon a road to prosperity. Such success may be a fantasy – but it is one which promotes attitudes very different from the frustrations of total unemployment.

The continuing significance of the informal sector in the third-world cities will have a marked effect on developments of political consciousness and behaviour. Large numbers of men and women will be involved in modes of production in which personal betterment is seen in terms of individual achievement and in which relationships of patronage are seen as the means of such achievement. Collective action to pursue common ends is but weakly developed, for the perceived foci of opposition are either government agencies, responsible for licences, or other forms of control or a myriad of employers – master craftsmen having their apprentices and journeymen, affluent families their domestic servants. In contrast to this category there are, indeed, equally large groups of poor wage earners – those in unskilled and often irregular employment. But these too tend to be weakly organized in their trade unions – partly because of the instability of their occupations, partly because, as individuals, they seek to enter the informal sector where, even with small savings, a route to prosperity appears to be open before them. These men in turn are differentiated from the skilled workers, usually well organized, whose trade unions are adept at bargaining to maintain or improve living styles. The support of these unions is eagerly wooed by the competing radical political parties, contributing to a politicization of the workers themselves.

The dichotomy between these two categories of wage employees in the formal sector is seen in two ways. One view postulates a clash of interest between the well-paid and poorer employees. The trade unions of the former are interested only in the welfare of their own members, not that of the entire mass of the poor. They seek to maintain the differential between their wages and the incomes of the unskilled. The latter cannot therefore see the former as their allies. Much depends here on the actual differential involved. Some industries, for instance oil, do pay very high wages, but the majority pay little more than the national minimum wage – though this itself is higher than the remuneration of many employees in small workshops in the informal sector, of domestic servants and of many self-employed petty traders. In contrast it is argued that the informal sector embraces those who provide goods and services for the poor and who can raise their own prices only when their customers have had wage increases, and also those whose bargaining for higher wages from a small employer is largely dependent upon nationally won increases for the unionized workers. They thus tend to support the wage demands of the skilled workers as an indirect means to their own higher incomes. Any political view of the poor must take account both of the diversity of the specific interests of different categories and of the conditions under which these categories might become political allies.

It is commonly assumed that political consciousness develops as a cumulative process. The recently arrived migrant from the rural area is passive because he is a stranger to the city, dazzled by the bright lights and anxious only to share in the glamour. With residence and experience he will grow more critical. Thus those who have lived for longer periods in the city and the second-generation migrants will be the more politically radical. Such a view overlooks the fact that many migrants now come from areas experiencing widespread and often violent peasant movements. Again the experiences of the city do not necessarily lead to radicalism. Successful establishment in the informal sector encourages attitudes of individual achievement. The failure of community associations to achieve the goals sought, either because of repression from without or dissension within, can produce feelings of disillusion with such collective action, again prompting the search for an individual solution to problems.

Underlying such empirical questions is, however, a deeper theoretical issue – how do we define and measure political consciousness? Two elements are involved. First the knowledge of the political process – how does government work? Clearly those with longer residence in the city are probably more knowledgeable. Leaders usually owe their status to their understanding of the bureaucracies, to their acquaintance with individual officials and a correct appraisal of their powers and duties. Secondly, consciousness implies an awareness of a structure. Categories of persons and activities are conceptually distinguished and related to each other. Events witnessed are seen to form a coherent pattern, not a series of random happenings. As thus defined, individuals sharing a similar level of political consciousness may hold very different views of their world. Political consciousness does not necessarily imply a radical view, though many writers do appear to measure levels of consciousness according to the actor's convergence with their own 'correct' view of reality.

Class-consciousness is one form of political consciousness. Marx distinguished the class-in-itself – the external observer perceives an identity of class interests which are not perceived by the members themselves – from the class-for-itself – the group conscious of its interests. Recent writers (for example H. F. Moorhouse, 1976) have sought to elaborate on the latter categorization. Class-consciousness can denote an awareness of a class identity; the recognition of common interests and their active pursuit; a belief that these class interests totally define one's position in society; a view of an alternative form of society which can be achieved through class action. These four elements represent an increasing scale of radicalism or revolutionary potential; but they are qualitatively different from one another, so that an increase in one does not necessarily lead to the next. Class-consciousness, as so defined, is an attribute of the underprivileged majority in a society. Attempts are made to raise the levels of their consciousness, so that by their collective action they may overthrow the dominant groups. The class-consciousness of the dominant groups takes a different form. They are probably more aware of the basis of their privileged position and are usually better organized for its protection. However, their activities must be cloaked by an ideology which stresses consensus and legitimacy.

Political-attitude surveys tend to explore not the level of political consciousness but the degree of political tension; not the type of model used by the actor to structure his society but his feelings towards his government or bosses. Tension can exist with a very low degree of political consciousness – a high degree of consciousness does not imply tension. The models used by the individual change over time but slowly, though he may use more than one model, varying his use according to situation, and one set of questions may evoke a description of one model while another set generates a different response. Tension however seems a much more variable quality. At one moment men may express an acceptance of their government, only to reverse their opinions a little later following a political crisis. Tension, without (working) class consciousness, will not generate any form of organized activity capable of bringing about a change in the structure of society. Tension alone, however, may be manipulated by outside groups to their own ends – a political party for instance may welcome unstructured violence in the shanty towns to demonstrate the lack of control exercised by the government and so enhance its claims for its downfall.

In assessing the possible changes in the political climate of the shanty towns we must, therefore, distinguish factors producing increases in tension from those which develop political consciousness.

Increased tension will result from any absolute decline in living standards, a consequence perhaps of adverse fluctuations in the principal export commodities upon which national wealth depends. But the determination to hold on to one's job in a period of rising unemployment is inimical to protest movements. Tension too will rise if the poor observe that the small improvements in their own living styles are exceeded by the benefits accruing to the higher strata. An increase in frustration is often predicted as migrants fail to achieve the goals to which they initially aspired. Many have stated that one of the principal attractions of the city was the availability of education for their children and the consequent opportunity for them to rise into the privileged sectors of the society. But the chances of success for the shanty-town children are slim. Their primary schools are generally poor; parents may not be able to afford secondary or higher education; or, if first primary education is free, the shanty-town youth are handicapped firstly in doing well and secondly in achieving the treasured qualifications, in competing for jobs with those from higher strata who have influential contacts. Mobility through education is likely to be slight. So too are the chances of upward mobility in the entrepreneurial sector. Yet both these channels are seen to be open and the individual shanty-town resident will be more cognizant of the career of the local boy who has made good than of national statistics indicating the improbability of such success. As we have seen in Chapter 7, the individual is more likely to explain his own lack of success in terms of personal feelings or bad luck than in terms of the structure of his society. And in so doing tension is reduced and the development of political consciousness is inhibited.

Perhaps we should look not to individual experiences but to collective activity as the principal factor for political consciousness. But here we have already noted the weaknes of trade-union activity among shanty-town members, and the neglect of such communities in almost every country by the radical political parties. Ethnic and community associations, given their present forms of organization and activity, will not encourage the growth of class-consciousness.

The poor are aware of the inequalities existing in their society. Their shanty towns are often built within the shadows of luxury apartment blocks. They feel too that the dominant groups control society to their own advantage, albeit casting some crumbs to the poor. But they find it difficult to articulate such a relationship of conflict. They have a diffuse view of the dominant groups and cannot identify the loci of decision-making or appreciate domains of competition with them. It is difficult for them to formulate an alternative structure of society. Attitudes of opposition to the rich and powerful are muted by the fact that the poor are related to them individually by ties of kinship or patronage. These ties, together with the perception of opportunities provided by education and within the informal sector, encourage the view of an open society; one does not attack privileges in which one hopes to share. Admiration is accorded to those who have reached positions of dominance through their own efforts.

Thus, while the mode of national economic development predicted for the coming decades will do little to change existing patterns of inequality and may bring little real improvement in living standards to the mass of the poor, the social forms generated by this development seem unlikely to generate of their own accord any social movements which will significantly alter this pattern of development.

The poverty of the shanty towns has been presented as a problem. It is a situation which one wishes to alleviate. But the argument presented here is that a solution lies not within the shanty town itself but in the larger society – that of the state and furthermore in its relationship with the industrialized nations. The variety of palliatives advocated by governments and aid-giving agencies may bring some immediate relief or may be quite ineffective; but they will do little to change the structure of society. Thus the presentation of solutions to the shanty-town problem lies far beyond the scope of this book. But any solution offered, whether it re-structures society or merely papers over the cracks, will affect those who live in the shanty town and will imply their acquiescence and perhaps active participation. The viability of our solution will depend upon the reliability of our own assessment of ongoing processes within the shanty town, both as we see them and as they are perceived by the residents themselves. It is to assist in this understanding and to eradicate some popular misconceptions that this book is written.

# Further Reading

The literature on shanty towns is vast; but the greater part of it deals with housing problems and is written by planners and for planners. Relatively little sets the problem in its wider social and economic context; even less gives us a picture of what life is like in a shanty town as seen from the inside. The books cited below will I hope help the reader to follow up the themes of this book; they are books on which I have relied, often heavily, though I have directly quoted from but a few. The works mentioned below are cited in full in the bibliography which follows this note.

Many readers will find useful a general introduction to the continents under discussion. Myrdal's (1968) *Asian Drama* is a classic, for a geographical perspective on Latin America I would suggest Gilbert (1974), an overview of West Africa is given by Lloyd (1967) and more recently of the entire continent south of the Sahara by Peil (1977). General introductions to social and economic problems of the third world are contained in two readers – those edited by Bernstein (1973) and Jolly *et al.* (1973), the latter focusing on employment problems; specific to Africa is that of Gutkind and Wallerstein (1976); Oxaal's (1975) symposium contains a useful critique of dependency theory by O'Brien. Two readers – those of Shanin (1971) and Potter *et al.* (1967) give a good picture of peasant society while that of Mangin (1970) has some vivid descriptions of the adaptation of rural migrants to city life.

The most fascinating reading is undoubtedly provided by monographs written about specific towns or communities; these tend to have a specific focus though each covers in some degree most of the issues with which I have been dealing. Oscar Lewis's (1959, 1961, 1967) works are certainly the most vivid in their portrayal of everyday life, though they lack analysis. In her study of a little squatter settlement in the heart of Mexico City Lomnitz (1975) discusses the social networks which bind the residents and enable them to survive poverty; Peattie (1968) lived in a settlement in Venezuela and describes *inter alia* the attempts to prevent the installation of a sewerage outfall on its beach. Roberts (1973) writing of Guatemala City and Safa (1974) of Puerto Rico each provides a comparison between a squatter settlement and a lower-class housing estate. The political consciousness of migrants is the theme of Cornelius's (1975) study of Mexico City and of Ray's (1969) monograph on Venezuela. Perlman's (1976) work on the *favelas* of Brazil explores the applicability of the term 'marginal'. Many influential and seminal articles have been written by Leeds, based upon his extensive research in the *favelas* of Brazil and his close acquaintance with other South American capitals, but to date, he has not produced a monograph.

Work on African towns seems to have had little influence on, or been influenced by, that in Latin America. There are fewer studies of small communities, that by Pons (1969) on a single street in Stanleyville, Congo, being exceptional. Plotnicov (1967) gives an unusual presentation of life in Jos, Nigeria, through the extensive biographies of eight individuals from different ethnic groups. Mayer's (1961) work on Xhosa migrants to East London, South Africa, is a classic which has had a very great influence on African urban studies. General descriptions of African cities which include sections on shanty towns include those of Leslie (1963) on Dar es Salaam, Tanzania; Southall and Gutkind (1956) on Kampala, Uganda; and Lloyd *et al.* (1967) on Ibadan, Nigeria. Hake (1977) deals specifically with the squatter settlements of Nairobi, Kenya – one of which has been studied intensively by the political scientist Ross (1973, 1975). Studies focusing more specifically on industrial workers are those of Epstein (1958) on a Zambia copperbelt mining community, Kapferer (1972) on a small textile factory in Lusaka, Zambia, Grillo (1973, 1974) on railway employees in Kampala, Uganda, Peace 1974, 1975) on factory workers living in a peripheral suburb of Lagos, Nigeria, and Peil's (1972) work on factory workers living in Ghana.

Two studies of Indian factory employees – those of Sheth (1968) and Holmström (1976) – provide comparable material. But whilst there are a vast number of statistical studies of poverty in Indian cities, such as Bhatt and Chawda (1972) and those surveyed in Bulsara (1964), few community studies exist. Gore (nd) gives a more sociological account than most; Lynch (1969) describes the position of a leather workers' caste in Agra; G. Moorhouse (1971), a journalist, provides a full and vivid contrast between affluence and poverty in Calcutta. Karpat (1976) has given a detailed description of the *gecekondu* of Turkey, Rew (1974) of the shanty towns of Port Moresby, Papua New Guinea. McGee (1967, 1971, 1973), a geographer, has worked extensively in East Asia, especially in Hong

Kong, focusing in particular on housing problems and the informal economy of petty traders. Jarvie's (1969) symposium on Hong Kong provides useful description of the urban development of this city which has reversed the usual pattern of shanty town growth.

The issues raised by these monographs on specific communities have been amplified in other works with a more thematic approach. The notion of a culture of poverty has been widely debated, for instance in Valentine (1968), Leacock (1970), Moynihan (1968) and Bloomberg and Schmandt (1968); Eames and Goode (1973) focus largely on third-world material and have an excellent chapter on the 'Coping responses of the urban poor'. Peattie (1974) and Perlman (1976) both attack the concept of cultural marginality; but its use in a more radical idiom is exemplified by the French geographer Castells (1973) and the Peruvian sociologist, Quijano (1972, 1974).

Studies of migration owe much to the very detailed surveys carried out by Caldwell (1969) in Ghana and by Balan *et al.* (1973) in their research into immigration into Monterrey, a steel town in the north of Mexico. Todaro (1976) provides an economic model useful in assessing the costs and benefits to the individual migrant. Connell *et al.* (1976) have surveyed village studies to abstract findings on the patterns of migration. Amin (1975), and du Toit and Safa (1975) and Safa and du Toit (1975) are three useful collections of essays – the first being of the papers presented at an International African Institute Seminar, the second two at the IXth Congress of Anthropological and of Ethnological Sciences.

Economists are increasingly turning to studies of the informal sector; much useful work has been stimulated by the International Labour Office under whose auspices the work of Bairoch (1973) on employment problems and the detailed field studies of Bose (1974) in India and Gerry (1974) in Senegal were conducted. The ILO (1972) also sponsored the study of the Kenyan economy in which the place of the informal sector was stressed; its findings have been strongly criticized by Leys (1975). King (1977) has given us some of the most detailed descriptions of artisans in his work on blacksmiths and others in Kenya. A Bulletin of the Institute of Development Studies, edited by Bell (1973) is devoted to the informal sector. Moser (1976) critically reviews recent theoretical models of this sector. (Lest anyone believe that the informal sector is a phenomenon peculiar to the third world, Jones's (1971) description of mid-nineteenth-century London provides a corrective). Wage earners in the formal sector are described in the monographs cited above; Sandbrook and Cohen (1975) provide however an excellent collection of articles on the development of trade-unionism and class consciousness in Africa. Worsley (1972) discusses the role of the lumpenproletariat, and the applicability of that term.

Political consciousness in shanty towns constitutes the theme of the works of Cornelius, Ray and Ross cited above. Huntington and Nelson (1976), Portes (1972) and Portes and Walton (1976) cogently explain the absence of revolutionary activity: their arguments are modified and amplified by the study of Eckstein (1977) of Mexico. Castells and his associates (in Castells 1973, Schteingart (1973)) have produced stimulating data and explanations of the varying levels of political activity in the squatter settlements of Chile. Nash and Corradi (1975) contains useful papers in the development of political consciousness in Latin America. It is significant that these themes have been so little developed in the literature on Africa and Asia.

Several good books analyse housing problems and policies. Abrams (1966) provided early stimulation. Dwyer (1975) and Juppenplatz (1970) have given us valuable surveys. Laquian (1969) advocates a humanistic approach in dealing with the problems of Manila, Philippines. Turner (1967, 1976) has been a leading advocate of self-help policies, though these have been critically reviewed by Brett (1974).

Clinard's (1966) book on modes of community development, with a detailed analysis of experience in India, is one of the most worthwhile works on this subject. With Abbott (Clinard and Abbott, 1973) he has given us an equally stimulating book on the distribution of crime.

Several symposia and readers are devoted largely to third-world shanty towns. Of these, that of Abu-Lughod and Hay (1977) is probably the best; those of Breese (1969), Field (1967), Horowitz (1970), Meadows and Mizruchi (1969), Southall (1973) and Weaver and White (1972) all contain useful articles, some of which are noted in the bibliography. Issues of the journal *Urban Anthropology*, and of *Latin American Urban Research*, provide a source of valuable material.

The bibliography of Buick (1975) is probably the most useful for our purposes since it covers all areas. Friedmann's and Wulff's (1976) bibliographic essay is excellent. Simms (1965), on Africa is now rather dated; Sable (1971) and Vaughan (1970) will provide the reader with leads into the earlier and more specialized literature on Latin America.

# Bibliography


Abrams, C. (1966), *Housing in the Modern World*, Faber.

Abu-Lughod, J., and Hay, R. (1977), *Third World Urbanization*, Maaroufa Press, Chicago.

Alberti, G., and Mayer, E. (1974), *Reciprocidad e intercambio en los Andes Peruanos*, Instituto de Estudios Peruanos, Lima.

Amin, S. (ed.) (1975), *Modern Migrations in Western Africa*, Oxford University Press.

Bairoch, P. (1973), *Urban Unemployment in Developing Countries*, International Labour Office, Geneva.

Balan, J., Browning, H. L., and Jelin, E. (1973), *Men in a Developing Society: Geographic and Social Mobility in Monterrey, Mexico*, University of Texas Press, Austin, Texas.

Banfield, E. C. (1958), *Moral Basis of a Backward Society*, Free-Press, Chicago.

Bejar, H. (1970), *Peru 1965: Notes on a Guerilla Experience*, Monthly Review Press, New York.

Bell, C. L. G. (ed.) (1973), *The Informal Sector and Marginal Groups*, Bulletin of Institute of Development Studies, Vol. 5, No. 2/3.

Berger, P. L., and Luckmann, T. (1971), *The Social Construction of Reality*, Penguin Books.

Bernstein, H. (ed.) (1973), *Underdevelopment and Development: The Third World Today*, Penguin Books.

Bhatt, M., and Chawda, V. K. (1972), *The Anatomy of Urban Poverty*, Gujarat University.

Bienefeld, M. A. (1974), *The Self-Employed of Urban Tanzania*, Institute of Development Studies, University of Sussex, Discussion Paper 54.

Bloomberg, W., and Schmandt, H. J. (eds.) (1968), *Power, Poverty and Urban Policy*, Sage, Beverly Hills, California.

Bohannan, P. J. (1957), *Justice and Judgement among the Tiv*, Oxford University Press.

Bose, A. N. (1974), *The Informal Sector in the Calcutta Metropolitan Economy*, International Labour Organization, Geneva.

Bowen, E. S. (1964), *Return to Laughter*, Doubleday, New York.

Breese, G. W. (ed.) (1969), *The City in Newly Developing Countries: Readings in Urbanism and Urbanization*, Prentice Hall, Englewood Cliffs, New Jersey.

Brett, S. (1974), 'Low-Income Urban Settlements in Latin America: The Turner Model', in E. de Kadt and G. Williams (eds.), *Sociology and Development*, Tavistock Publications.

Buick, B. (1975), *Squatter Settlements in Developing Countries: A Bibliography*, Research School of Pacific Studies, Australian National University, Canberra.

Bulsara, J. F. (1964), *Problems of Rapid Urbanisation in India*, Popular Prakashan, Bombay.

Caldwell, J. C. (1969), *African Rural-Urban Migration: The Movement to Ghana's Towns*, Australian National University Press, Canberra.

Castells, M. (ed.) (1973), *Imperialismo y urbanización en America Latina*, Editorial Gustavo Gili, Barcelona.

Clinard, M. B. (1966), *Slums and Community Development: Experiments in Self-Help*, Free Press, New York.

Clinard, M. B., and Abbott, D. J. (1973), *Crime in Developing Countries*, Wiley, New York.

Cohen, A. (1969), *Custom and Politics in Urban Africa*, Routledge and Kegan Paul.

Connell, J., Dasgupta, B., Lanshley, R., and Lipton, M. (1976), *Migration from Rural Areas: The Evidence from Village Studies*, Oxford University Press, Delhi.

Cornelius, W. A. (1970), 'Political Sociology of Cityward Migration in Latin America: Toward Empirical Theory', in F. R. Rabinouitz and F. M. Trueblood (eds.), *Latin American Urban Research*, Vol. 1, Sage, Beverly Hills, California.

Cornelius, W. A. (1975), *Politics and the Migrant Poor in Mexico City*, Stanford University Press, Stanford, California.

Davis, K. (1969), *World Urbanization 1950–1970*, Institute of International Studies, University of California Press, Berkeley.

Dwyer, D. J. (1975), *People and Housing in Third World Cities: Perspectives on the Problem of Spontaneous Settlements*, Longman.

Eames, E., and Goode, J. G. (1973), *Urban Poverty in a Cross Cultural Context*, Free Press, New York.

Eckstein, S. (1977), *The Poverty of Revolution*, Princeton University Press, Princeton, New Jersey.

Eddy, E. M. (ed.) (1968), *Urban Anthropology: Research Perspectives and Strategies*, Southern Anthropological Society Proceedings, 2, University of Georgia Press, Athens, Georgia.

Epstein, A. L. (1958), *Politics in an Urban African Community*, Manchester University Press.

Epstein, A. L. (1967), 'Urbanizations and Social Change in Africa', *Current Anthropology*, Vol. 8, No. 4.

Epstein, T. S. (1962), *Economic Development and Social Change in South India*, Manchester University Press.

Field, A. J. (ed.) (1967), *City and Country in the Third World*, Schenkman, Cambridge, Mass.

Foster, G. M. (1965), 'Peasant Society and the Image of Limited Good', *American Anthropologist*, Vol. 67, No. 2.

Friedmann, J., and Wulff, R. (1976), *The Urban Transition: Comparative Studies of Newly Industrializing Societies*, Edward Arnold.

Garbett, G. K. (1970), 'The Analysis of Social Situations', *Man*, (NS) Vol. 5, No. 2.

Garbett, G. K. (1976), 'Circulatory Migration in Rhodesia: Towards a Decision Model', in D. Parkin (ed.), *Town and Country in Central and East Africa*, Oxford University Press.

Gerry, C. (1974), *Petty Producers and the Urban Economy: A Case Study of Dakar*, World Employment Survey, International Labour Office, Geneva.

Gilbert, A. (1974), *Latin American Development: A Geographical Perspective*, Penguin Books.

Gluckman, M. (1955), *The Judicial Process among the Barotse of Northern Rhodesia*, Manchester University Press.

Gluckman, M. (1960), 'Tribalism in Modern British Central Africa', *Cahiers d'Etudes Africaines*, Vol. 1, No. 1.

Gore, M. S. (nd, *c.* 1970), *Immigrants and Neighbourhoods*, Tata Institute of Social Sciences, Bombay.

Grillo, R. D. (1973), *African Railwaymen: Solidarity and Opposition in an East African Labour Force*, Cambridge University Press.

Grillo, R. D. (1974), *Race, Class and Militancy: An African Trade Union 1939–1965*, Chandler, New York.

Gutkind, P. C. W., and Wallerstein, I. (eds.) (1976), *The Political Economy of Contemporary Africa*, Sage, Beverly Hills, California.

Hake, A. (1977), *African Metropolis*, Sussex University Press.

Handelman, H. (1975), 'The Political Mobilization of Urban Squatter Settlements: Santiago's Recent Experience and Its Implications for Urban Research', *Latin American Research Review*, Vol. 10, No. 2.

Hanna, W. J., and Hanna, J. (1971), *Urban Dynamics in Black Africa: An Interdisciplinary Approach*, Aldine, Chicago.

Hanson, R. C., and Simmons, D. G. (1969), 'Differential Experience Paths of Rural Migrants to the City', in E. B. Brody (ed.), *Behaviour in New Environments*, Sage, Beverly Hills, California.

Hobsbawm, E. J. (1973), 'Peasants and Politics', *Journal of Peasant Studies*, Vol. 1, No. 1.

Holmström, M. (1976), *South Indian Factory Workers: Their Life and Their World*, Cambridge University Press.

Horowitz, I. L. (ed.) (1970), *Masses in Latin America*, Oxford University Press, New York.

Huntington, S. P., and Nelson, J. M. (1976), *No Easy Choice: Political Participation in Developing Countries*, Harvard University Press, Cambridge, Mass.

International Labour Office (1972), *Employment, Incomes and Equality: A Strategy for Increasing Productive Employment in Kenya*, Geneva.

Jarvie, I. C. (ed.) (1969), *Hong Kong: A Society in Transition*, Routledge and Kegan Paul.

Jolly, R., de Kadt, E., Singer, H., and Wilson, F. (1973), *Third World Employment: Problems and Strategy*, Penguin Books.

Jones, G. S. (1971), *Outcast London: A Study in the Relationship between Classes in Victorian Society*, Clarendon Press.

Juppenlatz, M. (1970), *Cities in Transformation: The Urban Squatter Problem of the Developing World*, University of Queensland Press, St Lucia, Australia.

Kapferer, B. (1972), *Strategy and Transaction in an African Factory*, Manchester University Press.

Karpat, K. H. (1976), *The Gecekondu: Rural Migration and Urbanisation in Turkey*, Cambridge University Press.

King, K. J. (1977), *The African Artisan: Education and the Informal Sector in Kenya*, Heinemann.

Kravis, I. B. (1973), 'A World of Unequal Incomes', in *Income Equality, Annals of the American Academy of Political and Social Sciences*, Vol. 409, September.

Laquian, A. A. (1969), *Slums are for People: The Barrio Magsaysay Pilot Project in Urban Community Development*, University of the Philippines, Manila.

Leacock, E. (ed.) (1970), *The Culture of Poverty: Review and Critique*, Simon and Schuster, New York.

Leeds, A. (1969), 'The Significant Variables Determining the Character of Squatter Settlements', *America Latina*, Vol. 12, No. 3.

Leeds, A. and E. (1976), 'Accounting for Behavioural Differences: Three Political Systems and the Responses of Squatters in Brazil, Peru and Chile', in J. Walton and L. H. Masotti (eds.), *The City in Comparative Perspective: Cross National Research and New Directions in Theory*, Sage, Beverly Hills, California.

Leighton, A. A. *et al.* (1963), *Psychiatric Disorder among the Yoruba*, Cornell University Press, Ithaca, New York.

Lerner, D. (1967), 'Comparative Analysis of Processes of Modernization', in H. Miner (ed.), *The City in Modern Africa*, Pall Mall.

Leslie, J. A. K. (1963), *A Survey of Dar es Salaam*, Oxford University Press.

Lewis, O. (1951), *Life in a Mexican Village: Tepoztlan Revisited*, University of Illinois Press, Urbana.

Lewis, O. (1959), *Five Families: Mexican Case Studies in the Culture of Poverty*, Basic Books, New York.

Lewis, O. (1961), *The Children of Sanchez*, Random House, New York.

Lewis, O. (1967), *La Vida: A Puerto Rican Family in the Culture of Poverty – San Juan and New York*, Panther.

Leys, C. (1975), *Underdevelopment in Kenya: The Political Economy of Neo-Colonialism 1964–1971*, Heinemann.

Lloyd, P. C. (1953), 'Craft Organisation in Yoruba Towns,' *Africa*, XXIII, pp. 30–44.

Lloyd, P. C. (1967), *Africa in Social Change*, Penguin Books.

Lloyd, P. C. (1971), *Classes Crises and Coups: Themes in the Sociology of Developing Countries*, MacGibbon and Kee.

Lloyd, P. C. (1974), *Power and Independence: Urban Africans' Perceptions of Social Inequality*, Routledge and Kegan Paul.

Lloyd, P. C., Mabogunje, A. L., and Awe, B. (eds.) (1967), *The City of Ibadan: A Symposium on Its Structure and Development*, Cambridge University Press.

Lobo, S. B. (1976), 'Urban Adaptation among Peruvian Migrants', *Rice University Studies*, Vol. 62, No. 3.

Lomnitz, L. (1974), 'The Social and Economic Organisations of a Mexican Shanty Town', in W. A. Cornelius and F. M. Trueblood (eds.), *Latin American Urban Research*, Vol. 4, Sage, Beverly Hills, California. (A fuller version of this paper was given at the

13th International Congress of Anthropological and Ethnological Sciences, 1973.)

Lomnitz, L. (1975), *Como sobreviven los marginados*, Siglo XXI, Mexico City. English version (1977), *Networks and Marginality*, Academic Press.

Lopreato, J. (1967), *Peasants No More*, Chandler, San Francisco.

Lynch, O. M. (1969), *The Politics of Untouchability: Social Mobility and Social Change in a City of India*, Columbia University Press, New York.

Lynch, O. M. (1974), 'Political Mobilisation and Ethnicity among Adi-Dravidas in a Bombay Slum', *Economic and Political Weekly*, Vol. 9, No. 39, 28 September.

MacEwen, A. M. (1974), 'Differentiation among the Urban Poor: An Argentine Study', in E. de Kadt and G. Williams (eds.), *Sociology and Development*, Tavistock Publications.

McGee, T. G. (1967), *The Southeast Asian City: A Social Geography of the Primate Cities of Southeast Asia*, Bell.

McGee, T. G. (1971), *The Urbanisation Process in the Third World*, Bell.

McGee, T. G. (1973), *Hawkers in Hong Kong*, University of Hong Kong Press, Hong Kong.

Malinowski, B. (1922), *Argonauts of the Western Pacific.*

Mangin, W. (1960), 'Mental Health and Migration to Cities: A Peruvian Case', *Annals of the New York Academy of Sciences*, Vol. 84.

Mangin, W. (1967), 'Latin American Squatter Settlements: A Problem and a Solution', *Latin American Research Review*, Vol. 2, No. 3.

Mangin, W. (ed.) (1970), *Peasants in Cities: Readings in the Anthropology of Urbanization*, Houghton, Mifflin, Boston.

Matos Mar, J., *et al.* (1969), *Dominación y Cambios en el Peru rural*, Instituto de Estudios Peruanos, Lima.

Mayer, P. (1961), *Townsmen or Tribesmen*, Oxford University Press, Capetown.

Meadows, P., and Mizruchi, E. H. (1969), *Urbanism, Urbanization and Change: Comparative Perspectives*, Addison-Wesley, Reading, Mass.

Miller, G. A., Galanter, E., and Pribam, K. H. (1960), *Plans and the Structure of Behaviour*, New York.

Mitchell, J. C. (1966), 'Theoretical Orientations in African Urban Studies', in M. Banton (ed.), *The Social Anthropology of Complex Societies*, Tavistock Publications.

Moorhouse, G. (1971), *Calcutta*, Penguin Books.

Moorhouse, H. F. (1976), 'Attitudes to Class and Class Relationships in Britain', *Sociology*, Vol. 10, No. 3.

Moser, C. (1976), *The Informal Sector or Petty Commodity Production: Autonomy or Dependence in Urban Development*, Development Planning Unit, University College, London.

Moser, C. (1977), 'The Dual Economy and Marginality Debate and the Contribution of Micro-analysis: Market Sellers in Bogota', *Development and Change*, Vol. 8, No. 4.

Moynihan, D. P. (1968), *On Understanding Poverty*, Basic Books, New York.

Myrdal, G. (1968), *Asian Drama: An Enquiry into the Poverty of Nations*, Allen Lane, The Penguin Press.

Nash, J., and Corradi, J. (1975), *Ideology and Social Change in Latin America.*

Nolan, R. W. (1975), 'Labour Migration and the Bassari: A Case of Retrograde Development', *Man* (NS), Vol. 10, No. 4.

Ossowski, S. (1963), *Class Structure in the Social Consciousness*, Routledge and Kegan Paul.

Oxaal, I., Barnett, T., and Booth, D. (eds.) (1975), *Beyond the Sociology of Development: Economy and Society in Latin America and Africa*, Routledge and Kegan Paul.

Parkin, D. (ed.) (1976), *Town and Country in Central and East Africa*, Oxford University Press.

Peabody, N. S. (1970), 'Towards an Understanding of Backwardness and Change: A Critique of the Banfield Hypothesis', *Journal of Developing Areas*, Vol. 4, No. 3.

Peace, A. (1974), 'Industrial Protest in Nigeria', in E. de Kadt and G. Williams (eds.), *Sociology and Development*, Tavistock Publications.

Peace, A. J. (1975), 'The Lagos Proletariat: Labour Aristocrats or Populist Militants', in R. Sandbrook and R. Cohen (eds.), *The Development of an African Working Class*, Longman.

Peattie, L. R. (1968), *The View from the 'Barrio'*, University of Michigan Press, Ann Arbor.

Peattie, L. R. (1974), 'The Concept of 'Marginality' as Applied to Squatter Settlements', in W. A. Cornelius and F. M. Trueblood (eds.), *Latin American Urban Research*, Vol. 4, Sage, Beverly Hills, California.

Peil, M. (1972), *The Ghanaian Factory Worker: Industrial Man in Africa*, Cambridge University Press.

Peil, M. (1976), 'African Squatter Settlements: A Comparative Study', *Urban Studies*, 13.

Peil, M. (1977), *Consensus and Conflict in African Societies*, Longman.

Perlman, J. E. (1976), *Myths of Marginality: The Urban Squatter in Brazil*, University of California Press, Berkeley, California.

Plotnicov, L. (1967), *Strangers to the City: Urban Man in Jos, Nigeria*, University of Pittsburgh Press.

Pons, V. (1969), *Stanleyville*, Oxford University Press.

Portes, A. (1972), 'Rationality in the Slum: An Essay on Interpretive Sociology', *Comparative Studies in Society and History*, Vol. 14, No. 3.

Portes, A., and Walton, J. (1976), *Urban Latin America*, University of Texas Press, Austin, Texas.

Potter, J. M., Diaz, M., and Foster, G. M. (eds.) (1967), *Peasant Society: A Reader*, Little Brown, Boston.

Quijano, A. (1972), 'La constitución del 'Mundo' de la marginalidad urbana', *Revista Latin-Americana de estudios urbano-regionales*, Vol. 2, No. 5.

Quijano, A. (1974), 'The Marginal Pole of the Economy and the Marginalised Labour Force,' *Economy and Society*, Vol. 3, No. 4.

Ray, T. F. (1969), *The Politics of the Barrios of Venezuela*, University of California Press, Berkeley, California.

Redfield, R. (1930), *Tepoztlan: A Mexican Village*, Chicago University Press.

Rew, A. (1974), *Social Images and Process in Urban New Guinea: A Study of Port Moresby*, American Ethnological Society Monographs, West St Paul.

Roberts, B. R. (1973), *Organizing Strangers: Poor Families in Guatemala City*, University of Texas Press, Austin, Texas.

Roberts, B. R. (1974), 'The Inter-relationships of City and Provinces in Peru and Guatemala', in W. A. Cornelius and F. M. Trueblood (eds.), *Latin American Urban Research*, Vol. 4, Sage, Beverly Hills, California.

Rodman, H. (1963), 'The Lower-Class Value Stretch', *Social Forces*, Vol. 2.

Rodriguez, A., Riofrio, G., and Welsh, E. (1973), *De invasores a invadidos*, Desco, Lima.

Ross, M. H. (1973), *The Political Integration of Urban Squatters*, Northwestern University Press, Evanston, Ill.

Ross, M. H. (1975), *Grass Roots in an African City: Political Behaviour in Nairobi*, MIT Press, Cambridge, Mass.

Sable, M. H. (1971), *Latin American Urbanization: A Guide to the Literature, Organizations and Personnel*, Scarecrow Press, Metuchen, New Jersey.

Safa, H. I. (1974), *The Urban Poor of Puerto Rico: A Study in Development and Inequality*, Holt, Rinehart and Winston, New York.

Safa, H. I., and du Toit, B. M. (eds.) (1975), *Migration and Development: Implications for Ethnic Identity and Political Conflict*, Mouton, The Hague.

Salisbury, R. F. and M. E. (1972), 'Rural-Oriented Strategy of Urban Adaptation: Siane Migrants in Port Moresby', in T. Weaver and D. White (eds.), *The Anthropology of Urban Environments*, Society for Applied Anthropology, Monograph 11, Washington, DC.

Sandbrook, R., and Cohen, R. (eds.) (1975), *The Development of an African Working Class*, Longman.

Schteingart, M. (ed.) (1973), *Urbanización y dependencia en America Latina*, Ediciones Siap, Buenos Aires.

Seymour, T. (1975), 'Squatter Settlement and Class Relations in Zambia', *Review of African Political Economy*, No. 3.

Shack, W. A. (1976), 'Occupational Prestige, Status and Social Change in Modern Ethiopia, *Africa*, Vol. 46, No. 2.

Shanin, T. (ed.) (1971), *Peasants and Peasant Societies*, Penguin Books.

Sheth, N. R. (1968), *The Social Framework of an Indian Factory*, Oxford University Press, Bombay.

Silverman, D. (1970), *The Theory of Organisations*, Heinemann.

Simms, R. P. (1965), *Urbanization in West Africa: A Review of Current Literature*, Northwestern University Press, Evanston, Ill.

Southall, A. (ed.) (1973), *Urban Anthropology: Cross-Cultural Studies of Urbanization*, Oxford University Press.

Southall, A. W., and Gutkind, P. C. W. (1956), *Townsmen in the Making*, East African Institute of Social Research, Kampala.

Stokes, C. (1962), 'A Theory of Slums', *Land Economics*, Vol. 8, No. 3.

Strickon, A. (1967), 'Folk Models of Stratification', in P. Holmes (ed.), *Latin American Sociological Studies*, Sociological Review Monograph.

Thernstrom, S. (1975), *Poverty and Progress: Social Mobility in a Nineteenth Century City*, Atheneum, New York (first published 1964, Harvard University Press).

Todaro, M. P. (1976), *Internal Migration in Developing Countries*, International Labour Office, Geneva.

Toit, B. M. du, and Safa, H. I. (eds.) (1975), *Migration and Urbanization*, Mouton, The Hague.

Touraine, A., and Ragazzi, O. (1961), *Ouvriers d'origine agricole*, L'Ecole Pratique des Hautes Etudes, Paris.

Turner, J. F. C. (1967), 'Barriers and Channels for Housing Development in Modernizing Countries', *Journal of the American Institute of Planners*, Vol. 33, No. 3 (also in Mangin, 1970).

Turner, J. F. C. (1976), *Housing by People*, Marion Boyars.

Valentine, C. A. (1968), *Culture and Poverty: Critique and Counter Proposals*, Chicago University Press.

Vaughan, D. R. (1970), *Urbanization in Twentieth Century Latin America: Working Bibliography*, University of Texas Press, Austin, Texas.

Wallace, A. F. C. (1965), 'Driving to Work', in M. Spiro (ed.), *Context and Meaning in Cultural Anthropology*, Free Press, New York.

Weaver, T., and White D. (1972), *The Anthropology of Urban Environments*, Society for Applied Anthropology, Monograph 11, Washington, DC.

Whiteford, M. B. (1974), 'Neighbours at a Distance: Life in a Low-Income Colombian Barrio', in W. A. Cornelius and F. M. Trueblood (eds.), *Latin American Urban Research*, Vol. 4, Sage, Beverly Hills, California.

Williams, G. (1974), 'Political Consciousness among the Ibadan Poor', in E. de Kadt and G. Williams (eds.), *Sociology and Development*, Tavistock Publications.

Worsley, P. (1972), 'Franz Fanon and the Lumpenproletariat', in R. Miliband and J. Savile (eds.), *The Socialist Register 1972*, Martin Press.

# Index

## More About Penguins and Pelicans

*Penguinews*, which appears every month, contains details of all the new books issued by Penguins as they are published. From time to time it is supplemented by our stocklist, which includes around 5,000 titles.

A specimen copy of *Penguinews* will be sent to you free on request. Please write to Dept EP, Penguin Books Ltd, Harmondsworth, Middlesex, for your copy.

*In the U.S.A.*: For a complete list of books available from Penguins in the United States write to Dept CS, Penguin Books, 625 Madison Avenue, New York, New York 10022.

*In Canada*: For a complete list of books available from Penguins in Canada write to Penguin Books Canada Ltd, 2801 John Street, Markham, Ontario L3R 1B4.